At The Threshold

UFOs, Science and the New Age

by
Charles F. Emmons, Ph.D.

Wild Flower Press
P. O. Box 190
Mill Spring, NC 28756

Library of Congress Cataloging-in-Publication Data
Emmons, Charles F. 1942—
At The Threshold:
UFOs, Science and the New Age/
by Charles F. Emmons.
p. cm.
Includes bibliographical references (p.) and index.
ISBN 0-926524-38-0
1. Unidentified flying objects.
I. Title.
TL789.E44 1997
001.942--dc21
97-7719
CIP

The New Millenium Library
Volume II

Cover Artwork: Maynard Demmon
Manuscript editors: Brian Crissey, Amy Owen Demmon

Printed in the United States of America.

Address all inquiries to:
Wild Flower Press
an imprint of Blue Water Publishing, Inc.
P. O. Box 190
Mill Spring, NC 28756
U.S.A.

Blue Water Publishing, Inc., is committed
to using recycled paper.

Acknowledgments

Gettysburg College deserves thanks for awarding me sabbatical leave and a Faculty Research Grant for 1994-95 to conduct this research. I am grateful to Walter H. Andrus, Jr., Director of the Mutual UFO Network (MUFON), and to other members of MUFON, for their cooperation, and to the MUFON Journal for permission to include herein numerous extended references to cases published in the Journal.

I am also grateful to over one hundred people who provided me information and insights as interviewees or in other roles. Most but not all of them appear in the index to this book.

This book is dedicated to

Dr. R. Leo Sprinkle:

pioneering scholar,
therapist and
"arguably the nicest man in
North America"
(according to one of
his critics).

Table of Contents

Prologue

At the Threshold: UFOs, Science and the New Age is a story of deviance and conformity. UFO experiencers, especially abductees, are often considered psychologically deviant ("wacky") in scientific circles and in mainstream communications media. UFO cults, like Heaven's Gate, 39 members of which committed suicide together in late March, 1997, receive considerable media attention (far greater than their tiny numbers would justify) due to public fascination with what is labeled as bizarre and irrational. Academics who dare to examine the evidence for UFOs have often been labeled deviant as well, unless they take a strong debunking position. Such deviance is punishable by public ridicule and by on-the-job harassment or even dismissal. Conformity, on the other hand, may be seen in the smug rejection or ignoring of UFO reports, and in the preference of researchers to study "normal" science topics that stand a chance of being funded.

On the individual psychological level, people often go beyond a normal skepticism and deny their own strange experiences until they become too bizarre to explain away. Although many UFO experiencers find their encounters spiritually transforming, some would rather believe that they are "crazy" than consider their own apparent abductions to be real.

Why should UFOs be a deviant subject? If they represent extraterrestrial intelligence (and not all ufologists, i.e., people who study UFOs, agree that they do), then their presence should not be so surprising given the widespread opinion among astronomers that there ought to be a great many civilizations elsewhere in this and other galaxies. How they might get here across vast distances might pose a problem, but this point is debatable in modern physics. As we shall see, there are more than just objective scientific reasons that account for how ufology became a "deviant" science.

In spite of ufology's deviant label, and in spite of the lack of rewards for studying UFOs, there have been scholars like the late J. Allen

Hynek (astronomer at Northwestern University) who have taken the subject seriously for over forty years. And, in recent years, UFOs and other possibly related paranormal topics like out-of-body experiences (OBEs) and near-death experiences (NDEs) have been creeping closer to legitimacy with the publication of books by professors from major universities, e.g. *Abduction: Human Encounters with Aliens*, 1994, by John E. Mack, Pulitzer-Prize-winning professor of psychiatry at Harvard Medical School.

Since mainstream academic journals are largely closed to a consideration of UFOs, the debate over the legitimacy of ufology is going on mainly on TV talk shows and in newspapers, even when the advocates for ufology are respected academics like Dr. Mack. The outcome of this debate is uncertain. As John Mack put it at one UFO conference, there is a race between two tendencies: "My [Harvard] credentials convincing people, and my being discredited [because of the subject matter]."

It would be a mistake to assume that all of normal, mainstream science is firmly opposed to studying the "deviant science" of ufology. Some ufology articles are even starting to appear in academic journals (e.g., "Close Encounters: An Examination of UFO Experiences" by Nicholas P. Spanos and others, in the *Journal of Abnormal Psychology*, 1993). Nor do all researchers in the "UFO community" have a standard view of what the UFO phenomenon is all about or accept the methods and claims of other ufologists as legitimate.

Over the years, ufologists have progressed from "nuts-and-bolts" studies of lights and discs that make strange right-angle turns in the sky to increasingly stranger reports of landed craft with humanoid occupants, and of aliens who allegedly abduct humans for cross-breeding programs. It is common for ufologists to say that the more they learn about the phenomenon, the more perplexing the questions are that arise. Every door that opens in UFO research leads to stranger and more bizarre scenarios: telepathic communication with aliens, psychic experiences among the witnesses and New Age channels (mediums) who communicate with entities from the Pleiades.

It is no wonder that many serious ufologists become frustrated over the attempt to make their discipline acceptable in the academic community. In the effort to clean house and to set scientific standards within ufology, they draw boundaries that are just as exclusive as the boundaries drawn by outsiders between ufology and mainstream science. In other words, some perspectives (like channeling) are just as deviant to some ufologists as ufology is to UFO debunkers like the late astronomer Carl Sagan and science journalist Philip Klass.

In the meantime, mainstream academe has been generating perspectives that suggest that many of the strangest aspects of the UFO experience may be possible within (almost) normal science and not just as some paranormal phenomenon. New Physics theory gives us wormholes, hyperspace and holograms to get around the problems of faster-than-light travel, shape-shifting UFOs and the psychic and mythic dimensions of the experience.

Pandora's box has opened wide. Ufology is now a kaleidoscope of cosmic questions. Science and religion collide once again with a vengeance. It is no longer merely an issue of whether ufology can conform to normal science. It is now also a question of whether we can afford to label any "nonscientific" way of knowing as deviant if we hope to understand the whole phenomenon.

Chapter 1

The Strange Range of UFO Phenomena

Let us assume that you are willing to suspend judgment and to consider some UFO reports for what they might represent. Even UFO researchers (ufologists) generally agree with skeptics or debunkers that most UFO sightings represent misperception or misunderstanding of known phenomena like stars, planets, meteors, aircraft, weather balloons, flares, birds, insects etc. However, none of the cases in this chapter are apparently so easily identifiable, and none are obvious hoaxes to my knowledge.

For now let us take the following cases merely as illustrations, not proof, of several categories of observations that represent the range of allegedly UFO-related phenomena. Although "UFO" literally refers to any "Unidentified Flying Object," a better definition of "UFO" would be an "Unknown, intelligently guided vehicle,"[1] generally with the assumption that the intelligence is nonhuman, but not necessarily extraterrestrial (the plot thickens).

All of the cases in this chapter are strange in the sense that they seem to depart from normal experience, but the categories tend to get progressively stranger. Partly due to their increasingly bizarre nature, some categories of UFO experience are hard even for some ufologists to accept, no matter how apparently reliable the experiencers who report them. You are entitled to think, "Surely there must be some other explanation!" You may even turn your head away from this book and laugh, if you like. But if you care to learn what is happening in ufology, you must try to regain your composure and read open-mindedly on. There will be plenty of time for debunking later on, if you are so inclined.

The closer the phenomenon seems to get, from a distant nocturnal light to a humanoid staring into your face, eyeball to eyeball, the more information there appears to be, but the mystery is still far from solved. Conventional views of reality are progressively violated. In this state of

---

1. Richard L. Thompson, 1993, p. 42.

confusion, researchers are led to suspect that hoaxes, cover-ups, deception and disinformation may cloud the reality behind the phenomenon.

Nocturnal Lights

The father of ufology, astronomer J. Allen Hynek,[2] stated that nocturnal lights were the "most frequently reported and 'least strange' (UFO) events." Stars, planets, meteors and airplanes are also easily misidentified as UFOs by untrained watchers of the night skies. For these reasons, reports of nocturnal lights, unless observed at close range, are usually not very interesting to most ufologists these days.

However, in the following excerpt from a case collected by Richard F. Haines (Ph.D. in psychology),[3] there is an interesting *group* of lights suggesting manufactured objects under intelligent guidance. The pilot claimed that air traffic control observed the same lights and that the Air Force asked for his copy of the control-tower voice tape.

> A private pilot flying a single-engine plane north of Seattle, Washington, at 10:15 P.M. July 7, 1968 "saw eight small pulsating crimson-orange oval lights…in a roughly vertical formation on a collision course toward him…. He banked his airplane to avoid hitting them and they passed him on his left side…." The lights continued on and discharged "four smaller white lights simultaneously." Then "the formation…suddenly blinked out in perfect sequence…."

Daylight UFOs

The first illustration here of a daylight, as opposed to a night-time, UFO report is of particular historical interest. The pilot likened the objects to "manhole covers" twenty-one years before the press labeled as "flying saucers" the first really famous UFOs of the modern era, the ones reported by the pilot Kenneth Arnold over Mount Rainier Plateau in Washington State in 1947. Arnold actually said that the craft were crescent-shaped, but that they moved "like a saucer would if you skipped it across the water."[4]

> Richard F. Haines[5] reports that stunt pilot "Bert Acosta was flying…an open cockpit Ballanca [between Wichita, Kansas and Colorado Springs, Colorado in 1926] when he was startled

2. Hynek, 1972, p. 41.
3. Haines, 1994A, pp. 154-172.
4. Davenport, 1992B, p. 95.
5. Haines, 1994A, p. 158.

to see '...six things that looked like huge shiny manhole covers...' which circled his airplane."

In the next case, from 1993, investigated by Bill Hamilton,[6] a former National Guard radar operator and the Chief Investigator for Los Angeles MUFON (Mutual UFO Network), shape changes and unusual maneuvers suggest unfamiliar physics and even notions of hyperspace (see Chapter 7 on the New Physics).

> A former deputy sheriff in Antelope Valley, California, observed a round and white object in his binoculars "move north at a steadily increasing speed, changing from white to beige and flattening in shape. It moved with incredible speed and without slowing, swung a 'U' turn to the south and disappeared into the overcast."

Close Encounters of the First Kind (CE-I)

For convenience Hynek[7] referred to UFO sightings within 500 feet as "close encounters." Of course distance varies continuously, and one might discern the features of a larger craft beyond 500 feet more easily than those of a closer, smaller one. Hynek also subdivided close encounters into three types; only in the second type (CE-II) are there physical traces, and only in the third type (CE-III) are there reported humanoids. CE-I have neither feature.

Our first example of a CE-I is especially significant because it involves hundreds of witnesses to a very large craft flying close overhead at a speed so slow that, had it been a conventional airplane, it would have crashed. It is peculiar that witnesses reported a loud noise that began only when the object was directly over the house. In many UFO reports there is no noise. In this case the close, slow, noisy display seems to suggest that "it" wanted to be seen. The account below is derived from the investigation by Samuel D. Greco,[8] Ph.D., aerospace engineer and Major, USAF, retired, of sightings in and around Williamsport, Pennsylvania, on February 5, 1992.

> Generally between 6:05 and 6:30 P.M. witnesses heard a loud rumbling noise above the house that rattled the windows. After running outside, people would see a boomerang (77%) or other-shaped object (23%), usually 100-200 feet across, flying at a fast-walking or slow-running pace that they could keep

---

6. Hamilton, 1994, p. 10 ff.
7. Hynek, 1972, p. 98.
8. Greco and Gordon, 1992.

up with. The object was usually 50 to 200 feet above the ground, seldom (15%) estimated over 500 feet. Eight of the thirteen people in Greco's first set of interviews claimed to have been between 50 and 150 feet from the UFO. Most witnesses saw dull white lights, 1 to 14 of them, at the rear of the object. Some (31%) saw it hover, and many feared it would crash at first. It followed a straight line, at constant altitude relative to ground or tree level. Once it made a left turn over the Susquehanna River towards Williamsport. It is uncertain whether all witnesses saw the same object. No one thought it was an airplane. FAA and USAF sources claimed that there were no aircraft in the area at the time, and airports denied any sightings on radar.

Our next case, in addition to illustrating a CE-I, borders on a Close Encounter of the Second Kind as well because of the beam involved, except that there is no lasting evidence of a physical effect. For those who follow the Gulf Breeze, Florida case involving Ed and Frances Walters,[9] this report is one of many that supports the Walters in the debate over the possibility of a hoax in their UFO sightings and photographs, since the witnesses were neighbors of the Walters. The Walters' experiences began November 11, 1987. This incident occurred on April 3, 1988, but the report was not filed by investigators for a couple of years due to the heavy case load at that time.

Case investigators Vicki Lyons and Charles Flannigan[10] report that a teacher and her daughter were awakened at 2:45 A.M. by

> a dead tree falling across their backyard fence. [Looking out the window they] saw the object hovering about 50 feet above the ground. A circle of "porthole-like structures" emanated orange beams. [One beam striking the mother] made her feel "unique" as if she were being seen by the occupants.... The mother said she heard a throbbing sound, similar to a heart beating, during the entire sighting.

The daughter did not hear anything, but was afraid. Both lay in bed together for two hours until the light went away.

If the previous case suggests a psychological or physical effect from a beam, the next one does even more so. There is also a hint of a CE-III because of the apparent humanoid who does not abduct the human (CE-IV), but who gathers some information perhaps. Some abduction researchers would suspect that the witness had already been abducted because of his state of paralysis.

---

9. Walters and Walters, 1990 and 1994.
10. Ware, 1992A, pp. 17-19.

MUFON investigator Joe Nyman[11] filed this sighting report from a 34-year-old man in Framingham, Massachusetts. About 3:00 A.M. the witness awoke in his bedroom with a feeling of paralysis. He saw "a pencil-thin beam of green light coming through the open window behind his head, apparently 'reflecting' off the ceiling and entering his right eye. His eye burned as he struggled to move. When he was able to slightly move his head, the beam quickly re-entered his eye. He got the mental impression his mind was being read. He saw, 'somehow reflected' from the ceiling, the window behind him with a small head and hand pointing the light." In two minutes the light and a sine-wave, varied-pitch hum stopped, and his paralysis left him. "When he looked out the window, a green, self-illuminated cylinder about 3' by 18"-diameter with three orange legs was rising vertically." It was about 40 feet away and left in less than a second.

Close Encounters of the Second Kind (CE-II)

In a CE-II there should be clear evidence of a physical effect. Such is the case in another article about a pilot's experience studied by Richard F. Haines,[12] this one occurring over Siberia in December, 1989.

> Vladimir Kuzmin, pilot of a two-seat L-29 single-engine jet, at 3:30 P.M. "saw a dark gray, cigar-shaped object" for over eight minutes. It seemed about the size of an air transport plane [although Haines doubts his estimate], but nothing was picked up by ground radar. After landing, the pilot saw that "his face was becoming coated with a red crust of soft skin [something like a heat scald]." It was sensitive to touch, but not painful like a sunburn. Haines suggests microwave radiation that "cooked his facial tissue from the inside out."

Of course, there is still no "proof" that the burn was caused by the UFO, and no clear understanding how it might have been generated, although microwave effects are suggested in many UFO reports. Another commonly reported CE-II effect, that may also be caused by some type of electromagnetic phenomenon, is the temporary stalling of car engines and the disruption of a variety of electrical devices, as in this case from investigator Fearon L. Hicks.[13]

> "On March 11, 1992, at 3:52 A.M., a police officer near Haines City, Florida," saw a green-glowing object about 15-feet wide and 3-feet high with a white light on top. "The object

11. Ware, 1991, pp. 14-15.
12. Haines, 1991, pp. 12 ff.
13. Ware, 1993A, p. 16.

followed his car, moving from one side to the other, and then it moved in front, nearly filling the windshield.... [After reporting the sighting] he pulled the car to the side of the road, [and] the engine, lights and radio ceased to function.... A bright white light was shown into the vehicle...." The air around the vehicle was cold enough to fog the officer's breath. The UFO "sped away at tree-top level" after three minutes.

Two minutes later "another officer arrived and found him speechless, shaking and crying."

Close Encounters of the Third Kind (CE-III)

Such close-encounter experiences can be unsettling indeed, but the real watershed of credibility comes with the arrival of CE-III cases, i.e., ones involving UFO occupants. Especially "nuts-and-bolts" ufologists, ones who emphasize the study of UFO technology and physical traces, are suspicious of reports of humanoids. Why should this be? After all, if there are solid craft with apparently intelligent guidance, is it so difficult to imagine intelligent beings or robots driving or riding inside?

Probably the answer to this question is complex. However, the foundation of the problem is that most dominant scientific and religious conceptions are anthropocentric (human-centered). They do not allow for natural beings superior to humans. They may exist in faraway galaxies, but seeing them here is threatening, and those who claim to see them are more comfortably thought of as hoaxers or mental cases. There may be other good reasons for denying the existence of aliens or "visitors," e.g., governmental and military ones. (More on this later in Chapter 2).

Both CE-III cases presented below happen to be international ones, showing that UFO sightings, including ones with occupants, are seen around the world and not just in the U.S. The first occurred in Krefeld, Germany in September 1981.[14]

Driving home shortly after 1:00 A.M., a mailman stopped near a railroad track and saw about ten feet away in a field "a small humanoid (about four-and-a-half-feet tall) clad in a silvery jumpsuit. Some (90 feet) behind it was a bright object (12 to 15 feet) in diameter, about which bright colored lights were revolving." When the mailman asked what was the matter, the telepathic reply was, "'I see that you are afraid. I won't come any closer.... You are not ready, but we shall meet again.'" The humanoid returned to the object, the lights of which grew

---

14. von Ludwiger, 1993, pp. 240-301.

brighter. The mailman looked around for help, and looked back to see nothing but "a small bright dot...ascending towards the sky."

Experiencers in both the previous case and the following one were very upset by their encounters. In the next report two women and a six-year-old girl visit a park on the Dnieper River in Kiev, Ukraine, at dusk on July 4, 1989.[15] Notice that not all "aliens" are short, thin, hairless and gray.

> As the three witnesses approached the shore, they "saw a boat with three people in it. Their clothes were of silvery color, without collar and shaped like a night gown. Their faces were very pale, and similar like triplets, with long, wavy blond-golden hair and big shiny eyes." In a strange, archaic Russian accent these beings said that they intended to take the three humans on board their craft, a silvery, barrel-shaped object with a round antenna on top. When the humans begged not to be taken, the beings said that they would find someone else and departed in the craft which "flew up [until] it became a small star."

Abductions (CE-IV)

J. Allen Hynek's original typology of UFO experiences ended with Close Encounters of the Third Kind (CE-III). However, abduction cases are now often referred to as CE-IV. Notice that in each of the CE-III cases above, the humanoids allegedly were about to lead the experiencer(s) off for some purpose or other, but did not. If the experiencer is actually carried off, or perhaps examined or treated in place, then we have a CE-IV. Cynthia Hind, a ufologist from South Africa, says that the following is her best abduction case from southern Africa.[16]

> On July 19, 1988, at 3:30 A.M. a mother, age 60, and daughter, age 32, pulled their car over to park near the daughter's home. At this point a light, that had been following them, rapidly "overtook the car, at which time *both women heard a 'click' sound*. The next thing they recall is going up a ramp into a craft." Inside there were six beings, four males and two females, no taller than 4'8", "with very fine textured skin, oriental eyes and no hair," and wearing dark-colored jump suits. One of the females spoke in good but high-pitched and sing-song English, stating that she was "Meleelah from the Pleiades." Mother and daughter ended up on an examination table,

---

15. Huneeus, 1990, pp. 170-201.
16. Hind, 1993, pp. 17-25.

where at least the daughter underwent exam procedures, including a needle being inserted below her left breast. "A small, fading scar [could] be seen" there years later.

Neither woman could recall the entire episode, but hypnotic regression, a debated technique, was not used. Nor was it used in the next case, in which the woman who was the focus of the apparent abduction remembered nothing.[17]

Charles A. Gallella, case investigator, reports the following from a 29-year-old male witness in East Hampstead, New Hampshire.

At 4:00 A.M. in February, 1990, the witness and his girlfriend awoke to a "bright reddish light coming through the bedroom back window.... [He] got up, went to the window, and saw a large circular object about five feet above the ground and twenty feet away. Frightened, he tried to exit [the door and the side window, but neither would open]. He hid in the closet, [but] his friend said, 'It's no use. They are coming in.' He came out and found a fat, four-foot-tall, bluish-gray being standing next to his girlfriend. It had a big head with big eyes, a wide nose and a big mouth. He was very frightened, but when it grabbed his hand he felt calm. When it cocked its head and smiled at him, he lost all memory until he awoke in bed the next morning."

Attracting UFOs (CE-V)

It has been reported from time to time that people have thought about seeing UFOs, and suddenly they appear. Or in the middle of a sighting some action or thought by the witness seems to bring about a response from the UFO. Dr. Steven Greer, an M.D. in Asheville, NC, and founder of CSETI (Center for the Study of Extraterrestrial Intelligence), refers to such encounters as CE-V. Our first case, as told to case investigator Richard D. Seifried,[18] happened by accident.

At 10:30 P.M. on April 14, 1991, in Durant, Oklahoma, a young woman went outside to see a very large silver object "with a 'nipple' on top with a red light and antenna" plus windows and rows of blue and red lights. "She was frightened, extremely happy and crying. She began jumping and for some reason jumped two steps to the left. The object changed and it, too, seemed to respond by jerking two 'steps' to her left. She

17. Ware, 1992B, p. 15.
18. Coyne, 1992, p. 19.

thought this was wonderful so she jumped two steps to the right and the object responded by moving to the right. This was repeated several times so there was some sort of intelligent contact made."

By contrast with this report, the next one was preplanned, by Dr. Greer himself. It took place in Gulf Breeze, Florida, scene of the famous Ed Walters sightings, and was filed in a lengthy report by six investigators.[19]

On March 14, 1992, Dr. Greer led a group of 39 people "in a friendly invitation to the UFO folk. Recorded sounds were played, and powerful light-beam patterns were made in the sky just before four of the bright cherry-red UFOs appeared." Videos were taken from two separate locations, allowing triangulation measurements, the closest UFO being 2.1 miles away. "When a 500,000 candle power light was flashed at the UFOs…at least one of them blinked back in similar sequences. After many wished the UFOs to come closer, two of them moved about 0.8 miles closer before they dimmed out as they each climbed 400 or 500 feet from their original altitudes of 2200 and 3000 feet."

The close-encounter typology is useful, but it cannot indicate all of the strange features associated with the UFO phenomenon. An overview of a few other allegedly related topics will help complete the picture.

Probes

"Probes" are a somewhat dubious category, since the term presupposes more knowledge of their function than we might want to claim. Probes are small lights or objects, often seen around UFOs, that are apparently too small for humanoid occupants. They might gather information, like probes used in the U.S. space program, or they might take action of some kind. The first report below was investigated by Norma Croda[20] in Plainfield, Indiana.

Early in the morning, July 1988 a man "noticed a 'blinking' light on his bedroom wall…. He looked out his bedroom window to see five objects 1.5 to 2 feet in diameter 'floating' approximately 5 to 6 feet away from the window and about 6 to 7 feet off the ground. Somewhat frightened, he watched the

19. Gribble and Ware, 1992, pp. 18-19.
20. Ware, 1993B, p. 16.

objects change from white disks to 'big bubbles' with pulsing blue lights coming from within the objects [which] then changed color to orange and back to disc shapes with a 'flash.' They then 'shot up' and took off at a high rate of speed."

In the next case, investigated by Cynthia Newby Luce,[21] two Brazilian couples saw "small lights bobbing up and down on the horizon" near Sao Jose de Rio Preto, Brazil, after dark. It is uncertain whether those lights were the same as or associated with the following object that they saw after driving to a different field.

"A dull sphere, just smaller than a volleyball and no more than 30 feet above the heads of the witnesses, just appeared and glided silently toward the woods behind…fleeing animals [horses and cows]. It disappeared before it reached the trees, but from that direction issued 16 loud musical tones 'like an electronic flute wired to a very powerful amplifier.' One of the witnesses is a trained musician, and worked out the memorable pattern of notes as: A, F#, D, B, A repeated twice, then D, B, A repeated twice, coming from no visible source."

Animal Mutilations

Reports of animal mutilations involve mainly cattle found dead with genital, anal and other body parts excised with sharp instruments and high heat. Linda Moulton Howe is the best known researcher to find that many mutilation reports are associated with UFO sightings. She states, for example, that

A couple in Springfield, Missouri, in July 1983, "watched through binoculars while…two small, silver-suited beings [in a pasture at 11:00 A.M.] somehow paralyzed [a] black cow and then levitated it out of the pasture and into [a] cone-shaped craft and disappeared."[22]

Another UFO researcher, John S. Carpenter, argues against the popular satanist-cult explanation for animal mutilations and in favor of the UFO theory. In discussing the association between UFOs and mutilations in southwest Missouri, he refers to

"…reports of odd 'silver-suited children.' One rancher and his son observed a glowing, four-foot 'child' in 'tin foil' on their property after several horses were mutilated. Recently a report surfaced from years ago during a wave of studies of four

---

21. Jerold R. Johnson, 1994, p. 18.
22. Howe, 1993A, pp. 27-40.

'children wrapped in aluminum' crossing the road in front of the witnesses' car."[23]

Crop Circles

Like animal mutilations, crop circles are a study unto themselves, largely beyond the scope of this book. There are some good sources, such as *The Crop Circle Enigma*, edited by Ralph Noyes,[24] but research and controversy develop rapidly in this field. These complex patterns swirled into fields of grain, especially in England, have been analyzed chemically and in other ways to determine to what degree humans are capable of creating (hoaxing) them. George Wingfield, an English researcher, is one who argues for the UFO connection, although he points out that UFO landing traces, typically burnt circles on the ground are not very similar to most crop circles. "And yet," he states, "UFOs have on occasions been seen in close proximity to crop circles either shortly before or after the appearance of the latter."[25]

Too Strange to Study?

The purpose of this chapter has been to introduce the range of strange phenomena associated with UFO reports. The next question is whether the strangeness should make us curious to investigate or make us dismiss the reports as absurd. Although many scientists disagree, David Barclay and Therese Marie Barclay, both British ufologists, put it this way:

> "An impartial eye can immediately see from the documentation that there is certainly something begging an explanation; either that or it must be assumed that millions of credible witnesses, world-wide, have taken leave of their senses."[26]

Many scientists (astronomers and physicists that I have interviewed, for example) have decided that the documentation is not worth looking at; they have higher priorities. Other scientists have looked at some of the data and take an active debunking position. Then, of course, there are the ufologists, participants in a "deviant science." How ufology became deviant is the story of the next chapter.

For now, at the risk of dropping my mask of objectivity so early in the game, let me say that I have never (to my conscious recollection)

---

23. Carpenter, 1992, pp. 20-21.
24. Noyes, 1991.
25. Wingfield, 1994, pp. 257-274.
26. Barclay and Barclay, 1993, p. 15.

had a definitive UFO experience. Of course, I have heard experiencers
relate their own stories at UFO conferences and in interviews that I
have conducted. However, it is far more significant to me that six people I know well, relatives, friends and colleagues, have told me about
their own fairly close encounters (not just some dubious, far-off nocturnal lights). I seriously doubt that any of these people are lying, and I
hardly consider them likely to hallucinate. If I had heard just one or two
of these accounts, I would still be curious enough to consider the subject worthy of study.

Chapter 2

Labeling Ufology a "Deviant" Science

Studying the History of UFO Studies

Should UFO studies be considered a deviant science? By one reckoning the answer seems to be no. In a 1977 survey of 1,356 members of the American Astronomical Society, Peter Sturrock[1] asked whether "the UFO problem deserves scientific study." Only 20% responded negatively, another 27% said "possibly," and over half were supportive (23% said "certainly" and 30% "probably"). There is reason to believe that a survey conducted today would find even greater support from astronomers as individuals, because the trend in Sturrock's survey was toward greater support from younger respondents. Among those aged 21-30, 32% said "certainly" and 33% said "probably," whereas in the over-60 group only 5% and 18% gave these positive responses.

And yet, ironically, professional astronomers are virtually absent from involvement in the largest ufology organization, MUFON (The Mutual UFO Network), although there have been some prominent astronomer-ufologists like J. Allen Hynek and Jacques Vallée. Why? Because everyone knows that there is virtually no explicit government funding for UFO studies, and because astronomy as a discipline does not recognize the subject or publish the work of ufologists in its academic journals. Very few ufology courses are taught in American colleges and universities, and rarely are they found in departments of physics or astronomy.

In other words, ufology lacks official, institutional support in academic organizations in spite of the attitudinal support for the idea among astronomers and other academics as individuals. Recently there have been private funds available from the Fund for UFO Research (FUFOR) and from the Bigelow Foundation, for example, but not publicly advertised governmental funds. Such was not always the case. In the late 1960s, the Ad Hoc Committee to Review Project *Bluebook*, con-

---

1. Sturrock, 1994A, pp. 1-45.

sisting of physical and social scientists, recommended that the Air Force establish contract research on UFOs at universities.[2] In 1966 the Air Force did contract with the University of Colorado for the Condon study on UFOs and funded it for a final total of over $500,000.[3]

How then did ufology officially become labeled "deviant" (read "unfundable")? The answer must come from the history of UFO studies. One wonders if studying the history of UFO studies is also taboo. Fortunately we have the classic work by David M. Jacobs that was his Ph.D. dissertation in History at the University of Wisconsin: *The UFO Controversy in America*, published in 1975.[4] As of this writing, Michael D. Swords, Ph.D. in the History of Science and Technology, and Professor of Natural Sciences at Western Michigan University, had just finished a sabbatical leave to work on a history of ufology covering the past twenty years.

Let it be clear that this chapter is not an attempt at historical research, but rather a sociological look at factors that contributed to a labeling of ufology as deviant. It relies upon the historical research of others, such as Jacobs, who have examined primary sources and analyzed the evidence carefully. As Jacobs[5] points out in his scathing review of a 1994 publication by the Smithsonian Institution Press entitled *Watch the Skies!* by Curtis Peebles, a B.A. in history with no graduate work in history, "History, like modern art, is something that untrained people think they can do. Debunkers and UFO proponents alike have been guilty of this practice in recent years. Curtis Peebles is the latest culprit."

U.S. Government Investigations

Jacobs, an historian, explains in *The UFO Controversy* how modern UFO studies began in 1947 with governmental, and in particular U.S. Air Force analysis of reports, although there had already been many sightings of "foo-fighters" (UFOs) by pilots in World War II. The Air Force sent all reports to the Air Technical Intelligence Center (ATIC) at Wright Patterson Air Force Base in Dayton, Ohio for the next 22 years, at least officially.

From 1947 to early 1949, this investigation was carried on under the name Project *Sign*, from early until late 1949 as Project *Grudge*, and from 1951 until 1969 as Project *Bluebook*. Throughout this period, vari-

---

2. Richard L. Thompson, 1993, p. 90.
3. Jacobs, 1975, p. 184.
4. See also Randles and Warrington, 1985.
5. Jacobs and Swords, 1994, pp. 7-10, 23.

ous explanations for UFO sightings were advanced both inside and outside the Air Force, including misinterpretations of natural phenomena, mass hysteria, Soviet secret weapons and extraterrestrial craft or space animals.

At the same time, public interest in and reporting of UFO sightings came to be considered a problem in public relations and in national security (to be discussed further below). Although both Project *Sign* and Project *Grudge* had ended with claims of insignificance for the alleged phenomenon, there was enough concern about the reports themselves for the CIA to convene a panel of scientists, the Robertson panel, to discuss the matter January 14-17, 1953. The panel's conclusions led the Air Force to tighten security on their UFO data and to emphasize that "an impartial scientific body had examined the data thoroughly and found no evidence of anything unusual in the atmosphere."[6]

From that point Project *Bluebook* had a reduced staff and was directed to cover up and deny rather than to investigate. Ufologist Walter N. Webb, recalling his visit to Wright Patterson AFB just after graduating from college in 1956, reveals his conversation with Captain George T. Gregory, head of Project *Bluebook* at the time, a man Jacobs refers to as "a zealous UFO debunker." Gregory gave the young Webb, nephew of a civilian intelligence analyst who worked for ATIC, his debunking routine which included a look at the "crackpot file." Apparently aggravated when Webb then expressed the opinion that UFOs deserved more serious investigation, Gregory, in an unguarded moment, said, "We have some sightings in the files that would make your eyes pop out!"[7]

Air Force pronouncements about UFO reports, supported by academic authority represented by the Robertson panel, contributed to the labeling of UFO studies as trivial, if not deviant, especially from 1953 to 1965. Calls for Congressional investigations on the part of NICAP (National Investigations Committee on Aerial Phenomena) and other private UFO organizations were opposed by the Air Force, of course, and the issue generated only "fleeting interest" until the wave of UFO sightings that began in 1965. The momentum of the 1965-1967 wave led to the Condon committee study and report,[8] 1966-1969, the definitive showdown in which academe helped government to define UFO reality and to assign authoritative labels for UFO studies.

6. Jacobs, 1975, pp. 84-86.
7. Webb, 1992, pp. 3-5.
8. Jacobs, 1975, p. 171.

The Condon Report

According to Jacobs, sightings in Texas and elsewhere in 1965 began to revive the UFO issue in the press, and there were stirrings of concern over this publicity again in the Air Force. Then the infamous swamp-gas incident occurred in March, 1966, over sightings in Dexter and Hillsdale, Michigan. J. Allen Hynek, the astronomer who would later be known as a founder of ufology, representing the Air Force at that time, stated at a press conference that one explanation for some reported lights could be spontaneous combustion of marsh gas. In the press this one element was blown up into the "swamp gas" debunking theory, and the public reaction to Hynek from witnesses and cartoonists was generally hostility and ridicule.[9]

In the wake of such controversy, Gerald Ford, House Republican minority leader at the time, called for an investigation, which was held in April, 1966, by the House Armed Services Committee. One of those testifying in open hearings was Hynek, who countered his debunker image by arguing for scientific study of UFOs. These hearings were the impetus to the Condon study. Although it was difficult to find a university willing to host such a controversial project, the Air Force announced later that year that the University of Colorado had accepted and that the prominent physicist Dr. Edward U. Condon would be the director.

There are many secondary sources that make reference to Condon's bias and prejudice regarding the UFO subject. Most have borrowed directly or indirectly from Jacobs' *The UFO Controversy*, which should be read thoroughly by anyone interested in the Condon study. Suffice it to say here that Condon made it clear that he was interested in exploring only two explanations for UFO reports: misidentified natural events and sociocultural phenomena. Perhaps Condon's clearest statement of bias is reported by Jacobs as part of a speech Condon gave to "the Corning Section of the American Chemical Society on January 25, 1967…. 'It is my inclination right now to recommend that the government get out of this business. My attitude right now is that there's nothing to it.'"[10]

In a personal interview, Dr. Robert M. Wood, Ph.D. in physics and an aeronautical engineer who worked for McDonnell Douglas from 1956 to 1993, told me about his experience with Condon and the study committee. Having been encouraged both by Hynek and by Dr. James E. McDonald (physicist and major authority on UFOs) to go to the Con-

---

9. Jacobs, 1975, pp. 177-179.
10. Jacobs, 1975, p. 188.

don committee, Wood asked and was allowed to meet with Condon and the whole staff for a couple of hours in 1968. After Wood had explained the work he had done at McDonnell Douglas studying the feasibility of a UFO-type propulsion system, Condon stated categorically that such a thing was impossible. When Wood asked Condon whether he would change his mind if he saw such an object land on the lawn, Condon replied in the negative.

After this meeting, Wood thought, "These guys are in trouble with Condon in charge." Therefore, he wrote ten suggestions to Condon about how to broaden the inquiry, and sent copies to the Condon staff members. Two days later, according to Wood, Condon called up James S. McDonnell (of McDonnell Douglas) and asked him to fire Wood. McDonnell then checked on Wood, got back to Condon, told him that the company supported Wood's UFO-propulsion project, and essentially told Condon to go to hell.

Of course, the Condon report that appeared in January 1969, is well known for having Condon's conclusion at the beginning of the lengthy document (1,485 pages in hard cover, 965 in paperback). Although 30 of 91 cases in the main UFO sections of the report were unexplained, Condon concluded that "nothing has come from the study of UFOs in the past 21 years that has added to scientific knowledge" and that further investigation could not be justified.[11] According to Michael Swords (in his commentary at the 1995 MUFON International UFO Symposium), detailed historical analysis reveals that twelve of sixteen members of the Condon study group judged UFO studies to be worthwhile, in contrast to Condon's authoritative statement.

On one level this is an amusing "Emperor's New Clothes" tale, arguing for the view that science is often a matter of social conformity and not just an objective procedure (see ch. 6). Most scientists who commented, and some of the press, supported Condon. Condon had sent a pre-release copy of the report to the National Academy of Sciences who praised it as "a creditable effort to apply objectively the relevant techniques of science to the solution of the UFO problem."[12] As long as the report conformed to the normal science view of UFOs, the scientific establishment was not about to question the emperor's logic or methodology.

To ufologists who have read the entire report the inconsistency between Condon's conclusions and the body of the report are obvious. Ronald D. Story, who has more recently moved into the debunker

---

11. Jacobs, 1975, pp. 212-216; Condon, 1969.
12. Jacobs, 1975, p. 212.

camp, but who called himself "a very cautious UFO 'proponent'" in 1981, said then that Condon's conclusion did not fit the rest of the report, that some of the best cases were ignored, and noted that Condon never participated in a single on-site investigation.[13] Thornton Page, astrophysicist working for the National Aeronautics and Space Administration, who had been on the CIA's Robertson panel in 1953, criticized the Condon report as "unscientific and inconsistent."[14]

Jacques Vallée states that in 1967 Condon told him in private conversations that "he thought a study of UFOs was a waste of time not because the problem didn't exist, but because it was outside the realm of science."[15] Condon, in the report, stated that teachers should discourage students who wanted to read about UFOs and should get them interested in serious science.[16] Ironically, Jacobs thinks that having someone with Condon's prestige assigned to the committee "helped legitimize the (UFO) subject and made it easier for scientists to discuss the matter without fearing as much ridicule as they had before 1966."[17] In particular, Jacobs mentions four scientists who became interested in ufology during this period: Dr. Frank Salisbury, plant scientist at Utah State University; Dr. Leo Sprinkle, psychologist at University of Wyoming (who was actually involved before 1966; see his biography in Appendix); nuclear physicist Stanton Friedman at Westinghouse Astronuclear Laboratories; and Jacques Vallée, astronomer and computer expert at Northwestern University.

The Effects of Delegitimation

Although the Condon report was not the first statement by academe or government to declare UFO studies scientifically worthless, it was the most significant development in the labeling of ufology as a deviant science. It resulted in the official ending of Project *Bluebook* by the Air Force in 1969 and provided an authoritative model that any university or granting agency could use in rejecting scholarly proposals for UFO teaching or research.

Of course, ufology did not come to a screeching halt. As noted above, the Condon report did play a role in arousing the curiosity of professionals who became ufologists. J. Allen Hynek emerged as an advocate of more sophisticated study of UFOs, especially with the publication of his book *The UFO Experience: A Scientific Inquiry* in 1972.[18] And

13. Story, 1981, pp. 21, 69-70.
14. Story, 1981, p. 9.
15. Vallée, 1992C, pp. 56-67.
16. Condon, 1969, pp. 6-7.
17. Jacobs, 1975, p. 190.

Peter A. Sturrock, astronomer at Stanford University, worked with other scientists to establish the Society for Scientific Exploration with its *Journal of Scientific Exploration* after having an article he wrote on the Condon report turned down by six journals for six different reasons.[19]

However, Jacobs points out that the Condon report, along with the closing of Project *Bluebook* and the decline in UFO sightings after 1968, "definitely affected public interest in the subject."[20] Some popular UFO publications were discontinued, and UFO organizations lost membership. NICAP (National Investigations Committee on Aerial Phenomena) declined from 12,000 in 1967 to 4,000 in 1971. APRO (Aerial Phenomena Research Organization) declined from 4,000 members in 1967 to 2,000 in 1971. More recent efforts of UFO researchers and organizations to develop scientific standards and to attain legitimacy in academe are discussed in Chapter 10.

Although the situation was a mixed bag, it is clear that such a definitive rejection of ufology by a prestigious academic inquiry had a chilling effect. One consequence of the pseudoscience label is that there is virtually no funded and accepted academic community that can generate, publish, and debate the validity of research (or "knowledge").

If I get an article published in a refereed sociology journal, my sociology colleagues will assume, without reading it, that it is a useful contribution, as will the Provost of Gettysburg College and the members of the Faculty Personnel Committee. If I get an article published in a ufology journal, many people will suspect, without reading it, that it is nonsense.

Moreover, people who believe that UFO reports must be either misidentifications, hoaxes or hallucinations will probably reject ufology articles from the outset. Without an authoritative community of scholars to validate such claims, many people will have to have their own UFO experiences to be convinced that UFOs are "real." On the other hand, even if an article in a sociology journal were a total fabrication, based on a survey that was never taken, it would probably be accepted as legitimate.

Indeed, there have been many famous scholarly publications that turned out to be frauds, as in the case of Dr. Cyril Burt's twin studies that were never actually conducted, but were the basis of "knowledge" about I.Q. for many years. Burt even published other fraudulent articles under a pseudonym that apparently supported his findings, and he was knighted for his work.

---

18. Hynek, 1972.
19. Sturrock, 1994B.
20. Jacobs, 1975, p. 227.

More Recent Revelations on
U.S. Government Involvement

It seems peculiar that the UFO community of researchers, writers and conference speakers devotes so much attention to what the government may be hiding about UFOs. This is not the case with other unexplained or paranormal subjects. Can you imagine an *Omni* magazine series on "The Great Ghost Cover-Up," or a tabloid headline, "What the Government Knows about Astrology," to parallel what Stanton Friedman calls the Cosmic Watergate, the alleged government cover-up about UFOs?

Of course, the reason for concern about the government and UFOs is that certain elements in the U.S. government, including the Air Force, the CIA, etc., played a major role in de-legitimizing ufology as an academic subject. And in the Condon study especially the government co-opted authoritative members of academe to help label UFO studies as scientifically worthless and unfundable. Michael Swords has found clear evidence, including a signed letter from the Air Force, showing pressure put upon Condon by the Air Force to conclude that UFOs were not worth studying.

But if in fact there have been elements in the government that have taken UFOs seriously and have collected important data, perhaps even physical remains, this means that the major UFO-studies organization lies within the government itself. Certainly the "black-budget" funding, the expertise and the technical facilities are available, along with the security procedures, to keep it a secret. If this were the case, would "national security" be reason enough to have deceived the public and to have impeded scientific inquiry in the academic community?

Because of the difficulty in penetrating government security on this matter, there is a forest of rumor and conspiracy claims in the UFO community about crashed saucers, secret documents from secret study groups, underground bases for back-engineering extraterrestrial craft, alliances between aliens and the government, about which ufologists are working for the CIA, and about CIA spies at UFO conventions. It is all too bewildering and beyond the scope of this book. However, I have seen and heard enough to think that at least some of it must be true; although I'm not sure which parts! For example, I spoke with one very suspicious character at a UFO conference who seemed to have several humorous earmarks of being a low-level CIA agent, not that I could prove it. And considering the huge U.S. intelligence budget, not just the CIA's, it would not surprise me to find that several people are paid to attend conferences and maybe even to be ufologists and spread disinformation. Several well-informed ufologists have claimed as much.

Those who are interested in the cover-up issue should read, for example, books by Timothy Good on worldwide cover-up;[21] Kevin Randle and Donald Schmitt[22] on the alleged retrieval of a crashed saucer and alien bodies by the Air Force near Roswell, New Mexico, in July 1947; Stanton Friedman;[23] and the *Omni* magazine cover-up series.[24] For the purposes of this book it is not important to track down the truth on all these matters, but it is important to indicate that there is evidence that important elements in the government *did* consider UFOs worthy of study and in fact continued to study them and gathered important evidence in spite of the public labeling of ufology as a worthless scientific endeavor.

Bruce Maccabee, a Ph.D. in optical physics and chairman of the Fund for UFO Research, points out that information has been released in more recent years that was unavailable to David M. Jacobs when he wrote his classic history of *The UFO Controversy in America* in 1973.[25] In 1975, records of Projects *Sign, Grudge* and *Bluebook* were released. Also, since then people like Stanton Friedman (the persistent dean of such efforts) have invoked the Freedom of Information and Privacy Act (FOIA) to get documents from the FBI, CIA and other agencies.

Stanton Friedman, who has given over 600 college and university lectures on UFOs, tells amusing stories of his FOIA efforts, showing slides of document pages with the majority of the lines blackened out, indicating how difficult it is to get around the claim of "national security." Even such pages with little evidence left besides the word UFO are themselves a kind of evidence about the seriousness of the subject to the government.

One Top Secret document Maccabee refers to as evidence of government involvement is the Smith memorandum dated November 21, 1950. Wilbert B. Smith, senior radio engineer who worked with the Canadian government, learned the following from the Canadian Embassy staff in Washington: "Flying saucers are the most highly classified subject in the U.S. government; they exist; a special project under Vannevar Bush is studying them, and the subject is considered of tremendous importance."[26] Maccabee goes on to relate how Stanton Friedman lo-

21. Good, 1988.
22. Randle and Schmitt, 1991 and 1994.
23. e.g., Friedman and Berliner, 1992.
24. Stacy, 1994.
25. Maccabee, 1991C.
26. Maccabee, 1991C, p. 5.

cated Robert Sarbacher, the source of Smith's information, several
years after the Canadian government released the document in 1979.

Dr. Sarbacher, who evidently had told what he knew to Dr. Bren-
ner, Smith's contact at the embassy, told Maccabee in a 1985 interview
that "he was invited to travel to Wright-Patterson Air Force Base to
view the remains of a crashed UFO, but was unable to go at the time.
Several of his acquaintances…did go and…told him…that 'certain materials reported to have come from flying saucer crashes were extremely light and tough…. The "people" who operated these
things…seemed to be like insects. Maybe they were robots.'"[27]

Another strategy for uncovering what the U.S. government might
know about UFOs is to ask the Russians, since the Soviets had conducted espionage on the U.S. more effectively than American ufologists
ever could. UFO journalist George Knapp, on a trip to Russia in 1993,
was told by Colonel Boris Sokolov, who was put in charge of collecting
UFO reports for the Soviet military in 1978, that "the U.S. military had
constructed 30 tracking stations around the world for the express purpose of monitoring UFO activity."[28]

Knapp was also shown documents from the ongoing Russian Min-
istry of Defense UFO study named "Thread 3." One section "contains a
fairly detailed history of the U.S. government efforts to maintain a UFO
cover-up. It lists several examples…(with) titles and dates of official or-
ders concerning UFO secrecy. It notes that U.S. intelligence agencies
went to great lengths to find out what Russian agencies might know
about UFOs."[29]

While such reports are suggestive, it is, of course, difficult to assess
the overall picture without more complete evidence from U.S. government files. In 1994 Representative Steve Schiff from New Mexico managed to get Congress to order a GAO investigation into the alleged
cover-up of the 1947 Roswell saucer crash.[30] It was not surprising that
the U.S. Air Force, after looking into the matter, reported on September
8, 1994, that the debris that had been recovered on Mac Brazel's ranch
in 1947 came from a top-secret military balloon, not from a weather balloon as the Air Force had claimed in 1947, and not, of course, from a
"flying disc" as Lt. Walter Haut had first announced on July 8, 1947.[31]
Most ufologists were dubious to say the least.

---

27. Maccabee, 1991C, p. 5.
28. Knapp, 1994, pp. 276-306.
29. Knapp, 1994, pp. 292, 294.
30. Whiting, 1994, pp. 11-13.
31. Rodeghier and Chesney, 1994.

Why the U.S. Governmental/Military Concern over UFOs?

Along with questions about *what* the government might be covering up, there are also questions about *why* that are debated at every UFO conference and probably in every local UFO study group. It is all part of the rumor and lore of ufology.

Part of the answer has been obvious since World War II when the military was concerned about mysterious "foo-fighters" that appeared near U.S. military planes in flight. The Air Force, as noted earlier, considered the possibility that UFOs were Soviet secret weapons, or even U.S. Navy planes they hadn't heard about. And, of course, high-technology extraterrestrial craft could be a threat to national security as well. More recently the rumors about secret government projects to back-engineer alien craft rest on the idea that the possession of alien technology by the U.S. could provide a military advantage, and possession of this technology could benefit an earthly enemy.

But what sense would there be in secrecy about such projects since the end of the Cold War? As Stanton Friedman points out,[32] "black budgets" in the government provide huge amounts of money for secret military projects, and these constitute a great vested interest on the part of the organizations and individuals that are funded to do this work. Others have noted that anyone or any agency involved in previous secret projects or cover-ups could be worried about revealing previous lies, especially if illegal activities were involved (thus the comparison to Watergate in "Cosmic Watergate").

Another sociological, rather than logical, reason for secrecy lies in the incredibly complex governmental bureaucracy, especially when it comes to secret projects. Maccabee discusses the way in which knowledge of saucer remains may have been kept from people who were involved in collecting evidence from UFO sightings.[33] "Need-to-know" regulations keep all but a few, if any, people from knowing the structure of the entire operation. In a sense, no one may be in charge, and certainly a number of people in high places may know nothing at all. If this sounds hard to believe, just recall the 1970s Congressional investigations into the CIA that revealed Nixon's ignorance of the CIA spying on him while he was in the Oval Office, or President Reagan being deceived about happenings in Mexico by the CIA.

One "benevolent" reason for secrecy about UFOs that has often been mentioned is the need to prevent panic. A model for such panic

---

32. *Larry King Live*, 1994.
33. Maccabee, 1991C, pp. 7-8.

has been suggested in the 1938 "War of the Worlds" radio broadcast that was the subject of the social-psychological study by Hadley Cantril.[34] In a 1988 national survey of 475 psychologists and psychiatrists, Raymond W. Boeche found that 47% agreed or strongly agreed that if a government announcement were made of contact with ETs, "Mass panic may occur."[35] Even worse, 65% thought that "Financial chaos (would) result due to the culture shock." And 53% expected religious beliefs to be shattered. Boeche, an artist, was not especially alarmed by the findings and felt personally that panic would not occur.

Robert L. Hall, a Ph.D. in sociology and an expert in social psychology, argues that collective panic is very rare and would be very unlikely in the event of ET contact.[36] However, exaggerated journalistic accounts of panics and general folklore about panic seem to lead to governmental policy of secrecy to prevent foolish public reactions. Hall argues that a lack of previous authoritative information about UFOs would "almost surely...*increase* the risk of 'panicky' public reactions if a dramatic contact occurs."[37]

In 1953 the CIA's Robertson panel thought that public panic or mass hysteria over UFOs might confuse military intelligence and make them "misidentify or ignore 'actual enemy artifacts.'"[38] In other words, the public should not receive information about UFOs because it would encourage them to report more of them. Then the military would be so used to UFO reports that they would think an enemy attack was actually UFOs.

More recently, just the opposite argument has been made, namely that a lack of awareness of UFOs on the part of the military might make them misidentify a UFO as an enemy attack, leading to a nuclear exchange. Robert O. Dean claims that this nearly happened in Europe in 1961.[39] Bryan Gresh reports that an incident with a UFO near an ICBM base in the Ukraine, in which the missiles were somehow enabled, influenced the Soviets to argue for exchanging UFO information with the West to avoid accidental attack.[40] Of course, the argument in these cases was that the military should share UFO information with other countries, not with the public.

---

34. Cantril, 1966.
35. Boeche, 1988, pp. 73-85.
36. Robert L. Hall, Johnson and Rodeghier, 1990, pp. 61-71.
37. Hall, 1990, p. 70.
38. Jacobs, 1975, pp. 82-83.
39. Dean, 1994, pp. 91-107.
40. Gresh, 1993, pp. 3-7.

Governmental/Military Responses Outside the U.S.

Although the governments of other countries have generally been quiet about the UFO question, they have not always been as secretive as the U.S. government. As mentioned above, Knapp and Gresh have reported on the importance of UFO investigations in the Soviet Union and in Russia today. Knapp states that the Russian Academy of Sciences has been heavily involved with UFO studies, and that Russian scientists and generals have recently been opening up on the subject.[41]

Probably Belgium has been more officially open about UFOs than any other country. Major General Wilfried De Brouwer, Chief of Operations of the Belgian Air Force, cooperated with civilian UFO groups and with the police in providing radar and other data during the 1989-1991 wave of triangular UFOs, as J. Antonio Huneeus points out.[42]

Huneeus also finds the French rather open with an established system of report-collecting by the national police (Gendarmerie). Coordinated analysis is then done by the agency called SEPRA (Service of Expertise of Atmospheric Reentry Phenomena).

In Spain the Air Force gradually began to declassify some UFO documents in 1992 after a long process of negotiations that began in 1978. Spanish ufologist Vincente-Juan Ballester Olmos was largely responsible for this achievement.[43]

Japan's military has been very limited since World War II, and the JSDF (Japan Self-Defense Forces) is guided by the U.S. Pentagon and presumably, thinks Huneeus, follows "the official American line" regarding UFOs.[44] Interestingly, however, there is one government-funded UFO Museum and Archives in Hakui, Japan, perhaps founded in part through the efforts of former Prime Minister Toshiki Kaifu who stepped down in 1991.

Hoang-Yung Chiang, a Ph.D. in biotechnology from Taiwan, reports that the Taiwan government officially recognized ufology as a science in 1993, ten years after the founding of the Taiwan UFO Science Association.[45] In the People's Republic of China, the China UFO Research Organization was founded in 1988 and had about 4,000 members in 1993. Chiang does not mention any formal cooperation with or recognition of this organization by the PRC government.

In Australia there has been little involvement of professionals in ufology, compared to the United States, due to the conservatism of the

---

41. Knapp, 1994, pp. 296, 304.
42. Huneeus, 1992.
43. Ballester Olmos, 1993.
44. Huneeus, 1992, pp. 183-185.
45. Chiang, 1993, pp. 42-58.

academic community (also true in the United Kingdom), and because there were very few UFO sightings there in the 1980s.[46] And yet, unlike the alleged cover-up situation in the U.S., Australian ufologists have been given open access to Royal Australian Air Force UFO files.

Admittedly, international comparisons of government-ufology relations are a bit sketchy, but it does appear that UFO secrecy is largely a Cold War phenomenon. In the aftermath of the Cold War, Russia seems to be relaxing security about UFOs, although it has also experienced the subdivision of the Soviet state. Whether the U.S. government will reveal anything significant as time goes by remains to be seen.

---

46. Basterfield and others, 1990.

Chapter 3

Mass Media and UFOs

In the previous chapter we considered the history of government involvement in the defining of UFO studies as deviant, and the participation of academics like Dr. Condon in legitimizing this definition. In this chapter we shall see to what extent mass media of communications have contributed to this process.

In one sense it seems ironic to credit mass media with labeling a discipline as pseudoscientific, because the usual perception is that popular media are superficial and credulous in dealing with the paranormal. Wouldn't this tend to legitimate UFOs in the popular mind? Perhaps, but the issue here is the effect of mass media on academics who might consider studying UFOs. In Chapter 4 we shall see that academics outside of ufology tend to get a distorted view of ufology through mass media, and ufologists are most likely to get in trouble with their academic institutions when their work is distorted in popular media.

In other words, this chapter addresses the questions of how accurate media portrayals of UFO reports and UFO studies have been, how seriously or frivolously UFO studies have been treated, and how valid or respectable they have been made to appear. There is a tendency to think too stereotypically about mass media, when in fact there has been quite a variety of types of treatment.

Kenneth Arnold and the Media

One early and important case of media coverage was the reaction to Kenneth Arnold's sighting on June 24, 1947. Even in this one case there was a variety of treatments, and the definition of the situation changed over time. At first Arnold's report of nine crescent-shaped objects flying over Washington State was taken seriously in the press "because Arnold was such a reputable citizen (pilot, businessman, deputy sheriff)."[1] This contrasts with the current state of newspaper reporting in which UFO sightings are typically ignored or at best reported only in local or regional newspapers.

However, as the Arnold report spread around the world, it was attached to the term "flying saucer," based on Arnold's statement that they moved like "a saucer skipping over water," not that they were shaped that way.[2] As Jacobs points out,[3] the very term "flying saucer" sounds ludicrous, since saucers don't fly about by their own power, at least not according to the collective wisdom of the 1940s. This helps to attach a deviant label to "saucer" sightings and to invite ridicule of any UFO experiencer, and, of course, of any academic who would dare to take the subject seriously enough to investigate it.

According to Jacobs,[4] UFO sightings in 1947 were reported fairly objectively at first, but especially as some of the reports became increasingly strange, and since there was no clear explanation for UFOs, newspapers started to label witnesses as "crackpots" or "morons.".Kenneth Arnold himself began to be ridiculed to the point that he stated, "If I saw a ten-story building flying through the air I would never say a word about it."[5]

Media Models before Arnold

Although the Arnold sighting was the significant beginning of modern UFO cases covered in mass media, there were, of course, earlier sightings of unexplained aerial phenomena and nonfictional and fictional stories about them. For example, Raymond A. Palmer's *Amazing Stories*, a science fiction pulp magazine, published sensational stories in 1945 about underground beings called Deros who controlled humans with ray guns.[6] Many readers wrote letters to *Amazing Stories* supplementing and supporting these stories with their own claims of experiences with aliens and unidentified craft. *Fate* magazine, also initially a Palmer product, began carrying flying-saucer reports in 1948, the year after Arnold's sighting. Nowadays *Fate* is a mixture of responsible articles and other more dubious materials, including sensational advertising.

Whether such popular fiction created or influenced the experiences of UFO observers from Arnold on is an interesting question. There were already members of the Fortean Society for the study of anomalies

1. Jacobs, 1975, pp. 31-32.
2. Strentz, 1970, p. 2.
3. Jacobs, 1975, p. 32.
4. Jacobs, 1975, pp. 32-33.
5. Jacobs, 1975, p. 33.
6. Keel, 1989.

who thought that unidentified aerial sightings throughout history were evidence of extraterrestrial contact. And spiritualists had already been channeling outer-space entities before Arnold's sighting.[7]

Probably there has been an interaction between sightings and fiction in both directions rather than a simplistic creation of a flying saucer culture by popular media. Even if some UFO reports have been influenced by expectations from literature and folklore, this does not mean that *all* UFO experiencers are under this influence to the point that it distorts their observations. In fact, many investigators have found that witnesses are frequently unaware that what they have experienced is typical of what has happened to others.

Be that as it may, the important point of this book is that popular media have often created the impression that the entire subject of flying saucers or UFOs is "flaky." This view is supported not only by ignoring the subject or by condemning it, but also by treating the subject in a sensationalistic manner.

Popular Science: From Education to Sensational Entertainment

In an article about media treatment of UFOs, Don Berliner complains that "the American press has failed to treat the subject with the seriousness that the data and the reputations of the witnesses would demand if the subject were something other than UFOs," and notes that serious journalists avoid the topic in part because much of what does appear involves "the most preposterous claims (with) no concern for their validity."[8] This means that not only do mass media in general affect the legitimacy of ufology in other institutions like academe, but those parts of mass media that treat UFOs sensationally tend to delegitimize the subject for more respectable journalists.

All of this has its roots in the development of popular science. In the nineteenth century, scientific popularization was part of a crusade by academic scientists to wipe out "superstition" and "magical thinking" and to replace it with "skepticism and naturalism."[9] This was a very moralistic perspective, a kind of "religion of science," science with a mission to liberate the unenlightened from their ignorant past and from pseudoscience of the present. Of course, this was also a very elitist perspective, denying the validity of folk wisdom and of knowledge generated by researchers unrecognized by the academic establishment.

7. Keel, 1989, p. 142.
8. Berliner, 1992, pp. 16-18.
9. Burnham, 1987, pp. 6-8, 21-27.

However, by the end of the nineteenth century and increasingly in twentieth century America, popular science lost much of this enlightenment emphasis and began to be driven by a consumer culture, especially in newspapers and other media supported by advertising.[10] Yellow journalism in turn-of-the century newspapers included "Gee Whiz!" science with amazing, oversimplified stories and "facts." Popular science as religion became popular science as entertainment. The most notorious genre of popular "science" today is the supermarket tabloid.

Tabloids

Tabloid stories on UFOs are hilarious, except when one considers the damage they do to serious inquiry. If there were any truth in tabloid stories, would it be recognized in the middle of ludicrous composite pictures of President Clinton with B-movie-type aliens, or lists of U.S. Senators who are ETs?

Ronald D. Story agreed to minor editing of his book *UFOs and the Limits of Science*[11] when it was to be serialized in the *Weekly World News* in 1981. However, he was outraged when he discovered that not a single sentence he had written, except some quotes of other authors, was left intact, and that the work had been "rewritten to make the incidents seem more dramatic and mystifying."[12] Then in 1982, another tabloid, the *Globe*, quoted Story substantially. Although he had talked to a *Globe* reporter about a year before that, Story said that the quotations were a total fabrication and much more pro-UFO than anything he had said.[13]

Fabrication and distorted reworking of material are symptoms of the principle of popular science as entertainment taken to the sensationalized extreme. I have had my own experience with the same phenomenon. In 1982 the *National Enquirer* contacted me about doing a story on my book *Chinese Ghosts and ESP: A Study of Paranormal Beliefs and Experiences*.[14] At first I refused to be interviewed because I had heard horror stories about tabloid treatments of psychic topics. One parapsychologist had told me that he had considered a class action suit against a tabloid for damage to the careers and reputations of misquoted parapsychologists.

However, it occurred to me that having my own tabloid experience might be a wonderful case study to present to my sociology class in

10. Burnham, 1987, pp. 7-8.
11. Story, 1981.
12. Frazier, 1982, pp. 7-8.
13. Frazier, 1982.
14. Emmons, 1982.

popular culture. The reporter even agreed to read the text of his article to me over the phone before publication. When he did so, it didn't sound bad, but when it came out it received a sensationalized headline on the front page, "Startling New Evidence That Ghosts Really Exist!" Also the entire section on the methodology of the study had been edited out, and there were quotation marks around things I hadn't said, and exclamation marks that I couldn't hear on the phone. In essence, it was a beautiful example of how to sensationalize without even fabricating (except for the quotation marks), and using only omission and emphasis for effect.

Surprisingly the *National Enquirer*, when its format emphasized the paranormal rather than celebrities, was one of the more "scholarly" of the tabloids, at least in regard to UFOs. James A. Harder, a pioneering ufologist with a Ph.D. in fluid mechanics from the University of California, and a retired engineering professor from UC Berkeley, reports that he, Leo Sprinkle, Frank B. Salisbury and Robert Creegan, all from APRO (Aerial Phenomena Research Organization), and J. Allen Hynek himself formed the UFO consulting board for the *National Enquirer* in 1972.[15]

The publication established a reward of $50,000 for "the first person who can prove that a UFO came from outer space and is not a natural phenomenon." Not only did this statement contain the assumption that UFOs must be extraterrestrial and nonnatural, but it seemed so difficult to prove that another award of $5,000 was added for best evidence each year. In 1975, the editors of the *National Enquirer* were uncertain enough about the validity of the Travis Walton case (in which Walton was knocked down by a beam from a UFO in an Arizona forest and disappeared for five days) that they decided not to publish it, although later the consulting board decided to award Walton and five other witnesses in the case the $5,000 for 1975.[16] Three MUFON consultants were added to the board in 1978, but it was eliminated in 1979. Certainly this is an atypical chapter in the tabloid UFO story, but it also shows that mass media are not as uniform as one might think in spite of certain general patterns.

Films

Films are less directly relevant to ufology in the sense that Hollywood does not include the work of academic ufologists in its fictional

---

15. Harder, 1994.
16. Harder, 1994, p. 230.

portrayals. An exception of sorts to this statement can be found in *Close Encounters of the Third Kind*, the title of which is a concept from J. Allen Hynek's typology of sightings. Hynek himself appeared briefly in a cameo shot in the film, and the character of a French scientist was based on another ufologist Jacques Vallée.[17] When ufologists get themselves in trouble through media, it is typically due to popularizations or distortions of their work in the press, especially in tabloids, or in superficial TV coverage.

Nevertheless, fictional films are an important aspect of the pop culture of UFOs and aliens. In this sense they sometimes contribute to the definition of UFOs as a bizarre subject unworthy of serious study. As Forrest points out,[18] cinema aliens have tended to reflect the times. In the 1950s they paralleled a concern over the "red menace" as in *Invaders from Mars, War of the Worlds, The Thing, The Day the Earth Stood Still* and *Invasion of the Body Snatchers*.

This scare genre continued into the 1960s with *Atomic Submarine* and *Cape Canaveral Monster*.[19] However, films in this period also began to take on a greater complexity and variety of themes of good and evil contact. Some included psychic powers, like *Village of the Damned*, alien plants, as in *Day of the Triffids*, and long-term alien involvement in human evolution, as in *Five Million Years to Earth* and, of course, *2001, A Space Odyssey*.

Probably Stanley Kubrick's *2001*, released in 1968, was the most significant presentation of a more benevolent extraterrestrial influence on humans, although the message is subtle and mysterious. Then, of course, *Close Encounters of the Third Kind* (1977) and *ET* (1983) gave aliens a lovable image more consistent with New Age millennial expectations and with the view of alien contact as transformative for the human spirit and for the future of the planet. I suspect that all three of these quality productions are also more conducive to a more tolerant academic attitude toward ufology than are any of the absurd B movies about alien monsters.

In one other UFO film genre, famous close encounter or abduction cases have been dramatized. For example, the Betty and Barney Hill case that occurred in 1961, and became the first highly publicized abduction case in the book *The Interrupted Journey* by John G. Fuller in 1966,[20] was the basis for the film *The UFO Incident* (1975).

17. Keith Thompson, 1991, p. 99.
18. Forrest, 1987.
19. Forrest, 1987, p. 35.
20. Fuller, 1966.

Another such film was *Fire in the Sky* (1993) based on the 1975 Travis Walton case mentioned above. According to Travis Walton, although most of this film was fairly accurate, the scene portraying Walton's recalled experience inside a UFO was a total fabrication.[21] According to Tracy Torme of Cheyenne 7 Productions who worked on the film, *Fire* was in the early stages of pre-production when the CBS mini-series *Intruders* first aired. Paramount was alarmed at the similarities between classic abduction experiences and the beings Travis reported seeing. "They insisted that we fictionalize the alien sequences..." which they did in part in "a compromise."[22] Whatever the artistic or financial motivations involved, many ufologists were upset that a film generally construed as factual would be distorted by the bizarre cyberpunkish onboard scene.

The 1996 box-office hit *Independence Day* revived the invasion theme of the 1950s, this time with dazzling special effects, and the 1997 reissue of *Star Wars, The Return of the Jedi*, and *The Empire Strikes Back* promised to stimulate cosmic consciousness even more against a backdrop of the Hale-Bopp comet and the Heaven's Gate UFO cult suicide.

TV Treatments

Because popular media are primarily tools for making money through entertainment, scientific debunking of UFO claims is seldom treated on TV. One exception was the BBC NOVA production of *The Case of UFOs* first aired October 12, 1982. Debunkers James Oberg and Philip J. Klass were featured prominently on the show. Predictably *The Skeptical Inquirer* called it "a laudable treatment" in which "UFO claims (were considered) in a hard-nosed, scientific, investigative manner while at the same time avoiding personal criticism of those who may have honestly reported sightings they didn't understand."[23] To the credit of CSICOP (Committee for the Scientific Investigation of Claims of the Paranormal, the debunking organization that publishes *SI*), they printed a review of the same program in the next issue in which Ronald D. Story, erstwhile cautious UFO proponent heading toward debunker, criticized NOVA for editing out their entire long interview with J. Allen Hynek. He also said, "Despite my own inclination toward skepticism in UFO matters, I would like to have seen more of a forum, with representatives on both pro and con sides having their own say."[24]

---

21. Walton and Rogers, 1993.
22. Torme, 1993.
23. Frazier, 1982-83.
24. Story, 1983.

Fourteen years later NOVA aired another UFO program entitled *Kidnapped by UFOs?* (February 27, 1996). Although the appearances of CSICOP members Carl Sagan, Elizabeth Loftus and Robert A. Baker were "balanced" by the inclusion of UFO researchers Budd Hopkins and John Mack, it was clear to anyone familiar with UFO research on abductions (or to me at least) that the program's central argument rested upon a rather superficial treatment of the hypnosis issue in abduction research. UFO researchers are well aware of the issue of possible "false memories" under hypnosis, but many abduction accounts are collected without hypnosis, and many researchers have ways of testing for "confabulation" under hypnosis (see Chapter 9), none of which was mentioned in the program. Nor were there any examples given of physical-evidence correlates of abduction (body marks, implants, etc.) or of multiple-witness testimony.

What amazed me the most about the program was the inclusion of an apparently weak abduction case investigated by Budd Hopkins. Very little evidence was presented, and it appeared that Hopkins was grasping at straws. Certainly, I thought, they could have included some of his more evidential cases. In the March issue of the *MUFON UFO Journal* Budd Hopkins counterattacked, pointing out, among many other things, that the couple involved had testified on camera to a series of vivid memories recalled *without* hypnosis, none of which testimony was included in the program.[25] In response to the program narrator's obviously derisive comment that Budd Hopkins considered the case to represent "compelling evidence," Hopkins stated in the MUFON article, "As *Nova* well knows, no one on Earth would ever describe [what little was shown on the program] as 'compelling evidence'—unless their goal was a conscious attempt to make the individual look like a fool."[26] The program also contained a segment about the allegations against John Mack's abduction research from Donna Bassett (see page 39 in this chapter), but there was no mention of the creation of comparative data files from other researchers, only an apparent attack on Hopkins and Mack.

In his *Skeptics UFO Newsletter*, Philip J. Klass, the most active UFO debunker, countered Hopkins' attack on *Nova* as well as objections made by John Mack.[27] Klass pointed out that no alleged abductees were ridiculed, although the views of Hopkins and Mack were questioned. He also stated that Hopkins was in error about *Nova* falsely reporting an increase in UFO sightings after the release of the film *Close*

25. Hopkins, 1996A.
26. Hopkins, 1996A, p. 18.
27. Klass, 1996.

Encounters of the Third Kind. Points made by *Nova* regarding possible influences on subjects by Hopkins were reiterated in the Klass newsletter, as well as suggestions that John Mack was duped by Donna Bassett. Some or all of these arguments may be valid. However, Klass did not discuss Hopkins' central complaint that certain important types of evidence were not considered or that important testimony in the featured case was excluded. The interested reader may refer to the Maarch/April edition of *Contact Forum* for a comprehensive, in-depth analysis of the integrity of the PBS special, with commentary by both John Mack[28] and Budd Hopkins[29].

Most TV treatments of UFOs, however, whether documentaries or docu-dramas, suggest that they are real or at least worthy of study. Problems, from the point of view of ufologists, nevertheless arise from lack of knowledge and from the need to dramatize for entertainment purposes. Budd Hopkins served as consultant to the CBS mini-series *Intruders*, based loosely on his book with the same title,[30] in hopes of ameliorating these difficulties. When the program aired May 17 and 19, 1992, it contained minor distortions for dramatic effect, but Hopkins said that if he were a teacher, he would give it a "B+."[31]

One of the better documentaries in its representation of UFO cases has been *Unsolved Mysteries*. According to an editor at Wild Flower Press, publishers of Raymond E. Fowler's book *The Allagash Abductions*,[32] this abduction experience of four men in northern Maine in 1976 was handled in excellent fashion and portrayed "to the letter" in the program aired September 18, 1994.

Unsolved Mysteries has not gone without criticism however. Patrick Ferryn, an investigator of the mainly triangular UFO sightings in Belgium in 1989, gave a generally good review of their treatment of this case, but he noted one "big error": a portrayal of an object collapsing into a ball. This was apparently done in the interest of special effects, but was incorrect according to the script provided.[33]

Another episode was criticized more severely, one on the Bentwaters/Rendlesham Forest case of December 1980, in England that involved UFO sightings on U.S./U.K. air bases. This case was analyzed by prominent British ufologist Jenny Randles in the book *Sky Crash*.[34] However, much of the criticism of the *Unsolved Mysteries* treatment

---

28. Mack, 1996.
29. Hopkins, 1996B.
30. Hopkins, 1987.
31. Early, 1992.
32. Fowler, 1993.
33. Ferryn, 1992.
34. Randles and others, 1984.

(September 18, 1992) seems to be based on a disagreement among witnesses,[35] some of whom complained that their perspectives were not
adequately covered.

In one overview of TV documentaries on UFOs, Sherie Stark finds
a tendency toward "less-than-responsible" coverage based upon what
Howard Rosenberg, TV critic for the *L.A. Times*, calls a blurring of "the
line separating documentaries and entertainment."[36] This is reminiscent of the trend toward popular science as sensationalized entertainment referred to earlier in this chapter. She also paraphrases Rosenberg
stating that "The short attention span encouraged by successful shows
like *60 Minutes* and *20/20* has spawned the trend toward mini-
docs...making less and less room for really serious long-form documentaries."[37] This frustrating fact has probably not escaped the notice
of anyone who has been interviewed for TV or radio on any academic
subject, when the reporter is looking for good "sound bytes" (brief, interesting comments).

Robert Guenette, producer of documentaries for CBS, PBS and
HBO, admitted to Stark, "I don't think of myself as a journalist or a reporter, but as a filmmaker, and an entertainer.... I don't try to misin-
form, but I don't live by the rules of journalism."[38] One producer of
UFO documentaries related to me that it has been very difficult to get
TV networks to accept standards of truth because of the driving purpose to entertain.

Linda Moulton Howe, multiple Emmy Award winner for educa-
tional documentaries, and producer of the original *Sightings* special on
the Fox network in 1991, among many other things, states that "One of
the current challenges for the media in general is to handle this material
with any comprehension of its complexity and still get it onto radio/TV
news in any coherent way."[39] Howe is an example of a journalist with
the expertise and experience to do a highly competent job with topics
like animal mutilations and crop circles, but few producers of UFO programs have either the background or the time to do such research for a
project.

Although the popular fictional *X-Files* series, which often treats the
UFO phenomenon, cannot be critiqued in the same way as the nonfictional documentaries, at least it can be said to demonstrate significant
knowledge of themes in UFO reports. This cannot be claimed for a

---

35. Speiser, 1991.
36. Stark, 1988.
37. Stark, 1988, p. 19.
38. Stark, 1988, p. 23.
39. Linda Moulton Howe, personal interview, Oct. 5, 1994.

number of less serious programs that have jumped on the alien band-wagon in the wake of *X-Files'* success.

"Leno Laughs at UFOs"[40]

If entertainment is more important than information and analysis in popular media, it is not surprising that UFOs and those who claim to have experienced them would be laughed at from time to time. Laughter and ridicule are not ideal aspects of scientific method, but who cares, if entertainment is the goal? Certainly part of the appeal of B movies was their campy quality, being so poorly made that they were laughable.

Add to this the sociological perspective of deviance. Bizarre-looking monsters or aliens are pop culture icons of deviance due to their ugliness and strange and immoral behavior. Anyone who suggests that such absurd characters (and aliens are on the list) could be real is also in danger of being labeled as deviant. Whenever an anomalous story hits the TV or radio news, the well-worn standard joke is to roll the eyes and to "Do-do-do-do, do-do-do-do," the theme from *The Twilight Zone*.

Perhaps Patty Grant, producer of the *Tonight Show*, had something like this in mind when she took host Jay Leno to a UFO conference in Los Angeles. "We wanted to do something light-hearted to run as a segment on our show," she said.[41] In spite of the fact that organizers of the conference, UFO Expo West, asked Grant not to come on the grounds that researchers and experiencers might not appreciate the comedy angle, the Tonight Show staff got permission to set up in the hotel and interview participants.

Leno's approach was to ask people if they knew any aliens, then to show tabloid stories on aliens and Clinton, aliens and U.S. Senators. Several times he apologized and said, "I'm just trying to have fun with this."[42] When Yvonne Smith, a therapist who works with experiencers, referred to her abductee support groups, "Patty Grant looked at me and said that my stuff, as Grant called it, was way too serious." Although Grant and Leno were apparently very courteous, the point remains that such treatment of the subject of UFOs is hardly conducive to the definition of ufology as legitimate.

---

40. Stock, 1994.
41. Stock, 1994, p. 9.
42. Stock, 1994, p. 9.

Mack and the Media

As sensationalistic, distorted and ridiculing as popular media may be at times about the subject of UFOs, at least they are far less likely to ignore or condemn the subject than academic publications are. Consequently even serious academics like John E. Mack, Pulitzer-Prize winning Harvard psychiatrist, often have to go to popular media channels if they want their work to receive any significant attention.

Mack decided that it was hopeless to get his work with abductees published in academic journals in any reasonable length of time. Therefore, he had his book, *Abduction: Human Encounters with Aliens,*[43] published by Charles Scribner's Sons in 1994 and then went on a whirlwind tour of TV and radio talk shows and magazine-format news shows as part of the publisher's promotion campaign. Many of these programs gave very brief and superficial treatment, but Mack was undaunted by this, said that he had expected it, and looked forward to longer, more serious pieces that the initial publicity would help generate.[44]

Pieces in print media tended to treat *Abduction* with greater depth and seriousness. The *Washington Post* even featured a more than half-page article by Mack himself a month after the book was released.[45] This was highly significant, because the mainstream press seldom pays any attention to UFO stories except in small local or regional papers. Also important was the decision by the *New York Times* to print a mixed but fairly positive review of Mack's book by James S. Gordon,[46] a professor of psychiatry at Georgetown University School of Medicine. It is interesting that the information listed about Gordon failed to mention anything about his having written about abductees before, as in his positive piece about Leo Sprinkle's Rocky Mountain UFO Conference in *The Atlantic* in August 1991.

Nevertheless, such expertise on UFO subjects is often lacking in journalistic pieces. *Psychology Today* did a fairly long and generally negative article on Mack and his book.[47] Although some of the criticisms may have been valid, and in a sense the author, Jill Neimark, did a good job of research with mainstream skeptics at least, the casual reader would have a difficult time knowing enough about the subject to imagine the objections to this review that someone well versed in UFO studies might make.

43. Mack, 1994A.
44. John E. Mack, personal interview, June 25, 1994.
45. Mack, 1994B.
46. Gordon, 1994.
47. Neimark, 1994.

Probably the nastiest review of Mack's work appeared in *Time*, April 25, 1994.[48] The article was entitled "The Man From Outer Space" printed in large, sensational letters beside a picture of Mack eerily lit from behind. It claimed to debunk Mack's research largely based on the statements of Donna Bassett who allegedly convinced Mack that she was an abductee and told him wild stories about being in a UFO with Kennedy and Krushchev during the Cuban missile crisis. Bassett's case, incidentally, was not one of the thirteen included in *Abduction*. However, Philip Klass from his debunking perspective praised *Time* for engaging an investigative reporter, James Willwerth, for their article, and criticized the *Washington Post* for not doing the same before publishing Mack's article referred to above.[49]

The Media Message

What is the message about UFO studies generally presented in popular mass media of communications? Although it is a mixed bag, the subject of UFOs has usually been sensationalized if treated at all. The core of this matter is the profit motive that encourages popular science as entertainment rather than as education. More serious journalists would be inclined to avoid the subject altogether because of the association between UFOs and B movies and tabloids.

On the other hand, popular media coverage is one way that ufologists can circumvent the academic taboo on publication of UFO studies. When scholars like John Mack use media this way, they make their work more accessible to the public, and even to other academics who might never hear about it otherwise. They also run the risk of being treated sensationally in some stories and debunked in others.

Either way, the presentation of UFO material will usually be superficial. Even the use of ufologists as consultants, as with Budd Hopkins for the TV *Intruders*, does not guarantee sophisticated treatment, because there is still a tendency to produce dramatic effects. Producers like Linda Moulton Howe and authors like John E. Mack and James S. Gordon are needed for their expertise and knowledge of the subject.

Although their institutional goals are different, mass media, academe and government all generally contribute to a definition of ufology as deviant. Academe has a normal science perspective into which ufology does not yet fit very well. Government either has something to hide or is trying to protect the public or both. Mass media are simply

---

48. Willwerth, 1994.
49. Klass, 1994.

organized to make a profit, and until academe and government decide to legitimize the UFO subject and release information about it, it is more convenient and prudent for mass media to treat UFOs as crazy, though fascinating, pop culture than to take them that seriously.

Chapter 4

Daring to Study UFOs

The View From Normal Science

In light of the official condemnation of UFO studies as worthless, according to the 1969 Condon report as pointed out in Chapter 2, it is not surprising that academic and at least publicized governmental support for ufology has been virtually nonexistent. This means that trained researchers who want to initiate UFO studies are hampered by a lack of funding. Even if they do the research and write up their findings, mainstream academic journals will not publish them. If they write books, chances are that these will not be considered positively toward promotion or tenure.

If these obstacles are not sufficient to discourage the potential UFO researcher, there is still the issue of mass media coverage (see Ch. 3). Such publicity will probably be either irrelevant or embarrassing. Business and industry operate differently than academic institutions, but they also dislike degrading publicity for their employees. And, of course, no governmental agency wants its workers associated with UFOs in the media.

This is not to say that *individuals* in these institutions all condemn an open inquiry into the UFO question. In fact, most astronomers seem to favor the idea (see Ch. 2). The problem is "normal science" as an *institution*. Individuals will conform to what is defined as "normal" even if they see it differently themselves. This has been demonstrated in many classic social-psychological laboratory studies, e.g., in which people have claimed to believe that two lines obviously different in length are the same, just because confederates of the experimenter made the same claim first, and they were afraid to deviate from the group wisdom. If a granting agency receives an excellent proposal for UFO research, each member of the panel may give it a bad evaluation just because he/she is afraid the other members will consider it flaky, or that the agency will look bad to outsiders if such research is supported.

Ufology is, of course, not the only "deviant science" with this problem. Parapsychology is somewhat more legitimized in the sense that it is officially recognized by the American Academy for the Advancement of Science, and there are some graduate programs in parapsychology and other programs in which a parapsychological topic can be accepted for a dissertation. Nevertheless, ESP and other psychic phenomena are taboo subjects in psychology and in academe in general, and, of course, they are debunked as roundly by CSICOP and *The Skeptical Inquirer* as UFOs are.[1]

Even when a subject area is legitimate in academe, certain specific projects and interpretations may lie outside the acceptable paradigms. This is the case in what Michael A. Cremo and Richard L. Thompson call "forbidden archaeology."[2] If previous chemical dating evidence has been accepted for a culture, new contradictory evidence may not only be questioned, but bring ridicule on the upstart academic with the deviant claim. UFO researcher Philip Imbrogno found that archaeologists had little interest in the stone chambers of the Hudson Valley because the collective wisdom was that they were from the colonial period and "archaeologically sterile," in spite of indications that such chambers may have much earlier European connections and be of great ceremonial significance, not to mention the frequent UFO sightings around them.[3]

Given the rules of normal science and its punishment of, or at least lack of rewards for nonconformist researchers, who would dare to study UFOs? John Mack, the Harvard psychiatrist who wrote *Abduction*, said that some of his colleagues at Cambridge wondered if he was having a mid-life crisis, although he was a bit old for that at 63 and didn't think there was such a thing as an "early elderly crisis."[4] Maybe his upbringing in a New York intellectual community or his attendance at Oberlin College (where Budd Hopkins, another prominent abduction researcher, also graduated), a place of diversity and tolerance for nonconformist thinking, had something to do with it. At any rate, the risk-reward structure would seem to filter out the faint-hearted and many talented individuals who have hopes for mobility in the system.

1. Hess, 1993.
2. Cremo and Thompson, 1993.
3. Imbrogno, 1993.
4. Mack, 1993B.

"Where Are the Aliens? Where Are the Astronomers?"

Although not all ufologists would agree, it is usually assumed that if UFOs are "real," they must be extraterrestrial. Therefore, astronomers are the normal-science authorities into whose laps the UFO question is dropped first. There is a temptation to assume that if UFOs are absurd, then the possibility of intelligent ET life must also be absurd. Interestingly, this is not necessarily the case.

Most astronomers accept the possibility, if not the probability, that there is a very large number of high-technology civilizations in our own galaxy alone. Such estimates are based on the Drake Equation, a formula devised by Frank Drake[5] to multiply a list of probabilities for necessary conditions, such as stars having Earth-like planets, these planets actually developing life, and intelligence coming from such life. The late astronomer Carl Sagan was the leading popularizer of the notion that the possibility of other civilizations among the 400 billion stars in our Milky Way galaxy makes it worthwhile to try to contact them via radio through the SETI program (Search for Extra-Terrestrial Intelligence).[6]

If it is respectable in astronomy to speculate on the existence of ET civilizations, why is it not respectable to do ufology, i.e., to look for visitors who might be ETs? Astronomers present a number of objections, including the impracticality, if not impossibility, of interstellar travel, although ufologist Michael D. Swords argues that mainstream physics literature makes the distance argument weak, even just with extensions of current technologies.[7]

Surely, one might ask, would not the evidence of UFO sightings suggest that interstellar travel is indeed possible? Is it not worth a close look? Of course, the normal science answer in astronomy is "No." "It can't be, therefore it isn't." If they can't get here, or if they wouldn't be motivated to invest the time, effort and capital, then they must not be here.

Ironically, there is another normal-science argument that turns Drake and Sagan on their heads: the Fermi Paradox. Enrico Fermi is credited with asking, "Where are the aliens?" He and others, including Frank J. Tipler,[8] have reasoned that if there have been hi-tech ETs in the galaxy, they should have been able to colonize it all in short leaps by now.[9] Therefore, since they are obviously not here, there is something

5. Drake, 1976.
6. Sagan, 1993.
7. Swords, 1989.
8. Tipler, 1980.
9. Swords, 1989, p. 87.

wrong; they must not have existed in the first place. "It should be, but it isn't; therefore it never was." Both the Drake-Sagan and Fermi-Tipler arguments assume that the ufological evidence is invalid, but they use this assumption in contradictory ways.

Let us recall, however, that astronomer Peter Sturrock found in his 1977 survey that 53% of astronomers thought that UFOs deserved scientific study (23% "certainly" and 30% "probably"), and another 27% said "possibly."[10] Two years later a survey published in *Industrial Research/Development* of "1200 scientists and engineers in all fields of research and development" found 61% responding that UFOs probably or definitely exist, 28% saying they probably or definitely did not.[11] Respondents under 26 years of age were twice as likely as those over 65 to state that UFOs exist. This shows the same tendency toward acceptance of UFOs among younger scientists that Sturrock found among astronomers, among whom 65% of those 21-30, but only 23% of those over 60 agreed that UFOs certainly or probably deserved study. Because of this tendency for younger scientists in earlier decades to be more receptive, we may suspect that the overall percentage of scientists, including astronomers, who are open to the idea of UFO studies has increased since the late 1970s, as these scientists have aged and the era of somewhat greater openness continues.

We must be careful not to overinterpret such surveys. For one thing, the two questions referred to above were not the same, one asking about scientific study of the UFO problem, the other about whether UFOs exist. Also, as Robert J. Durant points out in regard to general public-opinion polls, belief that UFOs are "real" (rather than imaginary) is not the same as believing that they are extraterrestrial.[12] Gallup and Roper polls show an average of about 45% of the general public believing in ET intelligent life since the mid-1970s, 45-50% saying that UFOs are real, and generally about 30% saying that UFOs are alien spacecraft.[13]

Nonetheless, it is fairly clear that astronomers, like other scientists, as individuals are quite accepting of the general idea of UFO studies, and are probably not much different from the rest of the population in this regard. This is in spite of the orthodox position in astronomy that ETs are not here, whether one follows the Drake-Sagan model or its contrary, the Fermi-Tipler model. Could it be that the orthodox position exists not because of rational, logical argument, but because of the

10. Sturrock, 1994A.
11. Fowler, 1981; cited in Richard L. Thompson, 1993.
12. Durant, 1993.
13. Durant, 1993, pp. 10, 13.

deviant label that has been attached to ufology for other reasons, the reasons laid out in Chapters 2 and 3?

It is interesting that in spite of the survey results on astronomer beliefs, Sturrock found only 7 of 1,322 astronomers "were actively studying the UFO problem," although another 34 "offered to help investigate the problem."[14] Philip Klass, UFO debunker, did not fail to note this lack of involvement when Sturrock first released findings in 1977.[15] At this writing there is only one consultant to MUFON in astronomy, a very competent investigator and writer with good knowledge of the field, but without an advanced degree in astronomy.

There have been some professional astronomers in ufology, of course, especially the late J. Allen Hynek. Jacques Vallée had training in astronomy and worked with Hynek, although his Ph.D. is in computer science. Peter A. Sturrock, professor of space science and astrophysics at Stanford, author of the astronomer survey, and Brian O'Leary, Ph.D. in astronomy and former colleague of Carl Sagan, have also made contributions to UFO studies. Clyde Tombaugh, the astronomer who discovered Pluto, argued for the importance of ufology as well.[16]

In order to get greater insight into the position of astronomers on ufology, I interviewed five who were not involved in ufology. They work at four different academic institutions in the northeastern U.S., two of them at the same one. All were quite generous with their time and genuinely interested in discussing the subject. I would have interviewed more, but it soon became obvious that astronomers generally know almost nothing about ufology. In fact, their knowledge of UFOs seems to come mainly from supermarket tabloids, which is another reason for ufologists to be dismayed at popular media. This makes me very suspicious of Sturrock's finding that the median category of "number of hours...spent...informing (oneself) about the UFO problem" was 8-50 hours.[17]

About 40% in Sturrock's survey stated that publications by scientists were their main source of UFO information, and 35% stated newspapers and magazines.[18] This could be the case, but the scientific publications were probably not by ufologists, and the newspapers and magazines were perhaps not very scholarly. None of my five informants had read a single UFO book or journal article by a serious ufologist, and their ideas of what ufologists do were generally naïve. The

14. Sturrock, 1994A, p. 6.
15. Klass, 1983.
16. Christensen, 1986.
17. Sturrock, 1994A, p. 7.
18. Sturrock, 1994A, p. 13.

most involved and best informed of the five stated that he often received UFO books to review, but he never read any because he had much higher priorities.

This is indeed the point. How many astronomers are going to make UFOs a priority when ufology is an officially taboo subject in their discipline? And yet of the five I interviewed, three considered highly intelligent alien life to be very likely, one didn't know what probability to assess, and one said that it was a matter of faith without any evidence at this point. The consensus was that most astronomers would say that it was likely.

On the point of whether ETs have already observed or visited Earth, one found it likely (this person a graduate student, the only one without a Ph.D.), two found it possible, one unlikely, and one said no. Perhaps surprisingly, all five considered UFOs "worthy of scientific investigation." This supports the Sturrock finding, although the sample is very small. Tellingly, however, only the graduate student considered UFO studies worth *funding*, and he knew that most astronomers would disagree. The other four said that it was a matter of priorities. They uniformly saw it as low in priority, rather than as a taboo subject condemned by normal science. SETI, by contrast, was seen by all as of much higher priority, although one wondered whether it was economical. Another said that SETI was of higher priority than ufology because it involved proper methodology, instrumentation and legitimate researchers.

In summary, my interviews with nonufologist astronomers suggest, although the sample is small, that in spite of a belief in intelligent ET life, and in spite of only one person being fairly certain that ETs have not visited or observed Earth, there is very little support for the idea of *funding* UFO research. Stating that UFOs are a subject worthy of scientific investigation is not necessarily the same as thinking that it should be given any significant priority in funding.

And, of course, astronomers know that there is in fact little money available. If there is no financial support for astronomers to do ufology within their discipline, it is no wonder that they spend so little time reading ufology. If they did look at the data, they might consider it a subject not only worth studying (anything might be worth studying to some degree), but actually promising enough to warrant funding! Of course, a change of attitude among individual astronomers about funding still would not necessarily mean that the field of astronomy would start funding UFO studies. UFO debunker Philip J. Klass quipped in an interview with me that he thought the funding priority for projects on ET visitors should fit just below studies of Santa Claus, and added seriously that it would be appropriate to fund studies on why people *believe* in UFOs.[19]

Next I will be so bold as to suggest that my five informants were naïve not only about ufology, but also in their idea that ufology is not *taboo* in astronomy but is merely given low funding priority. Some astronomers, and, of course, debunkers in general, have stated that UFOs are only a myth, because if they were really there, astronomers who observe would have spotted them in the skies. It is, of course, taboo to study what is "only a myth" in serious hard science. It is "pseudo-science."

Richard Thompson has analyzed this issue in regard to the Condon report and how it was debated at that time.[20] He concludes that in spite of most telescopes not being ideally designed to photograph UFOs, and in spite of a tendency not to examine photographic records for UBOs (unidentified bright objects), astronomers do indeed observe UFOs, probably more than people in the general population. However, they avoid reporting them in order to avoid publicity. In other words, it is inappropriate (taboo) to see them. This is a reverse "Emperor's New Clothes" story; in the original, subjects were required to see what did *not* exist.

Jacques Vallée became interested in UFOs in 1961 "when I saw French astronomers erase a magnetic tape on which our satellite-tracking team had recorded...an unknown flying object.... 'People would laugh at us if we reported this!' was the answer I was given at the time."[21]

A friend of mine who is interested in ufology walked into a physics department (where astronomers are typically located) at a university in a western state. She asked a professor sitting in his office if anyone in the department knew about UFO studies. He looked frightened and said, "Nobody here would be interested in that."

The anecdote about astronomers most frequently told at UFO conferences allegedly comes from J. Allen Hynek. As astronomer Brian O'Leary tells it, "several hundred professional astronomers [were attending a meeting] in Victoria, British Columbia, during the summer of 1968. When word spread of UFO activity above the hotel where a reception was going on, not one astronomer went outside to look."[22]

Whether this legend precisely represents what happened or not, it illustrates an important point. There can be a difference between the at-

19. Philip J. Klass, personal interview, July 9, 1994.
20. Richard L. Thompson, 1993, pp. 25-27.
21. Vallée, 1979, p. 7.
22. O'Leary, 1989, pp. 86-87.

titudes of individuals and the behavior of people in groups. Even if astronomers find it likely that ET civilizations exist and think they may
have visited Earth, as members of a mainstream academic discipline
they will probably not examine UFO evidence for possible ET connections if their work is likely to be ignored or ridiculed.

How Ufologists Get Interested

Since UFOs are a taboo subject in normal science, not only in the
case of astronomy as explored above, but in other academic areas as
well, ufologists are recruited in nonstandard ways. They come from a
variety of disciplinary backgrounds, usually have to do their ufology as
a part-time or post-retirement or even hidden activity, and form a kind
of loosely structured community that lies outside of mainstream academic institutions and includes some people who are not academics at
all, but usually have advanced degrees nonetheless.

Who is a ufologist? This is hard to say, because there is no one particular degree or certification or academic department involved. As a
sociologist I would say that ufologists are not an easily defined "population" that I could sample. However, I chose to interview consultants
to the Mutual UFO Network (MUFON), the largest UFO organization
in the world with over 4,000 members. Members get the journal and
may not do anything else, but the consultants are mostly people with
the doctorate or other terminal degree in their fields and who are generally more involved. Since I was especially interested in academics, I
decided to skip the attorneys, M.D.s and those in certain other applied
areas less likely to be involved in academe.

There were 227 consultants on the overall list, and I tried to interview, mainly by phone, the 76 people in the fields I wanted who had a
listed phone in the U.S. I managed to complete depth, open-ended interviews with 62 of them from spring through fall of 1994. This is an
82% completion rate; only three refused (4% refusal rate), and the rest
of the noncompletions involved too many no-answer phone calls or
nonavailability of the respondent.

Twenty fields of study were represented among the consultants in
five general areas: physical sciences (27 people), psychological or psychic sciences (17), humanities (12), social sciences (5) and management
(1). The largest single disciplinary groups were physics (10), psychology (10), counseling (6), biology (5) and sociology (5). In addition to the
consultants, I interviewed or collected data at conferences on 29 other
ufologists, bringing my total sample to 91, not including my interviews
with experiencers and others who are not ufologists. My nonconsultant

ufologists were sometimes MUFON members and always showed some level of research, writing or speaking activity. These 29 people were spread over 13 disciplinary areas, the largest group in counseling (6), and 3 each in psychology, and communications or journalism.

Among the MUFON consultants 61 had doctorates, one a bachelor's degree. In the other group there were 15 doctorates, 8 master's, 4 bachelor's and 2 with no degrees. I did not have a random sample of all ufologists or even of all ufologists at the conferences I attended, but I certainly did not avoid people without degrees. I got every researcher I could, given the time demands on conference attenders; and almost everyone was gracious, even excited to talk with me. Therefore, I feel confident in saying that this high percentage of advanced degrees is typical among American ufologists.

Such is not the case in many other countries. Basterfield *et al.* state that in both England and Australia "professionals comparable in status and accomplishment to those [involved in ufology] in the United States have been far less visible," a situation they attribute to British and Australian "scientific communities [being] marked by an inherent conservatism."[23] We might be thinking, "American academics are not conservative?" but it is a matter of degree, of course. John L. Spencer notes that European ufologists also tend to be far more skeptical than American ufologists about the ET hypothesis, something reflected not only in a very conservative academe, but also in low belief in ET visitation in polls of the general public, often only 16 or 17%.[24]

Both the low percentage of professional degrees and the high level of skepticism referred to above can be illustrated in the British ufology book *UFOs: The Final Answer?* edited by David Barclay and Therese Marie Barclay.[25] Although this collection of essays is excellent, it is interesting that only the writer of the foreword, R.W. Shillitoe, is listed as having a Ph.D., and among the eight authors of chapters, only three have degrees listed, all at the bachelor's level. Out of nine chapters, one is highly skeptical, trying to explain UFOs away as natural or hoaxes or subjective (it would be acceptable in *The Skeptical Enquirer*), and two others suggest that UFOs and abductions are totally mental and not physical phenomena.

Among the MUFON consultants I interviewed, 7 of 62 portrayed themselves as skeptical or very skeptical about UFOs in general (of course there were others who were dubious about certain aspects, like abductions). None of the 29 other ufologists I studied could be consid-

---

23. Basterfield and others, 1990.
24. Spencer, 1990.
25. Barclay and Barclay, 1993.

ered seriously skeptical about the phenomenon. Among the skeptics, 4 were in physical sciences, which is an overrepresentation, although the sample is very small; 15% of MUFON consultants in physical sciences were skeptical vs. only 8% in all other areas combined.

I thought that these skeptics might be people who only buy the *MUFON Journal* and really do not accept ufology or at least do not do any research or communicate on the subject. Indeed, there are some MUFON consultants who have been very inactive. I developed an involvement scale based on levels of activity in UFO publishing, lecturing, consulting, investigation, conference and club attendance, and teaching. On a ten-point scale, I considered zero and one to be low. There are 8% of the consultants at zero and 11% at one. None of the 29 nonconsultant ufologists are at these levels, and the average involvement score for the consultants is only 3.7 compared to 6.9 for the nonconsultants. However, none of the consultant skeptics score zero or one, and their average score is 4.9.

At any rate, none of these "skeptics" could be called debunkers. They may emphasize "normal" explanations for UFOs, but at least they are willing to study the evidence and become involved in the enterprise of ufology, rather than merely going on a crusade to attack ufologists. It is remarkable that such a high percentage of the American ufologists in my overall sample of 91 have advanced degrees (84% doctorates, 9% master's degrees) considering the deviant status attached to UFO studies in American universities, even if academic institutions in other countries may be even more conservative.

How do these people become interested enough to do ufology in spite of the lack of rewards for such research in the mainstream? The most important single reason is having a UFO experience themselves. As one consultant put it, "Once I had this sighting [with my wife], it was no longer a question of whether UFOs existed or not. I just had to find out what they were." Of the 86 interviewees who answered questions about experiences, 48% thought they had had a UFO experience, and 8% thought they might have had one. This does not include questionable lights or other things that they thought were probably some mundane phenomenon. Not surprisingly, none of the 7 skeptics were among the 56%. Compared to the general population, between 5% and 14% of whom think they have seen a UFO in various polls in the U.S.,[26] 56% is a very high figure, especially for highly educated ufologists most of whom are well aware that about 95% of sightings can be identified as misperceptions of mundane phenomena.

26. Durant, 1993, p. 13.

And 38% of my ufologist sample are people who have had a sighting and also say that their sightings are the main reason for their interest in ufology (27%), or at least their sightings very significantly increased their interest (11%). The other 18% (56% minus 38%) were already interested for some other reason; 11% did significant study of UFOs before having their first experience. Randles and Warrington report that Shirley McIver, in her Ph.D. dissertation at York University, found that 19% of 218 members of the British UFO Research Association (BUFORA) reported being in ufology due to their own UFO experiences,[27] only half the 38% in my sample.

Although it is more difficult for researchers to admit to themselves and to others that they may have been abducted, partly because it may seriously reduce their credibility as researchers in the eyes of many, 9% of the 86 who answered experience questions said they thought they had been abducted, and 7% thought they might have been. I did not ask specifically about abduction, only about UFO experiences in general, and more might have mentioned it if I had. The abduction or contact experience is a strong motivator for investigation, and 12 of the 14 abductees or potential abductees said that their experiences were their main reason for becoming interested in ufology. I suspect that a higher percentage than 16% are at least subjectively experiencers of CE-IV, and I know of other researchers not in my sample who think they are abductees, but I did not go out of my way to put these ufologists into my sample, because this would have distorted the percentages.

Of course, there are other reasons for my ufologists becoming interested. Aside from the 29 who said the experiences were the main reason (leaving out the 2 experiencers who had significantly heightened interest), 17 mentioned reading, either specific UFO books or things about science, science fiction or the New Age; 6 were interested first in psychic topics like ESP; 6 had been interested since their early years for no special reason; 6 emphasized social influences from friends, relatives or clients; 5 were interested in anything that challenged scientific paradigms; 2 were interested in new energy sources, 2 in spiritual things, 1 had a spiritual experience; 5 mentioned other topics of interest including (one each) hyperspace, earthquake lights, chemical evolution, intercultural communication and astronomy; one had heard reports while in the military; 11 gave no answer or don't know responses. In many cases secondary reasons were given, especially the social influences of significant others who had had experiences or who had done extensive reading on UFOs.

---

27. Randles and Warrington, 1985, p. 187.

Some ufologists have not only become interested in the subject because of their own experiences, but in fact have written books about themselves. Three prominent examples are Leah Haley[28] and Karla Turner,[29] both of whom describe and analyze their own CE-IV, and Ellen Crystall[30] who describes her own CE-III and her many field observations and photographs of UFOs. All three of these women have advanced degrees.

Although it was not my real purpose to investigate reports, some ufologists gave me fascinating detailed accounts of their own experiences. Going over a couple of these should make it easier to appreciate the transformative effect that a paradigm-bending experience can have. Whether it is positive or negative for the experiencer, it creates a sense of awe as in a religious conversion experience.

One woman was sitting in her living room about dusk watching *Star Trek* on television with her family. Then the thought occurred to her that it would be neat to see a UFO. She got the feeling that she should go to the window, and when she did she saw a flattened-football shaped, whitish orange object in the sky. It moved twice from west to east and was gone. She felt elated and joyous, then went back to her chair to resume watching TV. She knows that she was the only one to see it, but oddly cannot remember much about what her family was doing.

Someone with the "reality tunnel" of a debunker would quite logically suspect that she wanted to see a UFO so badly, especially in the context of watching *Star Trek*, that she hallucinated the whole thing. A UFO researcher familiar with similar reports would note the possible telepathic signaling from UFO to experiencer. If this sighting was an intentional display, it may have been designed to impress the "chosen one" and set her on the path of UFO research (a "mission," to be discussed later). Sometimes experiencers oddly do not discuss what they have seen with others, and perhaps the family was not meant to be included. Setting such speculation aside, at least it can be said that this experience was a strong motivator.

In the next case, the individual was not the only witness but was apparently one of at least three. There is always the possibility of a hoax, since I did not investigate the case, but I see no earthly reason for it, because he is not trying to exploit it for gain and does not even want his name associated with it. It is clear that he was not observing some mundane astronomical or meteorological phenomenon, and if it was a

---

28. Haley, 1993.
29. Turner, 1994A and 1992.
30. Crystall, 1991.

hallucination, he must have shared this "apparition" with at least one other person.

Dr. X was driving his car, accompanied by his wife, sometime between 8:00 and 8:30 P.M. on a very dark evening in late fall. Both of them saw a white-amber object, about the size of a quarter at arm's length, rolling across the sky like a wheel on the horizon. Then it bent toward them, descended, diving and closing fast on them until it hovered momentarily over a parking lot across the highway. It was shaped like a two-rimmed, lighted Ferris wheel with lighted spokes joining the two rims. He said to me, "Imagine the biggest Ferris wheel you've ever seen, and multiply it by five." It was the most incredible sight either of them had ever seen. Then, from over the parking lot, the object headed directly for them and went right about 15 feet over the car. Dr. X and the driver in front of him both swerved off the road.

Dr. X and his wife ducked down. When they looked up again, the object was completely gone. They strangely do not remember driving the rest of the way home, but they arrived about 11:00 P.M., making an apparent "missing time" of about 60 to 90 minutes. Although they were never hypnotically regressed, and, of course, he knows whom he could contact for that, they realize that there is a suspicion that they were abducted at some point after the object swooped down on them. Dr. X and his wife could not talk about the incident for a year afterwards. Whenever he considered bringing it up, a voice went off in his mind saying, "You don't have anything to say about that." The standard ufological interpretation of this would be that they were programmed mentally not to remember or discuss what happened, and maybe not to go to a therapist or abduction researcher. He did file a report with a major UFO organization, but no investigation was ever done.

About three years later, Dr. X's wife was driving home on a back road when she noticed strange colored lights following her, darting around and rearranging themselves close to the ground. When she arrived, she ran into the house to get her husband, but when Dr. X came out the lights were gone. The next day they heard a loud rumbling and fluttering noise. Then they saw a black unmarked helicopter flying slowly just above the roof of the house. Many UFO experiencers have made similar reports of odd small, darting lights (sometimes called "probes," but it is unclear what they might be), and also of black, unmarked helicopters buzzing the house.

Both of the researchers who had the experiences related above were highly motivated by their sightings. The *Star Trek* experience was obviously more positive, but the Ferris wheel example was more awesome. As Dr. X put it, it was "too overwhelming to put into words."

The strong emotion of reality-shattering experiences (as they are commonly called in ufology, as in the title of the book by Alice Bryant and Linda Seebach, *Healing Shattered Reality*)[31] was enough to be the main reason for the involvement of 38% of the American ufologists in this study.

However, it is interesting that the UFO-experience-motivated ufologists are not any more involved in UFO studies than those primarily motivated by other reasons. The average involvement score of experience-motivated MUFON consultants is 3.5 compared to 3.8 for MUFON consultants with other main motivations. The average score among the nonconsultant ufologists who are experience-motivated is 6.5 compared to 7.3 for all others. This is slightly lower in each case, though not significantly so. In other words, there is no support here for the idea that all ufologists who have had their own UFO experiences are especially intensely involved because of some "chosen" status. On the other hand, debunkers might expect that ufologists who are intensely involved tend to be people with a distorted perspective caused by UFO hallucinations. This is not supported either, but more on this later.

Whatever the main reasons are for the interest that ufologists show in UFO studies—having had a UFO experience, having read about ufology and related fields, or having been influenced by significant others, these reasons have to be fairly strong ones, considering the lack of rewards offered by society in general. The social control system in academe, business and industry, government and professional communities rewards other activities more and in many cases punishes involvement in ufology.

The Support for and Harassment of Ufologists

If ufology is generally defined as a deviant science, it is not surprising that most ufologists are at least partly in-the-closet about their work. This means that they cover up their activity at least in certain social contexts, or they delay higher levels of involvement until they are more secure in their positions (or until after they retire). Government workers are the most likely to do ufology in the closet. Only 20% of the ufologists in my sample who worked two or more years full-time in government never hid or delayed their involvement. Among those who spent at least two full-time years in academic employment, 43% never hid or delayed their UFO studies; 48% of those in business or oth-

---

31. Bryant and Seebach, 1991.

er nonacademic private organizational employment, and 50% of free-lance or self-employed workers never did. Considering the official U.S. governmental/military position on UFOs, it is to be expected that government workers would be careful. One might expect even more secrecy among academics, considering the power of normal science, but I suspect that it is difficult for people who devote their lives to research and teaching to study something so interesting and keep it to themselves.

Covering up or delaying involvement helps avoid punishments for doing ufology, but it is difficult to get much done this way. In some work environments there is little to risk, and a few of my respondents claimed that it was not an issue, that there was little reaction, or even that reactions were overwhelmingly positive. However, sometimes just one enemy can cause serious problems, and it is difficult to judge the risk. One interviewee felt a "vague anxiety" about what it might mean to be more open. Another experienced "a little tension."

One solution to this dilemma is to be selective about whom to tell, as many of the interviewees said. This means discovering who is interested, and treating subgroups differently. Tell your friendly colleague, but maybe not the head of the department, and probably not the administration. One stock broker was open with co-workers and even management, but didn't risk discussing UFOs with conservative clients.

Academics seldom put any UFO research, conference presentations or publications on their vitas (résumés). Ufologists in business, and especially in government, may include disclaimers in their writings. Richard F. Haines, who works for a government agency, included the following at the end of one of his typically scholarly "nuts-and bolts" papers, "Disclaimer: The author's employer does not accept or otherwise support the facts of this paper. The report is entirely the work of the author."[32] Another prominent ufologist asks people to refrain from mentioning his specific place of employment with its military connection.

One way to avoid criticism is to present UFO material in a very serious, objective way without drawing any conclusions. This strategy is used frequently by college professors who seldom manage to teach courses on UFOs alone, but who are more likely to include them in a course like "Science and Pseudoscience" (taught by a physicist in my sample) or in a section of a course on "critical thinking."

---

32. Haines, 1986.

One ufologist said that although his work is in print and is well known, he is not likely to get in trouble because he takes a "very conservative position." The skeptics in ufology should be especially safe, but even skeptical work can raise eyebrows at times.

A ufologist who is an expert on earthquake lights told me that he gave his mundane explanation for some UFO sightings as lights caused by seismic activity only to find serious negative reactions from the audience at a meeting of the Seismological Society of America. Simply because his data base involved UFO sightings, it was considered tainted. He managed to quiet his detractors by telling them that his statistical correlations were better than those used for proof of the effectiveness of many medical treatments. The same talk at a UFO conference would probably have been considered debunking.

Anybody who gets involved in UFO studies, including some who make fairly conservative or even skeptical claims, can be open to negative social control. The safe strategy is to "keep a low profile," as some put it, or not to make an issue of it, or to stay at a low level of involvement. There are very few who manage to accomplish much by staying completely in the closet or leading a double life, but the farther out one comes, the greater the risk. As one ufologist said, who was being considered for a high-level award in science, you especially don't dare tell people you're an abductee or they'll think you're a kook.

Advertising oneself in popular mass media is particularly risky, although 53% of my sample have received at least some newspaper, TV or radio coverage. Of those appearing in mass media, 48% had at least some poor or problematic coverage. One scientist who got solid backing on his UFO studies from the company for which he worked was told nevertheless, "Don't embarrass us by talking to the media." Dr. Leo Sprinkle (see Appendix, page 235) especially found himself hassled as a result of his popular media involvement, the biggest problem arising from a poorly written newspaper article that made his work look ridiculous, leading to an ethics complaint that was thrown out by the American Psychological Association, but took a year to be resolved.

Several academics said that they had or would become more active after they got tenure, after they became a full professor, or after they retired. Some ufologists have taken voluntary early retirement or have resigned before becoming eligible for retirement. At least five people in my sample have done that already. Three of them were under no pressure to resign, but simply decided that the academic environment would not allow them to do enough ufology.

Although it is clear that there is little financial or even moral support for ufology, 24% of the academics in my sample felt that they had received at least minor support for their work, 34% of those in business and other private nonacademic organizations, 23% of free-lance and self-employed, and 15% in government. There is overlap among these samples because some individuals have worked in more than one of these areas full time for two years or more.

On the surface it would seem that academe would be the ideal location for a ufologist, since professors are partly researchers by trade, but, of course, the particular topic doesn't fit into normal science. It is less taboo to study UFO experiences as social or psychological phenomena, but even this kind of ufology is likely to be seen as a fringe or nonserious subject. Nevertheless, it is fairly easy to use one's yearly travel allowance for attendance at conferences, perhaps even at strictly UFO conferences, and extra funds may be available when giving one's own paper presentation. Sometimes professors can get small in-house grants, i.e., from the college or university, rather than from outside granting agencies.

One psychologist did use travel money and receive grants from the (well-respected) university to study what included UFO experiences and other phenomena that seem to involve altered states of consciousness. Dr. X was already tenured and continued to be treated well, although not especially rewarded for this work. Dr. X never felt hassled or discriminated against and said that it made a difference that the topic was treated academically without any attempts at proselytizing. However, once Dr. X received a rather insignificant raise after having a very good year that included a grant, a book and some articles. When Dr. X inquired about the size of the raise, the department head, who had evidently not read the book, said, "Well, stop doing religion and do psychology." This incident was an exception to generally good treatment.

Academics seldom get clear guidelines about whether ufology is acceptable or not. Most people know without asking. One of my interviewees reported that a physics professor who was scheduled to give a talk at a UFO conference was told by his department head not to do it, and the professor cancelled the engagement.

In another case, one of the ufologists in my sample actually went to the president and to the academic vice president of the university and put copies of a UFO research proposal on their desks asking, "Is this a responsible academic endeavor?" The answer came back, "This is fine, responsible, a good job. Enjoy yourself." This individual thinks that having performed well at the university and having good, nonthreatening interpersonal skills makes a big difference. I might say that interactive style and other social contextual factors make this process complex.

Another ufologist was not so lucky. Dr. Y asked the president of the university (a different place) about doing a UFO study for a sabbatical project, since final approval would have to come from the president anyway. The president turned it down cold on the grounds that the Condon report had said there was nothing to the UFO phenomenon.

Support for ufology in business and industry is usually of the moral type only, because it seldom has direct relevance to the organization. Robert Wood's work at McDonnell Douglas on the feasibility of UFO-type propulsion systems is a practical exception (see Ch. 2).

Most businesses are not going to want UFO media publicity for their employees just because of the "wacky" image the subject often has. In a probably unusual case, Walt Andrus (see Appendix, page 223), now International Director of MUFON, wrote UFO articles for the company newsletter, *Motorola Voice*, and was publicized by the company for his participation in the TV documentary, *UFOs: Do You Believe?* (1974).

Free-lance and self-employed persons who do ufology are less affected by workplace social control. However, their reputations among colleagues can be at stake. Therapists who deal with abductees can be supported by a community of nonufologists who at least recognize the psychological significance of the UFO experience. And, of course, some health professionals work at least part-time in agencies or hospitals.

Dr. Steven M. Greer, a ufologist who is an emergency-room M.D., related the story informally at a UFO conference that his hospital begged him to do a grand rounds presentation for the doctors on the subject of UFOs. At first he refused, a little wary of how they might handle the topic, but they convinced him to do it. It was well received, even by a conservative doctor who surprised Greer by saying that UFOs were the "most important issue facing our planet." Steve felt that his good reputation as a doctor at the hospital helped, and he was careful not to go too far-out in an introduction to the subject.

Moving from evidence of support to evidence for harassment or punishment, 32% of the academics in my sample felt that they had received at least minor harassment for their ufology work, 31% of business and other private organizational workers, 18% of free-lance and self-employed, and 15% of government workers. What constitutes harassment is partly subjective and a matter of symbolic interaction, as we know in the case of sexual harassment, but I went mostly by the interviewee's interpretation and did not count mild kidding as harassment.

Of course, there is a relationship between openness on the part of the ufologist and the amount of harassment. In some cases, people will be more open because they have tested the waters and can see that there is much support and little resistance. In other cases, people are so motivated that they are willing to pay the price for coming out of the closet.

Among the academics, 56% of those who were completely open reported being harassed, only 21% of those who were somewhat open, and 0% of those who were completely in the closet reported harassment. Among those in business, 50% of the completely open were harassed, 14% of the partly open, and 0% of those in the closet. In government, 25% of the completely open, 18% of the partly open, and 0% of those in the closet. In free-lance and self-employed, 25% of the completely open, 0% of the partly open, and 0% of the closeted. Sample sizes are small, but the association between openness and harassment is strong. Greater openness by individuals probably brings them greater harassment within the same organization, but the less threatening the organization is, the more open ufologists in it will probably be, until they are willing to risk no more and a kind of equilibrium is reached.

I am going to be very careful about naming names when giving examples of harassment, even when I have permission from the ufologist to do so. I want to protect both the individual and the institution, especially in recent cases that have been or may be under litigation. Neither do I want to hurt the innocent, nor do I presume to know everything about the cases, and a variety of interpretations may be possible. Sometimes I will leave out details that would make it easier to identify individuals. Some cases, like that of John Mack, are so well known and presented publicly by the individuals that it is pointless to conceal the names. General patterns are more important than particular cases.

Harassment in academe begins somewhere subjectively along the road from mild kidding to laughter to ridicule. One never knows when the laughter may accumulate among colleagues who will judge the ufologist for promotion or tenure on an anonymously voting committee.

I recall a university professor joking with me once in an airport, when I was heading for a UFO conference, about how I would soon see "those UFO nuts with antennae growing out of their heads." There was no malice in his tone, and I realized how acceptable it is to be prejudiced against certain groups. It reminded me how offended I was when some colleagues laughed at the polka band musicians I was studying for my Ph.D. dissertation in sociology. They didn't know these people as warm human beings like I did. I feel the same way about the ufologists and UFO experiencers I know. It is sad the way even some sociologists, who should know better, fall into stereotypic thinking about groups socially defined as "odd."

Laughter from colleagues may be supplemented by accusations of flakiness or even satanism from some students or local citizens who are opposed to the very idea of UFOs. No wonder many ufologists are hesitant to share their findings in the classroom or in mass media. Several of the interviewees mentioned such examples, but usually one or two complaints did not seem to be damaging, although the department head might ask the professor to tone it down a little.

Earlier I argued that the taboo against ufology has resulted in very few astronomers being involved, although there are a few prominent examples, such as the late J. Allen Hynek. Some would argue that Hynek was not punished for his involvement in ufology. Keith Thompson states that Hynek's "position as chair of Northwestern University's astronomy department signaled to scientists...that keeping company with flying saucers would not necessarily prove to be the kiss of death."[33] In one interview with a nonufologist astronomer, however, I was told that Hynek did his career no good by studying UFOs, because other astronomers would assume that he must believe in them in order to waste his time on such a low priority subject with such a low probability of discovering anything important.

Richard Thompson gives an excellent analysis of how Hynek waffled over the years and gradually came to argue that UFOs were more than mundane.[34] Hynek tended to go easy in a gradualist attempt to make ufology academically respectable, in contrast to James E. McDonald, senior physicist at the Institute of Atmospheric Physics and professor of meteorology at the University of Arizona. McDonald, who committed suicide in 1971, was highly respected as a scientist, but too intense for some in his condemnation of "the government foul-up" over UFOs to which he accused Hynek of contributing by not challenging the "absurd explanations" of many cases during Project *Bluebook*.[35] Some scientists who worked with McDonald stayed in the closet, "fearing loss of government grants, or loss of their jobs in government-funded aerospace corporations...(or) fearful of peer ridicule or diminished credibility."[36]

As mentioned earlier, a professor who reveals his/her own UFO experience takes a bigger risk than one who merely argues for the study

33. Keith Thompson, 1991, p. 114.
34. Richard L. Thompson, 1993, pp. 31-38.
35. Druffel, 1993; Vallée, 1992C.
36. Druffel, 1993, p. 6.

of UFOs. One professor who taught courses on UFOs and ETs, and who spoke about the positive effects of his/her own abduction experience, reported opposition from some professors at the university and has allegedly now been forced into early retirement. Leo Sprinkle is a well-known case of a psychology and counseling professor who was not forced out, but who became tired of the struggle over a long period and decided to retire early.

In another case, one that was pending court action at the time of our interview, a Professor Z claimed that he/she had been passed over for promotion twice based on trivial excuses, and had been cut off from computer usage, work-study student help, etc. Professor Z concluded that this treatment originated largely with his/her creative photo exhibit based on possible UFO landing traces outside the home and with some media coverage that put his/her experiences in an unfavorable light.

In Chapter 3 we looked at the media coverage of John E. Mack and his work on abduction. Of course, Mack's case is unusual since he is of such high academic status in psychiatry at Harvard and so respected in intellectual circles for his Pulitzer Prize and his social activism. Nevertheless, some of his colleagues are opposed to his work, and the head of his department said, "We wish John wasn't doing this."[37] At first there was no major controversy, and Dr. Mack said that Harvard just wanted to make sure that the right protocol was followed in his research. Later, however, a special faculty committee was convened at Harvard Medical School to investigate the case. No action was taken ultimately, but Mack incurred high legal defense fees (see Appendix, page 231).

Sometimes academics are faced with a mixed bag of positive and negative treatment. One social scientist reports no academic difficulty from his/her study of ufos, but says that it hasn't really helped with career mobility. Professor X never lists UFO investigations on the vita. He does list, however, other studies on the social science of the paranormal in general that are somewhat of a plus at the university, but until recently have been considered inappropriate or fringe work by colleagues in the same subfield at other universities. Professor X is considered "a little weird" for doing this research.

Another university professor has published two important books in ufology. Professor Y's first book was a positive, but more arm's-length treatment, and was considered academically acceptable. It helped him/her get tenure. The second book, however, was a contro-

---

37. Mack, 1994C.

versial treatment of UFO experiencers that considers their experiences to be real and not just some psychological pathology. Although recommended by the department for promotion, Professor Y was turned down by the faculty promotion committee allegedly on grounds of methodology used in the book. However, one member of the committee leaked information to a colleague that if Professor Y had declared that these UFO experiences were nonsense, he/she would have been promoted. Professor Y had predicted to the department members that doing this research would prevent him/her from getting promoted. They disagreed, but Professor Y told them they were living an illusion. Professor Y had decided that the research was important enough to do anyway. One clue that the university might not be very supportive of Professor Y's research is the fact that they never acknowledge any of the considerable media coverage that Professor Y gets, which is more than anyone else gets, outside of the athletic program.

Still another university professor, who expected to end up in the courtroom soon, was supported for tenure by the department, but rejected by the faculty tenure committee. The situation is complex, and Professor Z was frankly uncertain whether the real reason for the decision had anything to do with his/her involvement in ufology. The Dean did know about the ufology, which Professor Z kept rather quiet, had joked about it, and may have been influential in the committee's decision. The court case was expected to be tried on other grounds. At any rate, it is often difficult to know how decisions are made in academe, and unsubstantiated rumors and committee leaks are sometimes the only clues.

In one other case divided between support and opposition, Professor A is considered "nuts" by some of the people in the same department due to his/her research on abductees, research considered fascinating by many in surrounding departments. The department decided to deny tenure and not to defer the tenure decision for a year, but the faculty tenure committee overturned that decision, which was overturned by the dean, who was overruled by the vice president. Consequently the decision was deferred for one year.

Although psychologists and counselors often work in academic institutions, they may also work full or part-time in mental health agencies or in private practice where they still have professional colleagues to deal with. I attended one meeting of mental health professionals who were interested in helping abductees. Only 5 of 70 or 80 people in attendance raised their hands when asked if they were afraid of being ridiculed for their work, although it may just have been uncool to admit it. One person claimed that a certain debunking organization had written to a hospital asking them why they still kept a certain doctor on the staff who worked with abductees, this given as an example of the intimidation some people experience.

It was reported in *UFO* magazine that Dr. Scott Corder had his medical license suspended by the Kansas State Board of the Healing Arts in 1989 on account of "his claims to be in contact with the Apostle Peter, or Cephas...an alien representing God."[38] Corder blamed a tabloid for distorting his story. When he refused to submit to psychiatric testing or to attend further meetings of the board, the board suspended his license.

One therapist told me that his/her office lease was not renewed, allegedly on the grounds that other colleagues in the building didn't like the way a camera crew occupied the building when waiting to interview Dr. X. Dr. X suspected that the real reason was disapproval of the work he/she was doing with UFO experiencers, or that at least they didn't want to be associated publicly with this "flaky UFO thing."

Other than examples mentioned already elsewhere, I do not have many interesting cases of harassment of ufologists in other types of business. There are situations in which co-workers ridiculed or ostracized the individual, one in which a job interview went sour after the candidate mentioned being in MUFON, and one in which a supervisor tried to block someone's promotion. At one meeting of the Skysearch (pseudonym) study group, I heard two people say that they were careful never to tell anybody at work that they were going to a UFO meeting.

By contrast, harassment in government jobs and by the government is almost too interesting. I am very cautious in dealing with this, mainly to avoid danger to any individuals involved. I am also at a loss to know what to make of all the conspiracy claims involving the U.S. government and military, especially involving intelligence agencies. Consequently, I am concentrating on first-hand reports and mentioning names only when they have already been well publicized.

I have already pointed out above that very few ufologists in government said that they were completely open about their involvement (20%), and also that a low percentage (15%) claimed any harassment. Even those who do ufology publicly may give a disclaimer to make it clear that the government does not sanction their activity.

On the local level, Robert O. Dean accused the Pima County (Arizona) Sheriff's Department of passing him over for promotion in a job search for Emergency Services Coordinator when he rose to the top of

---

38. Corbin, 1989.

the candidate pool.[39] The alleged reason for his not being selected was
his interest in UFOs and his claim to have had a UFO experience. Dean
won a settlement of $100,000 plus $16,000 back pay in 1992, but at great
legal cost and only if he would retire.

Aside from harassment or punishment while working in the government, there are many claims that agents of the government have harassed ufologists, no matter where they work, in connection with the
UFO cover-up and the monitoring of ufologists' activities. One prominent ufologist, X, stated in a UFO conference that he/she has received
threats because of his/her work. Another person, who just might be in
a position to know, told me that he/she knows for certain that X is under surveillance by the government.

Three other ufologists have told me that they have been subjected
to dirty tricks and/or surveillance. These include an intelligence agent
trying to drum up phony malpractice claims against a therapist, mostly
minor vandalism, the frequent opening of mail that is then taped shut
in crude, obvious ways and then arrives very late, the tapping of phone
lines, and the cutting off of phone lines three times while the individual
was on talk radio discussing UFOs.

Who's Studying Whom?

Ufologists are often suspicious that there may be individuals or
subgroups within government agencies taking an interest in their
work. There are even rumors that certain well-known ufologists are on
the government payroll as spies or creators of disinformation. It is not
entirely a joke to say that anybody who is anybody in UFO studies has
been accused of working for the CIA. In addition to government attention, ufologists sometimes wonder if they are getting special attention
from the occupants of the very UFOs they are in the business of studying. Although this might seem absurd to outsiders, it is plausible if one
works under the assumption that UFOs are guided by a higher intelligence, extraterrestrial or otherwise. If humans are rats in an alien lab (a
common metaphor in ufology), ufologists are merely rats who pay
more attention to the experimenters.

There is reason to believe that some humans are more prone to see
UFOs than others, or to have multiple UFO experiences while others
have none. This suggests that UFOs are put on display to chosen people, although it may also simply indicate that some people have more
"encounter-prone personalities"[40] than others. If UFO experiences are

39. Dean, 1994.

more the former, i.e., displays directed by a higher intelligence, it is just conceivable that this intelligence (or some of these intelligences) might want to choose ufologists as experiencers.

We noted earlier that a very high percentage of the ufologists interviewed for this study say they may have had a UFO experience: 56% (48% yes, 8% maybe). My interpretation was that it took a strong motivator like this to get people to dare to study such a taboo subject. This may or may not have anything to do with some alien intention to get these people to do ufology.

Some ufologists claim that strange things started happening to them after they began to study the phenomenon, including UFO sightings or even abductions, but also a wider range of paranormal experiences. In my sample, 11% stated that they had UFO experiences only after getting into some significant study of UFOs. This might be a high figure, considering that it is probably somewhat higher than the percentage of UFO experiencers in the general population, and since they had not had any UFO experiences up through the adult years. However, it is very difficult to tell, because they may have forgotten or not recognized earlier experiences, and because they may have been especially open to and looking for experiences once they became ufologists, and because there was probably some "social-desirability response" in these interviews (my study was sanctioned by MUFON who gave me the consultant list) in favor of admitting UFO experiences.

There is always an undercurrent of expectation at a UFO conference that something strange might happen with all the ufologists and experiencers present, up to and including a UFO sighting. In fact the Gulf Breeze UFO Conference includes a beach cookout and skywatch because Gulf Breeze, Florida, is a UFO hot spot. At the 1994 conference held in Pensacola and Gulf Breeze, I was told by one of the organizers that two people reported sightings that night, one of them about 9:00 P.M., just about the time I left the beach. One of them was allegedly four red lights in a rectangular formation.

Short of actual sightings, people take notice of other occurrences that might be UFO-related, such as electrical or photographic anomalies, or synchronicities. At the reception on Friday evening, July 10, 1992, at the MUFON Conference in Albuquerque, New Mexico, I heard people "ooh" when the lights dimmed briefly. Someone explained to me that people were still thinking about how the power had failed for hours at the previous year's MUFON conference in Chicago, and, of

---

40. Ring, 1992, p. 39.

course, they wondered if such things might not be related to the electromagnetic effects associated with UFO sightings.

The next night, July 11, 1992, in Albuquerque, a fire alarm went off during the question-and-answer session at 10:19 P.M. after a question on crop circles. As people got up to leave, one ufologist said, probably half-jokingly, "I wonder if the aliens (did this)." There was only one other question-and-answer session at the conference, the next afternoon. About one-third of the way through, around 4:30 P.M., after a question on animal manipulation and AIDS, the fire alarm went off again. This time the chairperson quipped, "Aliens at work," and the session continued.

There was one other fire alarm incident that I am aware of. At the Gulf Breeze Conference in 1994 the elevators were stopped when the smoke-alarm system went off and fire fighters came to investigate. Keep in mind that I have attended nine major UFO conferences and two minor ones, and there is a certain probability that I would have experienced some situations like this during that time. However, it is at least subjectively important for ufologists who wonder if such incidents are meaningful and more frequent than expected.

At the 14th Rocky Mountain UFO Conference in Laramie, Wyoming, June 23-27, 1993, one person noticed that he was having unusual battery problems with his camera during the registration period on the afternoon of June 23, although the batteries worked fine later on. After the pictures were developed he noticed unusual overexposure problems and commented that he had had photographic malfunctions on several occasions, while photographing something anomalous, such as ghosts in a cemetery. Four people at the registration session talked about how they had all slept an unusually long time the night before, one of them thirteen hours, and they wondered whether people might have been examined or abducted that night since there were so many experiencers (abductees) at that particular conference. None of this was stated dogmatically, but people let themselves speculate.

Two days later, at a "closed" (no recording or note-taking) session I attended in which experiencers shared their stories from 2:00 to 4:00 P.M., the lights went off in the hall once, came back on again, then went off again later for good at 3:55 P.M., just before the scheduled end of the session. Someone told me that the lights had gone off in the same room the previous year at the conference, right after someone had related an anecdote including the idea "Give us a sign!" A tornado warning also came through at this time. Others confirmed this previous year's incident in general, but I did not hear anyone else mention the speaker's comment about a sign.

Synchronicities, i.e., coincidences that are seen as meaningful and perhaps too much of a coincidence to be interpreted as mere chance, are sometimes taken as a sign that something paranormal is going on, or as some kind of cosmic signal being delivered to the experiencer. One person attending the 14th Annual Rocky Mountain UFO Conference referred to above noticed that he had cut his chin in the same spot three days in a row while shaving. He thought, "If I were being foolish, I might look at this mark and think that I had been abducted the night before and that they had left this mark on me." But then he thought further, "That's silly. People don't get abduction marks on the chin." He had read a lot of UFO literature and could not remember this type of abduction scar being reported.

Then he went down to the conference meeting room just before it opened up for continental breakfast. In the few pages he had time to read while waiting he came across the famous Villas Boas case from Brazil in 1957 in which the abductee had blood samples taken from his chin. He thought, "It's as if they're telling me, 'You think you're so smart, but here's a case of a chin mark.'" Then, to make this a double synchronicity, in the very first session, Leo Sprinkle, organizer of the conference, brought up the Villas Boas case briefly in the course of an anecdote, the only UFO case mentioned during that session.

One example of a writer who reports strange experiences that began after he started investigating the subject is journalist Ed Conroy who looked into the story of Whitley Strieber, author of the best-selling book *Communion*.[41] In the Epilogue to Conroy's *Report on Communion*,[42] the author wonders if he has been visited by "UFO researcher's disease." The symptoms include his own apparent abduction experiences, a plague of various kinds of helicopters flying low and shining lights in his window, a tapped telephone and strange messages left on his answering machine, and a night-time UFO sighting with friends. In very much the same spirit related to me by other researchers, Conroy expresses both wonder over the experiences and concern that others will think that "My mind has taken me on a joyride."[43] Some ufologists keep such experiences to themselves to preserve credibility, but others feel compelled to share them.

Raymond Fowler, well known for his four books[44] on abductee Betty Andreasson Luca, the first of which, *The Andreasson Affair*, was published in 1979, began to have his own experiences and to report on

---

41. Strieber, 1987.
42. Conroy, 1989, p. 351-372.
43. Conroy, 1989, p. 369.
44. Fowler, 1979, 1982, 1990, 1995.

them in the subsequent books, *The Watchers* and *The Watchers II*. In spite of the disruptive effects on his family and church life, Fowler revealed his own abduction dreams and "punch biopsy-like scoop marks on my leg" similar to ones Betty Luca received about the same time.[45] Although Fowler insists that he remains skeptical about his memories, just as he is about other cases he investigates, he suspects that his "avid interest in UFOs and painstaking investigations, which I thought were of my own doing, are in reality part of an indoctrination process motivated by the phenomenon itself."[46] He thinks that many other ufologists may be involved unwittingly in the same complex plan and only hopes that it will be beneficial to humans.

It appears that some ufologists come to be aware that they are being chosen and perhaps directed by the UFO phenomenon. This has been called a "sense of mission." Of course, what we are observing here may be, at least in part, a conversion process similar to religious conversion. At least some ufologists to whom I attribute a sense of mission would probably not be offended by that explanation. In fact, they tend to see the UFO phenomenon as a kind of New Age awakening or transformation of humanity. But, of course, this interpretation causes problems within the debate over the scientific status of ufology and especially irritates ufologists who are more "nuts-and-bolts" oriented.

Although it is very tricky to interpret the qualitative material I have collected, I consider 9% of my sample of ufologists for whom I have the appropriate information on which to make a judgment (7 out of 77 of them) to have a high sense of mission, and another 8% (6 of 77) to have at least a moderate sense of mission, and the other 83% show no apparent sense of mission. All 13 in the high and moderate categories think they have had a UFO experience (no "maybes" here). Of the 7 rated "high" on mission, 6 think they are abductees; of the 6 "moderates," 1 thinks he/she is an abductee and 1 more is a maybe.

There seems to be a connection between UFO experiences, psychic experiences (ESP, psychokinesis, spirit voices, etc.), and the sense of mission. The association between UFO experiences and other paranormal, especially psychic experiences, has been discussed in the literature.[47] In my sample, 86% of abducted ufologists reported significant psychic experiences, 50% of the "maybe" abductees, 39% of UFO experiencers altogether, 14% of "maybe" UFO experiencers and 13% of those with no UFO experiences reported psychic experiences.

---

45. Casteel, 1991A.
46. Casteel, 1991A, p. 29.
47. Ring, 1992; Schwarz, 1983; K.W.C. Phillips, 1993; Dormer, 1993.

Remembering that a total of 17% of the ufologists had at least a moderate sense of mission, more specifically 36% of the UFO experiencers had a sense of mission, and 0% of all those saying either "maybe" or "no" to whether they had had a UFO experience had a sense of mission. And to round out the set of associations, 91% of those with a sense of mission (for whom the information is available, 10 of 11) reported psychic experiences, and conversely 42% of those with psychic experiences had a sense of mission (10 of 24). It may be that a UFO experience (preferably an abduction) plus psychic experiences are almost necessary, but not sufficient, conditions for this sense of mission.

Now to illustrate. Perhaps I should not have considered this person to have a "sense of mission," because there is no apparent spiritual transformation involved, but he/she definitely claimed to be directed by alien intelligences. This individual remembers without the aid of hypnotic regression at least part of a childhood abduction involving a little blue man and typical abduction examination marks. Dr. X is now a very successful inventor and has been guided in the invention process by the "others," as they call themselves. These beings, the "others," do not give the entire set of plans, but suggest things that lead to a wide variety of excellent inventions. Although Dr. X did not say so, it may be that some of the anti-pollution technology he/she has helped develop could be interpreted as "saving the planet," one element that has often been claimed by abductees to be part of the alien mission.

More typically, the ufologists on a mission, especially the ones rated "high" on mission, see themselves as spiritually transformed, although not usually in a traditionally religious sense, but in more of a New Age sense. One very popular recent book that outlines this New Age spiritual transformation, one that is of special interest to some of these ufologists in fact, is *The Celestine Prophecy: An Adventure* by James Redfield.[48] Although the subtitle and the style of the book would seem to make it clear enough that this book is a novel, there is a rumor among many that it is somehow based on something real. Essentially the adventure is a quest for fragmented copies of a manuscript from 600 B.C. in Peru.

This document presents Nine Insights that represent rather nicely a version of today's New Age principles of an impending transformation of humans and their world. It explains that we should pay attention to coincidences (synchronicities) in our lives that are guides to the paths we should be taking to spiritual evolution. In the last half of the twentieth century, people are gradually coming to develop their con-

48. Redfield, 1993.

sciousness beyond scientific materialism. Through meditation, humans will learn to give spiritual energy to others from the limitless universal supply, and live in harmony instead of conflict. Through new energy technologies and ecological harmony, society will be able to meet all people's physical needs by the middle of the twenty-first century, giving people free time for seeking spiritual truth.

In broad terms, *The Celestine Prophecy* exemplifies the New Age context within which the alien/visitor mission falls, at least as seen by most people who take a positive, transformative perspective on UFO close-encounter or contactee experiences ("abductions" is considered a negative term). In their book *Close Extraterrestrial Encounters,*[49] Richard J. Boylan and Lee K. Boylan state that "having an obsessive sense of mission" instilled by "intense telepathic communication" with ETs is a potential indicator of having had a close ET encounter, and they mention as one product of the sense of mission the writing of their own book.

Dr. Richard Boylan's (see Appendix, page 224) own ET encounter experiences and development of psychic abilities are related in one chapter.[50] In a personal interview, Dr. Boylan, a clinical psychologist, elaborated on his mission. Through psychic communication he has learned that he has a role in preparing people for increased ET presence among us, involving ambassadorial contact and cultural exchanges on a global scale. This sounds very much like the work being done by Dr. Steven M. Greer at the Center for the Study of Extraterrestrial Intelligence (CSETI) involving CE-V (inviting contact with ETs) to establish universal communication and peace.[51]

Another feature of the sense of mission mentioned by Dr. Boylan is his compulsive reading in new physics and in mathematics at a time when he saw no connection with UFOs.[52] He said that ETs may pick people to read things with which they have no familiarity, a kind of cross-training to stretch us. One of the four artists abducted in *The All-agash Abductions* stated at a UFO conference that after his experience, which was buried in his memory for years, he started devouring mathematics, which he had failed in school, and math became a major theme in his new artwork.[53]

The idea of having a compulsion to read, research, write and publish has been discussed not only by Dr. Boylan, but by several other ufologists as well. The Boylans state as another example of people with

49. Boylan and Boylan, 1994, pp. 42-43.
50. Boylan and Boylan, 1994, pp. 135-148.
51. Greer, 1992.
52. Dr. Richard J. Boylan, personal interview, Oct. 30, 1994.
53. Weiner and others, 1994.

a sense of mission the following, "Certain brave persons, like R. Leo Sprinkle, Ph.D., have dedicated much of their professional career and reputation to the task of spreading awareness of the ET presence. This is clearly Leo's mission."[54]

Leo Sprinkle discovered through hypnotic regression in 1980 that he had had an experience on a craft in his youth in which he was told, "Leo, learn to read and write well; when you grow up you can help other people learn more about their purpose in life."[55] For sixteen years Dr. Sprinkle organized the Rocky Mountain UFO Conference for experiencers and researchers, with emphasis on programs to help the former share and cope with their puzzling encounters.

Marc Davenport (see Appendix, page 225) is another ufologist who reports feeling compelled to write about the phenomenon, a fact that he attributes to his UFO experiences.[56] In fact, he thinks that the UFO presence is engaging in social engineering, some of which brings couples together, such as him and his wife, Leah Haley, who wrote about her own abduction experiences in her book *Lost Was the Key*.[57] Marc has been gathering data on other such couples. Budd Hopkins has referred to couples that think they have been brought together many times in their lives on UFOs, sometimes from great distances, in a kind of alien sociological observation of romantic relationships.[58]

In addition to these alleged examples of people brought together by ET/visitor design, I have noticed a few other couples who seem to work together in the development of a sense of mission, however they were brought together. The pattern involved in these relationships is that the male has a traditional academic background and is somewhat skeptical until the female influences him with her psychic or spiritual perspective, and then the male starts doing UFO research from a somewhat New Age point of view. The same pattern has occurred with a couple who both work with spirit possession rather than ufology. Although ufology has been heavily male in the past, there are signs that women are becoming more involved and influential, and we may expect more of this influence in the New Age aspects of ufology in particular, paralleling the gender phenomena in the New Age movement in general as discussed by David J. Hess in *Science in the New Age*.[59]

---

54. Boylan and Boylan, 1994, p. 42.
55. Sprinkle, 1994B.
56. Marc Davenport, personal interview, Oct. 15, 1994.
57. Haley, 1993.
58. Hopkins, 1994B.
59. Hess, 1993.

Chapter 5

Debunkers, Skeptics and True Believers

Evidence, Proof and "Extraordinary Proof"

It is obvious from previous chapters that the subject of UFOs is taboo in normal science. Part of the justification for this position is that "extraordinary claims require extraordinary evidence." Anything like UFOs that is outside of accepted, normal-scientific paradigms is "extraordinary." Probably the best known scientist associated with this view is astronomer Carl Sagan (of *Parade* magazine and public TV fame, and a member of CSICOP).

According to Topher Cooper, the aphorism "Extraordinary claims require extraordinary proof" is popularly attributed to eighteenth-century Scottish philosopher David Hume in his essay "On Miracles," although these exact words do not appear in the essay.[1] Cooper points out that there are some difficulties with this principle.[2] Is a claim extraordinary because it contradicts accumulated evidence, or only because it contradicts authoritative assumptions? Should there be different rules of evidence for ordinary (generally accepted) and extraordinary (generally unaccepted) claims?

Cooper warns against the "false complement: 'Extraordinary claims are refutable by extraordinarily weak arguments.'"[3] David M. Jacobs points out that J. Allen Hynek complained about the Condon report doing just this in its facile arguments that operated on the assumption that all UFO reports must have natural causes.[4] Hynek stated that "a possible natural, even though farfetched, explanation can always be adduced."[5] As an example of such a farfetched and weak argument, Hynek quoted the following from the Condon report, "This unusual sighting should therefore be assigned to the category of some almost

---

1. Cooper, 1994B.
2. Cooper, 1994A.
3. Cooper, 1994A, p. 123.
4. Jacobs, 1975, pp. 219-220.
5. Hynek, 1969, pp. 39-42.

certainly natural phenomenon which is so rare that it apparently has
never been reported before or since."[6]

One of the ways in which the UFO phenomenon has been dismissed by normal science has been to assign as many UFO reports as
possible to various categories of natural causes (like aircraft or stars),
and then to attribute the rest to hoaxes or to subjective factors (illusion,
hallucination, etc.). Of course, the Condon report did this to some degree, although many of the cases in the body of the report were left unexplained. A recent example of this strategy can be found in Robert
Moore's "Mundane-Synthesistic Hypothesis," meaning that a synthe-
sis of mundane explanations combines to reduce the possible unknowns to a very small percentage of all reports.[7] Then it may be
assumed from the perspective of normal science that further investigation would eventually provide a mundane explanation for *all* reports.

Ufologists complain that debunkers often use this procedure in an
absurd fashion; for example, explaining a huge light over a police car
that moves away and is chased for a great distance as the planet Venus,
or discounting the testimony of apparently reliable witnesses as hallucination without any "proof" of mental disturbance. Of course, the concept of "proof" is a very demanding one.

What constitutes "proof" of UFOs (in the sense of craft guided by
nonhuman occupants whether extraterrestrial or not)? If the only acceptable proof consists of an intact craft that could not have been constructed by humans with present technology, then no such proof is at
least publicly available. On the other hand, how can UFO debunkers be
expected to prove that all UFO reports have mundane causes? It is impossible to prove a negative of this type, i.e., it is not possible to prove
that there are no UFOs, or no fairies or sea monsters. It is even unreasonable to expect debunkers to account for all *known* reports, even if the
mundane-synthesistic hypothesis should happen to be correct.

As Michael Baigent and others say in their book, *Holy Blood, Holy
Grail*, when talking about interpretations of the New Testament, "Of
course, we could not 'prove' our conclusions.... But what...*would* constitute proof? ...The question of 'proof' is ultimately beside the point....
The most one can honestly do is deal with *evidence* [suggesting] greater
or lesser possibilities."[8] At this point the UFO question is of similar status. There is evidence rather than absolute proof in either direction.

Consequently, it is more appropriate at this stage to ask whether
the subject should be investigated and funded rather than to ask for

6. Condon, 1969, p. 140.
7. Moore, 1993.
8. Baigent and others, 1982, p. 16.

proof. As ufologist Stanton Friedman likes to say, "Extraordinary claims require extraordinary investigation." Debunkers like Philip Klass, however, question whether the subject has sufficient scientific merit to investigate and do their own investigations only to defend science against the claims of the ufologists.

Skepticism vs. Debunking

Although the distinction is often obscured, there is an important difference between skepticism and debunking. As will be discussed in the next chapter, skepticism or doubting is an important part of the scientific method. It is only by doubting and testing that science can claim to be an objective method. Debunking, however, goes beyond doubting to rejection.

Whether this rejection is appropriate or not depends upon your point of view. CSICOP purports to reject false claims or pseudoscience, thereby protecting the gullible who might embrace these claims. From the point of view of ufologists and other practitioners of "deviant science," debunkers reject evidence and even refuse to allow others to examine evidence without fear of ridicule.

Sometimes, however, ufologists recognize that debunkers can serve a useful scientific function. Chris Rutkowski states that debunkers "fill the niche of peer review, and...their comments help refine ufological theories.... Debunkers certainly have their specific biases and mindsets, but so do believers."[9]

Having a mind-set would not seem to be appropriate for scientific methodology, but it is reasonable for sociologists to expect it in human beings, even in human beings who claim to be scientists. Another word for "mind-set" is, of course, "prejudice." Taken at their stereotypical extremes, both debunkers and true believers are prejudiced, i.e., they both refuse to look at evidence. Debunkers refuse to examine evidence because they already know it is false. ("It can't be; therefore it isn't.") True believers refuse to examine evidence because they already know it is true. ("Blessed are those who believe but have not seen.")

Of course, this is not quite fair either to debunkers or to believers. After all, scientists cannot investigate every claim with equal vigor, and there must be priorities set on which studies are worth funding. Nor can people who have accepted certain claims be expected to test them forever. Calling them "true believers" is unfair if they have some evi-

---

9. Rutkowski, 1990, pp. 166-168.

dence for their beliefs, even if their evidence involves ways of knowing other than science.

Part of the controversy lies with the issue of how much acceptance or rejection of claims is really based on some kind of evidence as opposed to prejudice or mind-set. Sturrock found that the longer astronomers studied the UFO problem the more likely they were to give greater weight to exotic hypotheses and less weight to hoaxes and more mundane hypotheses.[10] This might mean that the evidence is convincing, but it might also mean that astronomers who have more belief in the first place are more likely to look at the evidence.

One of the nonufologist astronomers I interviewed said that most astronomers would assume that J. Allen Hynek must have believed in UFOs to begin with, or he would never have bothered to study a subject with such a low probability of discovering anything worthwhile. Of course, this statement overlooks the fact that Hynek seemed genuinely to be highly skeptical at first. And many ufologists get irritated by the question of whether they "believe" in UFOs. They like to say that they find the *evidence* compelling.

However, perhaps the most important point is that the social structure of normal science, especially in academe and in government, makes it so difficult for people to study UFOs that it takes a powerful personal incentive to do so. The most powerful incentive derives from having one's own UFO experience. Should this experience be considered evidence, or conversion to a belief?

"Reality-Tunnels" and the Illogic of Debunking

Science journalist Robert Anton Wilson writes about "reality-tunnels," paradigms that provide an understanding of reality but which, of course, restrict us from appreciating other perspectives at the same time. Under the influence of a particular reality-tunnel, a "crusading skeptic" (debunker) may deny that something like UFOs is possible. However, Wilson points out, such dogmatism assumes "that you already know *the full spectrum of the possible*. In a century in which every decade has brought new and astonishing scientific shocks, that [requires] a huge, brave and audacious faith indeed."[11]

One might presume that anyone who begins to examine the evidence that lies outside the old reality-tunnel will begin to entertain other reality-tunnels. Yet seeing is not always believing. Sturrock, in his

10. Sturrock, 1994A.
11. Robert A. Wilson, 1991, p. 36.

survey of astronomers, asked respondents to assign "prior probabilities" to a list of possible explanations for UFO reports, including hoaxes, known and unknown natural and technological devices, etc. If they
had had their own UFO experiences, they were asked to assign "post
probabilities" to possible explanations for their own sightings. An examination of the cases he presents shows an interesting tendency even
for the experiencers to give still rather low probabilities to ET devices
and other unknown causes.[12]

What I am suggesting is that nonastronomers would probably
have assigned a much higher probability of ET devices to any such
strange sightings they might have had. Perhaps astronomers are too
skeptical, or perhaps nonastronomers are too gullible. Nevertheless,
old reality-tunnels seem to retain great influence even under discon-
firming conditions. It may be just too threatening for many astronomers to embrace the ET explanation for their own experiences because
they are used to certain assumptions in their field about the difficulties
of traveling at such great speeds over such great distances.

It amuses me to hear people say that "ESP is a fraud," as one astronomer did in an interview, and then give me several personal examples of what could only be described either as ESP or as truly
astonishing coincidence. One tavern owner in a TV documentary said
that he didn't believe in ghosts, but also stated emphatically that his
tavern was haunted and gave several detailed examples.

I have observed another type of inconsistency between reality-tunnel and experience. One can accept a new reality-tunnel on an intellectual level and still deny one's own experiences because they violate an
old reality-tunnel that hangs on at the emotional level. Some people
who accept the idea of UFOs or ESP engage in extreme denial when
they are jolted by an apparent UFO or ESP experience. I think that this
is a type of prejudice that parallels racial prejudice. Many people who
have gone through a liberalizing higher-educational system know on
an intellectual level that prejudice is wrong, but experience their own
racist emotional responses in quick, everyday encounters before they
have a chance to think about them rationally.

Dogmatic defense of a reality-tunnel does not fit the ideal of science as an objective method (see next chapter). Although some debunking may be done fairly and find targets that deserve to be
debunked, ufologists are frustrated by what they see as debunking
based on propagandistic methods designed to support normal science.
Daniel Drasin presents an entertaining critique of unfair and illogical

---

12. Sturrock, 1994B.

debunking in "Ridicule Is No Laughing Matter: The Anatomy of Debunking."[13]

Essentially Drasin elaborates on classic propaganda techniques that are employed by debunkers not in the interests of scientific inquiry but to defend the sacred reality-tunnel. Of course, there are a great many possible deceptions and logical fallacies, but to a great extent such debunking is based upon the deviant status of the discipline, in this case ufology. Ridicule is an especially effective method of social control, since it emphasizes the lack of respect due to people who would dare to study something so preposterous, thereby labeling them oddballs or weirdos. Few academics can afford such a label. In addition to portraying the subject matter as ridiculous, the debunker can subject anyone who provides evidence for the phenomenon to *ad hominem* attack, pointing out any history of counseling or legal problems, or suggesting that they may profit financially from their claims.

Since this type of debunking is based so much on deviant labeling, it is not surprising that stereotyping is applied not only to the deviant scientists and experiencers, but to the arguments involved as well. Perhaps the most common use of stereotyping is the illogical extension of one bit of hoaxing or faulty evidence to the entire phenomenon. If one crop circle is a hoax, those who are comfortable with normal-science explanations may leap to the conclusion that all crop circles are hoaxes. If one UFO sighting turns out to be a misidentification of a planet, maybe similar sightings will be easily dismissed as planets without looking carefully at the evidence. Another problem is the possibility that even a person hoaxing in one instance might also have reported many genuine experiences, but few ufologists would dare to say so. Hoaxes are not so damaging in fields that are considered legitimate. For example, if one alleged Van Gogh painting is discovered to be a forgery, this does not easily lead the art world to the conclusion that all Van Gogh paintings are forgeries (or that Van Gogh never existed).

One outstanding example of debunking involves the "face on Mars," which is not a UFO case *per se*, but is of considerable interest to many ufologists because it suggests extraterrestrial civilization elsewhere in the solar system. Stanley V. McDaniel, professor emeritus, department of philosophy at Sonoma State University, has investigated and documented this case thoroughly.[14]

Photographs taken by the 1976 Viking Mars mission appear to some analysts to indicate artificial landform structures in the Martian

13. Drasin, 1992.
14. McDaniel, 1993.

region called Cydonia. These include especially a mile-wide mesa that appears to some to be a humanoid face, but also pyramids and a "city." NASA denied that there was any "credible evidence" of artificiality, and claimed that they had a later photograph that revealed that the apparent face was just an illusion of light and shadow. However, NASA failed to produce the later photo, and McDaniel states that there never could have been one since the surface was in darkness at the time it was supposedly taken.[15] McDaniel accuses NASA of avoiding evidence, refusing to examine evidence scientifically, making false statements, and condoning the ridicule of independent researchers who have done scientific analysis of the photographs.[16]

Perhaps the best insight into the reasons for the debunking of the face by NASA and establishment scientists comes from Brian O'Leary, because he was originally in the role of skeptical astronomer and gradually came to see the face as an important research topic. O'Leary states that when Richard Hoagland, one of the top investigators of the face on Mars, first talked to him about the subject, he didn't *want* to believe him.[17] O'Leary's reasons for being negative were his memory of previous exaggerated claims about life on Mars, his knowledge that his NASA colleagues had labeled the face a trick of light and shadow, and his fear of losing credibility professionally.

It is interesting that in spite of some previous fallacies, such as the reported canals on Mars that turned out to be astronomer Percival Lowell's imagination, there have been suggestions by other reputable astronomers that there might be evidence of ET visitors to this solar system. Astronomer Carl Sagan, of all people, had suggested in 1963 that space travelers may have visited the solar system about once every 10,000 years and that they may have left bases on the Moon or on other planets.[18] However, who is going to dare to be the first astronomer to claim that such evidence has actually been found, remembering the classic blunder by Percival Lowell? Once NASA has pooh-poohed the "face," who is going to risk asking for a second look?

O'Leary goes on to document the subsequent ridicule that he and other investigators suffered once he started to take the face seriously. Planetary geologist Michael Carr went on TV to point out a Martian feature that he said looked like Kermit the Frog from Sesame Street. "One could see on Carr's face an expression of sarcasm, and his condescending chuckles and an attitude of disdain...."[19] He compared the

15. McDaniel, 1993, pp. 11-12.
16. McDaniel, 1993, pp. xix-xx.
17. O'Leary, 1989, pp. 70-71.
18. Sagan, 1980, p. 211.
19. O'Leary, 1989, pp. 71-72.

face to New Hampshire's Old Man of the Mountain, which O'Leary says looks artificial only in profile, whereas the face retains its "face-ness" at all angles. Carl Sagan joined the fun by producing a potato chip that appeared to contain a likeness of Jesus Christ.

O'Leary expresses his dismay at the attitudes of his colleagues who laugh, but refuse to look at the mathematical data that argue strongly that the Cydonia features are not fractal (varying in a random natural way), but rather are artificial and contain an elegant geometry. He suggests two possible reasons for the debunking attitude: the threat to personal careers in academe, and a conspiracy on the part of the government to discourage such inquiry.[20] He finds the latter credible based on experiences with colleagues who seemed enthusiastic at first, but did a sudden about-face.

CSICOP and *The Skeptical Inquirer*

The Committee for the Scientific Investigation of Claims of the Paranormal (CSICOP) is an organization mainly of academics, led by Chairman Paul Kurtz, professor emeritus of philosophy, SUNY Buffalo. Beginning in 1976, it has published *The Skeptical Inquirer* to help in "the critical investigation of paranormal and fringe-science claims from a responsible, scientific point of view." Sociologist of science Marcello Truzzi broke away from the group early because he objected to its debunking bias that prevented a legitimate inquiry into the paranormal. Truzzi then founded the journal *Zetetic Scholar* in order to encourage such inquiry. Philip J. Klass (see Appendix, page 229) argued strongly against Truzzi's position in 1976 on the grounds that there were already groups promoting belief (in UFOs specifically) and that CSICOP should provide a skeptical counterbalance.

One astronomer who rejects ufology nevertheless told me that CSICOP and *SI* are too negatively biased in his opinion. To a great many ufologists CSICOP represents the archenemy, and Philip Klass is seen as the biggest and the most negative of the debunkers with his many books on UFOs and his articles and book reviews in *The Skeptical Enquirer*. An examination of the evidence reveals that this view is only partly justified.

Ufologist Jerome Clark stated in 1988 that Philip J. Klass was "the only would-be UFO debunker willing to take on the hard cases."[21] Mr. Klass also told me that he looks for the allegedly best cases. Clark's nice

---

20. O'Leary, 1989, p. 77.
21. Clark, 1988, pp. 59-72.

compliment, however, was sandwiched into the following statement, "As ufology has matured and standards have risen, investigations generally have become more professional, the evidence coming out of those investigations holding up and reducing Philip J. Klass...to the hurling of McCarthyite charges against the character of ufologists and foregoing rational discourse altogether."

My reading of the UFO articles and reviews in *The Skeptical Inquirer* over the years impresses me as follows. Although there is little attempt to investigate the phenomenon thoroughly, except in Klass's work, most pieces in *SI* are mostly fair although from a very skeptical perspective. One such example is a convincing critique by Taylor and Dennett of a photograph contained in a CUFOS traveling exhibit.[22] Other such "fair" articles are one by Philip Klass on the decline in radar UFO reports due to improvement in radar and computer technology,[23] a review of the literature on psychology and UFOs by Armando Simon,[24] and some harsh, but apparently reasonable, book reviews by Robert Sheaffer[25] and by David A. Schroth.[26]

Once in a great while there is even a (shock) positive article, such as Armando Simon's review of Richard F. Haines' book, *Observing UFOs*, in 1980.[27] Simon states that "Although Haines is open-minded to the possibility that UFOs may be something highly unusual, his feet are planted firmly on the ground, and he refuses to confuse speculation and wishful thinking with facts."

However, even many of the "fair" articles contain at some point the propagandistic technique of the sweeping negative statement. For example, the Taylor and Dennett piece referred to above states that "Chief among [the flaws in UFO studies, as pointed out in *SI* articles] is the failure of UFO proponents to use proper scientific methodology— or, for that matter, any methodology at all. Ufology has thus established itself as a counterfeit science—or...pseudoscience."[28] In the Schroth review there is the generalization that "UFO proponents do not enjoy having their claims questioned."[29] This can be seen either as a stereotype or as a truism that fits just about any author or scholar.

Erik Vaughn refers to Jacques Vallée's discussion of problems in the documentation of Soviet UFO cases and of methodology that was untested by independent sources, and then says that "Vallée [uninten-

22. Taylor and Dennett, 1985.
23. Klass, 1985.
24. Simon, 1984.
25. Sheaffer, 1982.
26. Schroth, 1980.
27. Simon, 1980.
28. Taylor and Dennett, 1985, p. 69.
29. Schroth, 1980, p. 75.

tionally] reveals [Soviet ufologists] to be as inept and credulous as their Western colleagues."[30] In 1978, Robert Sheaffer reviewed *The Hynek UFO Report*, gave four specific criticisms, giving most attention to what he perhaps fairly concluded to be a statistical misinterpretation by Hynek of Air Force Bluebook statistics, and then stated, "Any lingering suspicions the reader may have that ufology might be a legitimate protoscience should be safely dispelled by the unscientific behavior of the leading ufologist of our day."[31]

Although the sweeping negative statement seems to be the most common debunking technique in *SI*, there is also some use of ridicule in the sense of laughing at ufologists, making them appear gullible or unreasonable. At the very end of his "fair" article on radar, Philip Klass includes the following, "It would not be surprising, after publication of this article, if some UFO-promoters should charge that the U.S. government has installed this new [radar and computer] equipment, at great taxpayer expense, simply to filter out 'legitimate UFOs' as part of a massive cover-up."[32] Robert Sheaffer provides an update on the latest in the paranormal in his regular feature "Psychic Vibrations," which in recent years is mostly about ufology, a low-key satire consisting mainly of developments that are evidently supposed to be absurd, largely quoted or paraphrased from ufologists and experiencers themselves, complete with cartoons.

Another debunking technique is the emphasis on more easily refuted cases, some of which might be said to be included in "Psychic Vibrations." There is not a great deal of this in *SI*, but one such case is the coverage of a tabloid account of a supposed UFO that was easily explained as a hot-air balloon hoax.[33] No ufologists are mentioned in the story, but since *SI* is dedicated to examining "fringe-science claims," are readers expected to associate tabloid absurdities with ufology?

Another activity of CSICOP is their annual conference. The 1994 CSICOP Conference was held in Seattle and included a session on alien abductions on June 23. There were to be four speakers: psychologist Robert Baker, a CSICOP Fellow; ufologists Thomas Bullard (a folklorist) and John E. Mack (psychiatrist); and psychologist Nicholas P. Spanos. Because Spanos died tragically in a plane crash shortly before the event, Philip Klass was asked to take his place. Instead, Klass suggested Donna Bassett, who had appeared in a *Time* article as a phony abductee who had tried to fool Mack, and who was attending the conference any-

30. Vaughn, 1993, pp. 82-85.
31. Sheaffer, 1978, pp. 64-67.
32. Klass, 1985, p. 260.
33. Nickell, 1993.

way. Paul Kurtz, moderator of the session, decided to let Bassett speak, along with an abductee that Mack was bringing with him.

However, Dr. Mack was never told in advance that Bassett was going to appear. When it became known that Mack had not been informed, two members of the audience complained that this was unethical (Mack only mentioned one, but Klass said it was two). Mr. Klass told me that this was not intended to be an ambush, but had been settled upon for practical reasons in the emergency. Dr. Mack said that it shocked him that this was done, and he considered it a new low for debunkers.[34] One disadvantage that Mack had was his inability to say much about her claims due to doctor/patient ethics. Mack also commented that the statements by CSICOP members in that session led him to keep telling them, "You're ridiculing."

Counter-debunking

Before launching into the counterattack from ufologists against debunking, let me point out that it takes more detailed reading in the material produced by CSICOP and *SI* and in the books by Philip J. Klass and other skeptics/debunkers than can be represented here before someone can decide whether they are fair or convincing. Examples emphasized by counter-debunkers are bound to be selective in a search for ludicrous examples. And there are bound to be some weak examples if debunkers stick to the reality-tunnel in which all UFO reports are expected to fit into mundane-cause categories. Some are going to be force-fit, even if the mundane hypothesis is substantially correct.

Of course, debunkers often do the same thing to ufologists, nipping at the heels of the weakest members of the flock. Yet I have already shown that *SI* is *not* totally involved in debunking in the worst sense of the term, although the collective wisdom in ufological circles tends to be that it is, as I have discovered in many discussions with ufologists, as well as from reading ufological books and journals. I should also repeat, however, that *SI* does contain many sweeping negative generalizations, even in the generally fair articles.

It would certainly help if more ufologists read *SI* carefully, and if more debunkers read ufology journals carefully (at least two debunkers apparently do: Philip J. Klass and Robert Sheaffer). But still their respective reality-tunnels get in the way of understanding. One rarely sees a positive statement about *SI* in ufology journals, and *SI* chooses to give a smirking slant that discredits ufologists as scientists, rather

---

34. Mack, 1994C.

than pointing out the many scientific debates that occur in the ufology journals. As I shall point out shortly, ufologists can be just as critical of each other as debunkers can be of ufologists.

For people who are unfamiliar with academic journals, let me point out that even within mainstream disciplines the debates often get vicious. A conflict orientation within the accepted boundaries of conceivable theories is typical in male-dominated academe. Cooperating and agreeing with everyone does not advance one's status. It is no wonder that the conflicts are even worse when normal science attacks a discipline like ufology that has been labeled deviant.

David M. Jacobs sums up rather nicely the general attitude in ufology about debunkers. "Debunkers are not open-minded skeptics. The combination of ignorance of the subject, a messianic sense of defending science from the forces of superstition, an ego-charged idea that they know the answer to whatever UFO problem is being discussed, and a streak of mean-spiritedness are the necessary ingredients for debunking."[35]

Speaking more directly to CSICOP in particular, since its name is nearly synonymous with debunking to ufologists, Jerome Clark states, "CSICOP's ability to influence media is legendary. Its *Manual for Local, Regional and National Groups* devotes 17 pages to 'Handling the Media' and 'Public Relations' and, tellingly, a mere three to 'Scientific Investigations.' Early on, Dennis Rawlins, a CSICOP founder who later became bitterly disillusioned, observed that CSICOP had less interest in 'open-ended scientific research' than in 'media wheeling and dealing.'"[36]

In a review of two books by CSICOP Fellow Robert Baker on hypnosis and false memories, which are at issue in UFO abductions, ufologist Stuart Appelle quotes the following, "Throughout the history of science...progress has been made by the dedicated rebels and amateurs, those who swam against the stream and challenged the prevailing paradigm....The power and prestige of the academic establishment...has, in many instances, retarded...the gaining of knowledge."[37] Ironically, Appelle says, this was written by Baker "in defense of his own position against hypnosis," an ironic statement from a member of CSICOP, an organization that functions to protect the academic establishment.

---

35. Jacobs, 1991.
36. Clark, 1992.
37. Appelle, 1992.

Some of the counter-debunking critiques are long and involved, requiring not only a careful reading in their entirety, but, also, in fairness, a chance for the targeted debunker to respond, as happens in academic journals. After that there should be rejoinders to the responses, and even then the issue would probably not be settled, and few people would have changed their minds. Two examples of extended critiques of Philip Klass for those who would like to examine them come from Jennie Zeidman on the Mansfield helicopter case,[38] and from William L. Moore and Stanton T. Friedman on the MJ-12 document.[39]

There is also an extended section on the debunking of Harvard astronomer Donald Menzel in a paper by Bruce Maccabee,[40] some of which is short enough for inclusion here. One interesting characteristic in Menzel's debunking was his tendency to list multiple mundane explanations, each one more infuriating to ufologists than the last. Menzel gave a total of six different possible explanations in three different publications for Kenneth Arnold's June 24, 1947 sighting of nine crescent-shaped objects flying near Mt. Rainier, Washington, all six of which explanations Maccabee counter-debunks.

In 1953 Menzel thought that the most obvious explanation was that "Arnold saw 'billowing blasts of snow ballooning up from the tops of ridges.... These rapidly shifting, tilting clouds of snow would reflect the sun like a mirror. And the rocking surfaces would make the chain sweep along something like a wave, with only a momentary reflection from each crest.'"[41] Maccabee's response to this explanation is that it "might convince someone who is impressed by Menzel's scientific credentials, but who knows little or nothing about atmospheric optics. However, it is wrong because snow clouds do not reflect the sun specularly 'like a mirror,' but rather they provide a diffuse reflection. Such a cloud could be bright, but typically not more than 10 times brighter than the surrounding sky, whereas a mirror reflection of the sun from a large metallic surface [for example] could be hundreds or thousands of times brighter than the surrounding sky."

And so it goes through all six explanations through the last one published in 1977 after Menzel's death. "This time he suggested that Arnold saw the reflection off water drops on his windshield.... This explanation completely overlooks numerous details of the sighting including the following: according to Arnold's report to the Air Force, which Menzel had evidently read many years earlier, he turned his

---

38. Zeidman, 1989.
39. Moore and Friedman, 1989.
40. Maccabee, 1986.
41. Maccabee, 1986, p. 139.

plane sideways, opened his window, and then took off his glasses to be sure that he was not seeing some unusual reflection from a glass surface. (Anyone want to propose water drops on his eyeballs?)"[42]

Richard L. Thompson discusses another debunking explanation given by Menzel, this one of a sighting by astronomer Clyde Tombaugh, discoverer of the planet Pluto, from his back yard. Menzel thought that the moving object consisting of "illuminated rectangles" was "the lighted windows of a house reflected by a ripple in the boundary of an atmospheric haze layer. As this ripple progressed with a wavelike motion, the reflected house would have seemed to move like a flying saucer."[43]

James McDonald, senior physicist at the Institute of Atmospheric Physics and professor of meteorology at the University of Arizona (see Ch. 4), reacted as follows, "Now this might go down with a layman, but to anyone who is at all familiar with the physics of reflection and particularly with the properties of the atmosphere...the suggestion that there are 'haze layers' with sufficiently strong refractive index gradients to yield visible reflections of window lights is absurd."[44]

Keith Thompson refers to a 1952 sighting near Norfolk, Virginia, about which "debunker Donald Menzel [made the] straight-faced assertion that pilots Nash and Fortenberry had mistaken lightning bugs trapped between panes of the cockpit window for something more remarkable."[45] In typical fashion, however, Menzel had another possibility, hedging his bet, and he soon changed his explanation to temperature inversion.

In another case, the famous New Guinea report in 1959 by two Anglican missionaries and over thirty parishioners of a large disc with humanoid occupants hovering about 500 feet overhead, Keith Thompson discusses the explanations of both Menzel and his successor to the top debunker role, Philip Klass. "Menzel wondered why [Rev.] Gill [one of the Anglican priests] had failed to mention Venus as a point of reference, suggesting Gill had mistaken the planet for a spaceship...[even though] Gill's account specifically stated: 'I saw Venus, but I also saw this sparkling object [the large UFO]...above Venus.'"[46]

But Menzel thought that "Gill, who suffered from myopia and an astigmatism, had mistaken an out-of-focus, elongated image of Venus for his mother ship. 'The slight irregularities on the "hairs" of the lashes, perhaps dust or moisture, could easily be interpreted as activity of

42. Maccabee, 1986, p. 141.
43. Richard L. Thompson, 1993, pp. 24, 37; Menzel and Boyd, 1963, p. 269.
44. McDonald, 1967, p. 8.
45. Keith Thompson, 1991, p. 24.
46. Keith Thompson, 1991, p. 53.

the "beings" inhabiting the saucer.'" It turned out that Gill had been wearing proper glasses.

Thompson notes two criticisms from Philip Klass on this sighting. One was that another observer, Stephen Gill Moi, could not be considered a reliable independent witness because his name suggests a close friendship with Rev. Gill. Rev. Gill, however, "responded that he had known Stephen Gill Moi for only nineteen months prior to the sighting," and Moi had been named over thirty years before that.[47] Klass also expressed disbelief over the part of the report that stated that Gill had gone inside to eat in the middle of the second night's sighting of the same object. However, Gill replied that he had already seen it for four hours the night before and had lost interest, not really realizing how strange the object was until later. He had assumed that it was an American or Australian hovercraft of some kind.

In a further discussion of Klass's efforts at debunking other cases, Thompson concludes that "it is unlikely that [Klass] appreciated the extent to which his attempted debunkings [and those of his role model Donald Menzel] played into a growing conviction among the public at large that UFOs could not be explained away, especially not through byzantine theories requiring the seeming unlikely convergence of numerous ideal factors.... [Such explanations] seemed to many observers to be as nonsensical—if not more so—as the details of the [UFO reports themselves].... "[48]

Perhaps this principle could be called the "swamp-gas effect"; see Ch. 2 in which Hynek's suggested marsh-gas explanation led to an outcry in Michigan in 1966 and indirectly led to the Condon study. Thompson's conclusion may or may not be true in general. After all, how would the layperson be able to doubt the explanations in Menzel's books? And among the science-educated ufologists, who would need convincing? Among the science-educated nonufologists, who would be willing to be convinced that UFOs were worth studying? For one, Robert Wood (see Appendix, page 239) said he became interested in UFOs after being suspicious about a Menzel book he read in 1967.

Alleged Hoaxes

I should point out, just as I did in the section on counter-debunking, that alleged hoax cases often require a great deal of reading or investigation before an informed opinion is possible, except in the most

---

47. Keith Thompson, 1991, p. 54.
48. Keith Thompson, 1991, p. 77.

obvious balloon and pie-plate examples. It is difficult enough to debate issues in mainstream academe where the subject matter is considered legitimate by consensus, but when ufologist and debunker alike are dubious about the evidence, the issue can take on the proportions of a protracted court case too involved to settle, at least in this book.

Although I will give an outline of a few such cases, I think it is more important to consider the overall implications of hoaxes and rumors of hoaxes for ufology and the scientific process. It is difficult or impossible to prove such an assertion, but it is my impression that hoaxes in ufology are rare, just as they are in parapsychology, and for the same reason.

Most people are very reluctant to report UFOs, ghosts and other "paranormal" experiences because they are afraid of ridicule. Even if most Americans accept UFOs in principle, there is a substantial minority who do not, and anyone can doubt particular reports, any of which *might* be a hoax or an indicator of mental instability. Hynek discussed this reluctance to report UFOs and noted that the main reason people came to him, often in confidence, about their sightings was that they were stunned by them and needed an explanation to restore their equilibrium.[49] Today this principle can be extended to UFO experiencers/abductees who are troubled by their reality-shattering experiences.

Since a UFO sighting is still suspect enough in this culture potentially to label the experiencer as deviant, there are strong motivations in most people either to deny their own experiences to themselves and everyone else, or to report them quietly to investigators who will preserve their anonymity. As Therese M. Barclay points out, these quiet ones are the best witnesses, at least in terms of personal credibility,[50] although their reports could still be flawed in other ways. It is very instructive to meet a large number of experiencers at UFO conferences and elsewhere, and especially to have friends, acquaintances and relatives tell you about their sightings, as I have. This gives a much different picture of UFO witnesses than you get from tabloids and prominent media cases. Ufology has a great deal to study based on such witnesses without considering any of the several prominent cases that have been accused, rightly or wrongly, of being hoaxes.

Nevertheless, the alleged hoaxes in ufology gain a great deal of media coverage and probably do a lot of damage to the scientific process, although some of these sensational cases may be basically valid and contain valuable information as well. Jacques Vallée discusses the

49. Hynek, 1972, pp. 19-21.
50. Barclay and Barclay, 1993, p. 114.

role of various processes in hoaxes, including folklore, media and belief systems.[51] Conditions that make hoaxing possible, although far from inevitable, include financial gain for the witness and for the investigator, and a desire for extensive media coverage. From my research investigating apparitions and other paranormal experiences in Chinese culture,[52] I suspected hoax or exaggeration most in people who had a role to uphold, such as spirit medium or monk, in which they had to have such experiences regularly in order to be considered authentic. This does not seem to apply in the case of UFO experiencers, except in the case of some contactees who may have had some kind of UFO experience and then feel the need to claim others or to embellish their accounts.

It is quite possible that some prominent alleged UFO hoax cases are partly true and partly hoaxed, but many analysts are uncomfortable with such ambiguity and prefer to throw an entire case out if it seems to be tainted. It would seem more reasonable to me to asterisk such cases, keep an open mind and go on to other business, since it is virtually impossible to prove a complex case to be either completely a hoax or completely valid. It is in the interests of debunkers like Philip Klass to insist on the "best case" approach to UFOs rather than looking for patterns in a great many cases, because demands for absolute verification are always inconclusive. There can probably always be some doubt imagined in any case.

Let us take George Adamski[53] as one example of a case that by consensus of most ufologists is probably considered a hoax. Adamski is the most famous of the "contactees" of the 1950s. On November 20, 1952, near Desert Center, California, he allegedly met a spaceman from Venus who warned about the dangers of nuclear testing. Later Adamski lectured about his contacts with Space Brothers whom he sometimes met in Los Angeles. I have talked with ufologists who think that there was a kernel of truth to Adamski's stories, and it would be difficult to prove otherwise.

A more recent, complex and intriguing case is that of Eduard (Billy) Meier, who claims he began to see UFOs from the Pleiades beginning in 1975 in Switzerland. His evidence consists of photographs, films, sound recordings, crystals and metal from the occupants. Gary Kinder[54] and Keith Thompson[55] both consider this case a puzzling one, seemingly containing elements of both hoax and high strangeness, al-

51. Vallée, 1994.
52. Emmons, 1982.
53. Adamski, 1955.
54. Kinder, 1987.
55. Keith Thompson, 1991, pp. 135-139.

though there are allegedly a couple dozen named witnesses who attest to its reality. For a skeptical/debunking perspective, see Schroth's review of a pro-Meier book by Elders *et al.*[56]

To broaden the application of the hoax argument beyond UFOs, Uri Geller, the spoon-bender, may have embellished what started as a psychokinetic effect, just as Meier may have gilded a genuine UFO case. Even if they did cheat, this does not necessarily negate the authenticity of the original phenomenon or event.

Probably no allegedly UFO-related phenomenon has been so plagued by hoaxing as crop circles, those designs formed in grain fields, the most intricate of which have appeared in recent years in southern England. Even worse than a hoax is a hoaxed hoax, in this case the claims of Douglas Bower and David Chorley. "Doug and Dave," two British artists in their 60s, announced in September of 1991 that they had been making the circles with planks since 1978.[57] Although they later reduced their claims about how many they had done, and they could not possibly have created them by the thousands worldwide, media coverage of crop circles declined greatly as if the mystery had been solved. This is not to say that Doug and Dave may not have made several circles, but the magnitude of their initial claims is evidently a hoax.

Later that year, however, prominent British ufologist Jenny Randles argued that there have been many other hoaxes all along, and she estimated that the percentage of genuine circles in 1991 might be as low as 10% or even lower.[58] The following summer an ingenious hoax contest was held, from which ufologist Dennis Stacy concluded that "it's now obvious that many features of many formations can indeed be done by human hoaxers."[59]

In 1993 Chris Rutkowski stated that "most modern crop circles really are man-made hoaxes," referred to there being many more hoaxers than just Doug and Dave and called for a re-evaluation of a variety of hypotheses about the alleged physical processes involved in genuine circle formation.[60] Linda Moulton Howe has a long, well-illustrated section in her 1993 book that examines crop-circle evidence after Doug and Dave, and includes analysis of physical differences in hoaxed vs. genuine-circle grain by biophysicist W. C. Levengood.[61] George Wingfield maintains that there is still eye-witness evidence both for crop cir-

56. Schroth, 1980.
57. *UFO*, 1991.
58. Randles, 1991.
59. Stacy, 1992.
60. Rutkowski, 1993.
61. Howe, 1993B, pp. 4-93.

cles being formed with no human agency and for UFOs closely associated with circle formation.[62]

Beginning November 11, 1987, Ed Walters, a building contractor in Gulf Breeze, Florida, saw and photographed UFOs on many occasions. His sightings, mental phenomena like voices in his head, an encounter with a humanoid, and many spectacular, detailed color pictures of craft with windows and a bright ring at the bottom were published in a book co-authored with his wife Frances in 1990.[63] After Ed underwent hypnotic regression by psychologist Dr. Dan C. Overlade, former president of the Florida State Board of Examiners of Psychology, they published a book centering on Ed's abductions in 1994.[64]

As Richard L. Thompson points out, many people are suspicious of Ed Walters' case because the photographs are too good and too many.[65] Unless people accept the UFO "reality-tunnel," almost any kind of evidence is suspect. If someone sees a lot of UFOs, it is too much evidence. Those who do not accept the principle that some individuals do seem to be UFO magnets (because they have been chosen or are being visited multiple times) may assume that no one would see that many by chance. If the witness never takes a photograph, people will say, "Why didn't he/she ever take a picture?" If, like Ed, he/she takes several good ones, then surely they must be fakes.

Dr. Bruce Maccabee (see Appendix, page 230), optical physicist and photoanalyst, has done extensive analysis of Ed's photographs, directed him to use a Nimslo four-lens camera to get distance estimates, and has published his findings that the pictures are genuine not only in the first Walters book, but in several papers and journal articles.[66] Nevertheless, Ed and his photography have been the object of considerable debate among ufologists and, of course, Philip J. Klass.

Keith Thompson devotes an interesting eight-page section to this case,[67] but it would be difficult to do it justice in a whole volume. Ed was suspected of taking double exposures with his Polaroid camera, he admitted having spent nearly three years in jail for check forgery in his youth, and then in 1990 a model UFO was found in the attic of the Walters' former home. A week later, Tommy Smith claimed that he had helped Ed hoax his photographs as a high school student in 1987.

To my eyes, however, the model is a rather ludicrous construction of styrofoam plates, and it doesn't even look like the photographs.[68]

---

62. Wingfield, 1994.
63. Walters and Walters, 1990.
64. Walters and Walters, 1994.
65. Richard L. Thompson, 1993, pp. 8-9.
66. Maccabee, 1988.
67. Keith Thompson, 1991, pp. 210-217.

Some drafting paper included in the model was shown to belong to a house plan Ed had made in 1989, over a year after the photographs had been taken,[69] although Keith Thompson notes that Philip Klass thought that the paper could have come from a preliminary plan made in 1986.[70] UFO investigator Dan Wright concluded that the model was a plant set up after the Walters moved out of the house; "*Someone* crimped the water pipe leading to the refrigerator...then planted the model along the pipe in the attic in the hope that the new owner would find and report it."[71] It has also been wondered whether Ed would be so stupid as to leave such incriminating evidence lying around.

Tommy Smith's story was also attacked, e.g., by Bruce Maccabee, who stated that "many of the statements Tommy made about how Ed supposedly faked the photos made no sense."[72] But Maccabee also pointed out that even without Ed Walters' testimony, a great many others reported seeing UFOs in Gulf Breeze, some of them seeing and photographing the same type of UFO that Ed had seen and photographed.[73]

In a re-opening of the Gulf Breeze case by MUFON after the 1990 hoax allegations, Carol and Rex Salisberry stated that "we arrived at the conclusion that the Walters' photos were probably faked" and went on to disagree with some of Maccabee's analysis.[74] In the same issue of the *MUFON UFO Journal* that contained this statement, Walt Andrus, International Director of MUFON, complained that Rex Salisberry had violated the agreement that "the reopened investigation was to be confidential until a final report was prepared and released" by giving his findings to the press some months before, and that a final report had still not been submitted.[75] Although Gulf Breeze, Florida, is still a "hot spot" for UFO sightings, Ed Walters, who has more recent photographs, has been withdrawing from public attendance at UFO conferences. Now there is another case that has risen into a focus of controversy: the "Linda Cortile" (pseudonym) abduction case.

At the annual MUFON conference held in Albuquerque in 1992, Budd Hopkins shared information on what he thought could be "the case of the century," involving multiple independent witnesses of a woman who was abducted and floated through a closed window in her twelfth-story apartment in New York City and drawn up in a column

68. *UFO*, 1990.
69. Art Hufford, 1993.
70. Keith Thompson, 1991, p. 215.
71. Wright, 1991, pp. 8, 22.
72. Maccabee, 1991A.
73. Maccabee, 1991B.
74. Salisberry and Salisberry, 1991.
75. Andrus, 1991.

of light with three small creatures into a craft hovering above the build-ing.[76] Among the witnesses were "Dan and Richard" who were in a car below escorting "an important political figure."

Rather than taking a wait-and-see attitude, putting an asterisk be-side this sensational sounding report until Budd finished his book, and evaluating his evidence after that, many ufologists wasted an incredi-ble amount of breath and ink debating the merits of the claims made to date. Some "investigators" violated Linda Cortile's privacy by reveal-ing information about her that jeopardized her anonymity. Conse-quently, part of the debate centered on the ethics of these rogue investigators, accusing them of defamation of character among other things. *International UFO Reporter* has a 19-page debate about the "Lin-da case" and the ethics of the critique.[77]

Witness Ridicule

Although a good case can be made for independent critical inves-tigation of UFO claims, there are also serious ethical considerations in-volving the protection of witnesses. As mentioned above, witness ridicule is a strong disincentive against hoaxing, and such negative so-cial control can also make genuine experiencers wish they had kept si-lent.

In March, 1966, Frank Mannor of Dexter, Michigan, reported what he at first thought was a meteor landing and taking off again, but then appeared to be like a pyramid with lights on it.[78] Many others, includ-ing 87 women students at Hillsdale College the next night, had UFO sightings about that time, and this became the infamous "swamp gas" flap (see section on the Condon report in Ch. 2).

Mannor said that he was sorry he had ever told anyone. "They think you're a nut.... And I'm not going to take it no more.... And if the thing lands right here...I'd never say a word.... What would you think if somebody was throwing beer bottles at your house...screaming, 'You nut, you fanatic,' and all that?"[79]

In Budd Hopkins' "Linda case" mentioned above, Linda Cortile experienced harassment not only from other ufologists, but also from other witnesses in the case. At any rate, as is the situation with many other people involved in UFO sightings, Linda was concerned about her job. "I didn't want him [another witness] to show up at my place of

76. Hopkins, 1992C.
77. Clark and others, 1993.
78. Keith Thompson, 1991, p. 81.
79. Keith Thompson, 1991, p. 84.

employment. To think that my co-workers would find out about my involvement with UFOs was unnerving. If I were to be fired because of it, I couldn't get a good reference."[80] Then in late 1992 "three debunkers exposed my real family name. Thereafter, my name and address, etc., was put on electronic bulletin boards. They tried to take from me, what was most precious of all, and what Budd worked so hard to achieve, the safety of my children, my husband and me. They exposed us to the many crackpots out there. *It won't be forgotten.*"[81]

Ed and Frances Walters, the famous UFO experiencers in Gulf Breeze, Florida, complain, "The scales of justice are reversed. The witness is expected to prove that the UFO sighting happened. It is generally accepted that a skeptic need not prove that it did not happen—merely offer a standard explanation of 'heat inversion,' 'helicopter,' 'Venus,' 'hoax,' etc."[82] This brings us back to the principle of "extraordinary claims demanding extraordinary evidence" again; it also reveals the contrary frame of reference of a court trial in which the accused is innocent until proven guilty. The way the two are actually combined often results in the UFO experiencer being presumed to be either unbalanced or dishonest, without much of a look at the evidence.

Issues Within Ufology

From the literature reviewed in the alleged hoax cases above, it is obvious that there are serious debates within ufology over which cases are genuine and which are not. However, ufologists debate a great deal more than just hoax accusations. At this point, my purpose is not to explore issues in detail, but merely to show that ufologists can be just as critical or skeptical of each other's positions as outside debunkers can be of ufology. In fact, ufologists often complain about the divisiveness and bickering that goes on within the field. Perhaps many people in the "UFO community" are unfamiliar with the conflicts that occur in regular academic disciplines. Since there are so many academics in ufology, it is not surprising that they should have imported much of the conflict orientation from their own disciplines.

One example of such a ufological debate occurred in the *MUFON UFO Journal* over the extraterrestrial hypothesis (ETH). Jacques Vallée, computer scientist also trained in astronomy, who is generally a critic of the ETH, wrote the following in regard to a paper on the subject that had been delivered by Michael Swords, historian and professor of nat-

---

80. Cortile, 1994.
81. Cortile, 1994, p. 253.
82. Walters and Walters, 1994, p. 217.

ural sciences, at the 1991 MUFON Symposium in Chicago, "It is an unfair oversimplification to state, as Dr. Swords does, that I regard the ETH as absurd...."[83] Swords, replying in the same issue stated, "Whether Vallée concludes that the ETH is absurd...or not...his public presentation...at the Society for Scientific Exploration left little doubt that he regarded the ETH as 'dead meat.'"[84]

Vallée also commented that Swords "gives the impression that those who have critiqued the ETH on biological grounds have missed the point that alien life might very well be humanoid in shape.... However, in my own formulation the biological discussion was only one of five arguments against the ETH."[85] On this issue Swords wrote, "This is puzzling to me in the extreme. Please read Vallée's comments about the need to not only explain bioform similarity but [other factors as well]. Then please read my paper which speaks [about the same other factors as well].... I can only assume that the respondent must have been reading a copy which was missing several pages. Since I personally sent him a copy as a courtesy, I know that the copy was complete [when mailed].... I would like to ask for the minimal courtesy of actually reading the complete text before crying foul."[86]

On a third point Vallée stated, "When Dr. Swords states categorically that...we could never interbreed with [aliens], he may be experiencing the same 'difficulty in keeping up with all the scientific thinking necessary to make competent pronouncements' which he observes among his colleagues."[87] Again Swords wondered if Vallée had thoroughly read and understood his paper, since Swords had anticipated "Super ET Biotechnicians" who could overcome normal interbreeding problems. In summation, he accused Vallée of raising issues without reading the entire article and of trying to close the door on a major theory (the ETH),[88] although Vallée had stated that a healthy debate was still continuing on the matter.

Another example of a scientific issue in ufology, this time a methodological one, involves the nationwide Roper survey directed by Budd Hopkins and David Jacobs and published in a booklet called *Unusual Personal Experiences* in 1992.[89] Sociologists Robert L. Hall and Mark Rodeghier, along with psychologist Donald A. Johnson, made the positive comment (which would not have been made in *The Skepti-*

83. Vallée, 1992B, pp. 11-12.
84. Swords, 1992B, pp. 12-13.
85. Vallée, 1992B, p. 11.
86. Swords, 1992B, p. 13.
87. Vallée, 1992B, p. 11.
88. Swords, 1992B, p. 13.
89. Hopkins, and others, 1992.

cal Inquirer) that Hopkins and Jacobs had made "prior important contributions," but then tore into the booklet by saying that its "conclusion that as many as 3.7 million American adults may have been abducted is totally unjustified."[90]

Hall *et al.* focused on the methodological issue of the validity of the five abduction indicator questions on the survey, dealing with paralysis, missing time, a feeling of flying, unusual lights and unexplained scars. Although about 2% of respondents scored positive on at least four of the five indicators, and thus were considered possible abductees, "There are many alternative reasons why people might answer the indicator questions positively. [Hopkins and Jacobs] simply assume all other possibilities wrong."[91] Other possibilities being considered among ufologists include hypnagogic or hypnopompic hallucinations (visions occurring in dreamlike states going into or out of sleep) and the sleep paralysis associated with these states.

Noting that the researchers had not pretested their survey systematically, and that there was no discussion in the booklet of any statistical calculation of the reliability of the scale items, Hall, Johnson and Rodeghier argued that better research must be done to make the study of UFO abductions credible. "Our fellow scientists say, 'So this is the kind of evidence you take seriously?' A bad piece of research has the opposite of the intended effect: it reinforces their prior opinion that the whole phenomenon is lacking in evidence and that people who take it seriously are simply being fools."[92]

Cults and Study Groups

By now it should be obvious that many ufologists are academics who play the typical academic games of arguing among themselves about proper methodology, theories and, of course, about particular cases. Do not forget, however, that many nonufologist academics know virtually nothing about UFO studies and entertain a stereotype that is fed by tabloid UFO stories and popular culture notions of UFO cultists.

When I asked one nonufologist astronomer whether he considered ufology a pseudoscience, he replied that it probably was not even a pseudoscience, because it was "kookier," more of a cult, and not even claiming much of a scientific orientation to begin with. He guessed that most astronomers would mistakenly think that ufologists have a quasi-scientific orientation and stand out on mountains observing, whereas

---

90. Robert L. Hall and others, 1993.
91. Robert L. Hall and others, 1993, p. 11.
92. Robert L. Hall and others, 1993, p. 14.

he himself thought that there are probably only a few "serious" ufologists. I bit my tongue and wrote it down at that point, although I shared some ufology material with him later on.

The late J. Allen Hynek spoke against the misconception that only "UFO buffs and 'believers' of the cultist variety" report UFO sightings, and he was dismayed when scientists held that view. Dr. Fred Whipple, director of the Smithsonian Astrophysical Observatory, when asked by the press about UFOs said, "I do not make public statements about the beliefs of religious cults." To which Hynek relied, "Neither do I."[93]

In late March, 1997, 39 members of the UFO cult "Heaven's Gate" committed suicide in San Diego. One official of a UFO research organization, just as this book was going to press, bemoaned the damage it would do to ufology to have the media create an association in people's minds between UFO cultism and UFO research. More such reaction can be expected soon.

In his 1993, book *Science and Anti-Science*, CSICOP Fellow Gerald Holton, who is professor of physics and of the history of science at Harvard, has only this to say about UFOs in the entire book: "surface phenomena" [nonserious phenomena] in pseudoscience include "tabloid sensationalism involving UFOs [that] is merely hucksterism feeding on primitive ignorance [unless, as with the reputed recent inauguration of a section on 'UFO-logy' in the Russian Academy of Sciences, the craze gets official backing]."[94] Speaking of ignorance, one would think that a Harvard professor who claims to know enough to write a book on the anti-science issue and who is a CSICOP member would surely have read at least some articles in *The Skeptical Inquirer* about American ufology and would, therefore, have had some knowledge of it worth including in his book.

Nevertheless, the tabloids and UFO cults have been part of the popular culture. Cults in particular are relevant to ufology because of the New Age issues involved, e.g., when it comes to interpretations of UFO abductions/experiences as spiritually transformative. Although Hynek himself was grounded in a nuts-and-bolts view of UFOs, he increasingly began to realize that they might have some paranormal/ psychic importance.

For ufologists like Hynek, the problem with UFO cultists was that they were influenced by religious rather than scientific motives, and, of course, they were not interested in UFO observations. Instead they did

---

93. Hynek, 1972, pp. 10-11.
94. Holton, 1993, pp. 146-147.

and still do practice "channeling," i.e., psychic communication with extraterrestrial entities.[95] The classic sociological study *When Prophecy Fails* by Festinger *et al.* (1956) documents a Midwestern UFO cult that prepared to be saved by flying saucers from the end of the world in 1952.[96] The medical doctor who led this group had been influenced by a lengthy discussion with contactee George Adamski and was assisted in prophecy by a woman who communicated with an entity named Sananda through automatic writing (writing down material that comes to one's mind or hand psychically), a form of channeling.

Robert Sheaffer discusses a more recent UFO cult founded by Claude Vorhilon who claimed to meet aliens in France in 1973.[97] By 1994 this group reported 27,000 international members. Although its culture was based upon a 1960s counterculture of peace and sexuality, it has now asked for land in Israel on the grounds that their leader Rael is the Jewish Messiah.

In what is termed "the UFO community," which is centered around UFO organizations and conferences, there are certainly New Age religious interests, but UFO cults as such are somewhat peripheral. Much more significant are local UFO study groups or clubs mainly for people whom Hynek called "UFO buffs." Many ufologists in my interviews with them reported attending meetings of such local organizations.

There is evidently quite a variety of UFO study groups. Many are at least loosely affiliated with the Mutual UFO Network or at least contain MUFON members. Since there are typically no formal guidelines for these local groups, the personal characteristics of the leaders seem to have a great influence on particular groups. My interviewees sometimes expressed concern over factionalism in the groups and tended to be less involved if they thought that there was an unscientific or gullible emphasis.

For over two years I have belonged to and observed a local study group called "Skyscan" (pseudonym; all names given for participants will be pseudonyms as well). Skyscan meets monthly for about two and one-half hours for discussion and sometimes has an outside speaker or video. Attendance varies widely from about ten to fifty, with usually about twenty on average, and with about equal numbers of males and females. Education and occupation also vary widely. There are a few MUFON members, including the organizer, and a few are avid UFO conference attendees. Aside from me, there is one other researcher/au-

---

95. Emmons, 1993.
96. Festinger and others, 1956.
97. Sheaffer, 1994.

thor, and a few other members do UFO investigations. Skyscan holds its own small yearly conference and takes occasional field trips to UFO hotspots or to other small conferences.

To me the most fascinating aspect of the group is its orientation toward science and the evaluation of truth claims. I suspect that the stereotype of such groups in both popular and academic minds would be that they are full of cultists and gullible true believers. Nothing could be further from the truth in Skysearch, although I cannot claim that other UFO study groups are like Skysearch. My impression from my interviews with ufologists is that UFO study groups vary widely in how scientific they are, and that they are usually somewhat less tolerant of diversity within the group than Skysearch is.

In Skyscan, only one or two people seem willing to accept almost any UFO claim, nearly all have some skepticism, and a few are extremely skeptical. However, the unspoken norm is that everyone in the group is respected, although they may be mildly kidded for their beliefs. Just as in mainstream academe, they argue over the boundaries of what is proper methodology and what is to be accepted as truth. In other words, the process of labeling some forms of knowledge as deviant continues from CSICOP and mainstream academe, right down through MUFON ufologists, and even down to an organization of amateur UFO buffs in Skyscan! I did not expect this, but as a sociologist I probably should have known that debates over the definition of legitimate knowledge occur in all groups.

In Skyscan meetings, people have made skeptical remarks about, among other things, the Philadelphia Experiment (an allegedly UFO-related Navy experiment in invisibility in summer 1943),[98] the supposed sabotaging of the Mars mission in 1993, particular authors who might be frauds, and the sightings in Gulf Breeze. One member went to Gulf Breeze for two years in a row hoping to see a UFO, but was disappointed. He talked to skeptics in Gulf Breeze and saw literature there that tried to debunk the Ed Walters case. After these experiences he said that he was dubious about Gulf Breeze, but still believed in UFOs. Another member who had been there and had seen a credible video of Ed Walters defended the case.

Two members, Al, a tough skeptic, and Bill, who is as close to a true believer as there is in Skysearch, frequently go at each other. One time Bill talked about there being U.S. planes on the moon, evidence for which was a tabloid photo. This brought the usual good-natured scorn from Al. There is no apparent antagonism between the two men, and

---

98. Vallée, 1994.

they are both comfortable joining the congenial group for a snack at a nearby restaurant after the meeting.

Dot, who has had her own close encounters and has even drawn detailed pictures of the craft she has seen, nevertheless has shown disgust over the many UFO rumors one hears. Once she said, "I don't know what to believe." At another meeting she responded to one claim by saying, "I would look into that. I'm very skeptical."

Tony, a professional researcher and writer about the paranormal who has appeared on national television, is very open to all kinds of phenomena, but is also very cautious about drawing conclusions. At one meeting he reported on his investigation of a local crop circle possibility and suggested that it was probably caused by wind damage or some other mundane phenomenon.

Tom, the organizer, commented negatively on the credibility of one abductee by saying, "She believes in the New Age...crystals, seances, all kinds of weird things we're not interested in." I popped up with, "We're not?" Tom came right back, "Maybe *you* are; we're interested in hard evidence." For a moment I wondered if I was in trouble, but obviously not. The norm is to express one's opinion and to live and let live.

The same is true of "standard" religious beliefs; the group contains Christian fundamentalists and agnostics, and contrary opinions on UFOs and religion are expressed without rancor. If this sounds dubious, it must be seen to be appreciated. Ironically, the only important conflict I have seen in the group has been over things like whether a member could charge for distributing some materials and over the activities in the yearly conference—nothing ideological about UFOs.

However, in spite of the great tolerance for the expression of contrary opinions by other members, there is less tolerance concerning outsiders. I have noticed that the credibility of experiencers is an important issue, and that often they are labeled deviant for reasons that go beyond their claims. Some experiencers were doubted just because they seemed to be unambitious, or too revealing and extroverted, or for dressing provocatively.

The most interesting case of a doubted experiencer involves Will. On the different occasions that Will has come to the Skyscan meetings as a guest, he has shared the most varied and strong claims of paranormal activity, including many UFO experiences and accounts of helicopters that follow him, psychic experiences including out-of-body and near-death experiences, healing and religious experiences like stigmata (marks like Christ's crucifixion wounds). And they keep on happening to him.

Some people can be seen hiding smiles when he speaks, and when he is not at the meeting people express serious doubts about whether he is believable and whether that much could happen to one person. Tony, the researcher, said once that there was not enough information to judge him, but that what he said was plausible according to the paranormal literature. In fact, Will has been studied extensively by a respected psychic research organization.

During one of the debates about Will, one woman said, "You'd better not laugh at him. He may be one of us soon." This makes more explicit the usually implicit group norm that insiders are to be respected so that they will feel comfortable expressing their opinions and engaging in debate. While Will is an outsider who comes only as a guest, he can be the object of skeptical/debunking attack when he is not present; once he joins the group as a regular member, however, he deserves protection under the norm of tolerance.

And so it is that the "UFO buffs" that one might expect to be the true believers turn out sometimes to be skeptics and debunkers. And ufologists, as we have seen, are not merely the unscientific objects of scorn from CSICOP, the defenders of normal science; they often engage in scientific debates among themselves. But what is "normal" science really?

Chapter 6

Normal Science Under Attack

"It can't be. Therefore, it isn't."

Normal science, represented explicitly by the Committee for the Scientific Investigation of Claims of the Paranormal (CSICOP), and more implicitly by academics who work in higher education and sit on research grant-giving committees, is certain that UFOs cannot or do not exist. How do they know this? (This is a "sociology of knowledge" question, by the way.) One approved answer would be that CSICOP authority Philip J. Klass has investigated the whole thing and says it's nonsense. Another possible answer is that academics know without asking that anything that gets so much attention in tabloids is not going to get funded as a research project and, therefore, for all practical purposes, does not exist.

Should we accept this? Well, we already know that many ufologists in academe do not accept it, even though by studying UFOs they risk negative social control in terms of promotion and tenure. And, of course, (if you leave out the "don't knows") a plurality or majority of opinion-poll respondents think that UFOs are something "real" rather than imaginary (although not necessarily extraterrestrial). It may be an overstatement to consider these ufologists and poll respondents "anti-scientific" (a point to be discussed later), but at least they provide one indication that normal science is losing some of its authoritative grip over the definition of reality.

This chapter and the next present two reasons for doubting normal-scientific pronouncements about UFOs (and many other things). One reason is that the authority of science and even of scientific method is under attack. The other is that the New Physics, or at least some interpretations of it, suggest that UFOs may be much easier to accept and to explain than previously thought, even within a scientific framework.

Keep in mind that these two chapters deal with the *social* issue of whether UFO studies should be considered legitimate. Many individuals have had their own UFO experiences that are so reality-shaking that they accept them even without social approval, although they may be careful about sharing these experiences with others. There is nothing quite like a close encounter with a porthole-encircled craft or a bug-eyed visitor to make one wonder if science isn't missing something.

The Myth of Objective Science

It seems heretical in this modern age to question the objectivity of science. Americans are used to the norm of tolerance in religious matters: we are supposed to allow individuals to believe whatever they like about religion, including nothing, as long as they don't foist their beliefs on others. But claiming to doubt science makes one sound ignorant. If there is any reliable, objective institution in the 1990s, surely it is science.

Compared to other institutions that are in greater crisis, e.g., politics, law and medicine, science is still relatively highly respected and legitimate, although there are popular-culture stereotypes of mad scientists and absent-minded professors. Nevertheless, there have been signs of rebellion against science on both intellectual and popular levels. How could science, the cornerstone of modernity, be challenged?

To begin with, the myth of objective science rests upon the idea that science is a method rather than an institution with an ideology or doctrine. Instead of finding truth through faith or acceptance of the beliefs of some social group, scientists are supposed to go through rational methods of collecting data and letting the evidence reveal what is *really* real. Who can doubt lab instruments and statistics properly applied? This makes it "objective" rather than subjective or socially influenced.

If it is objective, then it must be valid, true, beyond question. Oh, but some scientists cheat or make mistakes, you say. Yes, but other scientists will catch them or correct them by replicating their studies. Science as a method remains unquestioned. It is our only hope for unbiased truth. If there is anything wrong with science, the scientists will make the proper adjustments.

In the 1940s, prominent sociologist Robert K. Merton challenged the notion that science was merely a method insulated from social factors. He said that science was a social institution like any other, *except* that it had an "ethos" that allowed it to generate knowledge in a special way.[1] This ethos included the values of "universalism" (treating all truth claims in the same unbiased way), "communality" (sharing infor-

---

1. Merton, 1949.

mation with other scientists), "organized skepticism" (putting hypotheses through tests), and "disinterestedness" (doing science for the sake of truth instead of for personal gain).

Thus Merton took the first step of pointing out that all organized human activity, including science, occurs within the influence of social values and norms. However, being a functionalist (i.e., not very radical) sociologist, he accepted the idea that science was a "special" institution because it had an ethos that was directed toward the goal of objective knowledge. Scientists actually have rules and procedures for getting the unvarnished truth.

More recently the "interests approach"[2] in the sociology of science treats this ethos as more of an ideology (a glorious statement of what *should* be) than as a realistic set of norms (rules that might actually be followed). In practice, it is the interests of authoritative actors and groups (e.g., prominent professors and funding agencies) more than some objective set of norms that construct scientific knowledge. Feminist critiques have been especially effective in examining implicit biases in male-controlled science in terms of both methodology and opportunities for social mobility by gender.[3]

Although I am a sociologist and see the biases in normal science as more of a social than a psychological problem, there is also a literature that questions whether individual scientists are really as objective and open-minded as they are supposed to be.[4] As I pointed out in Chapter 4, even though astronomers as individuals are frequently open to the concept of UFO studies, they know that astronomy as an institution defines it as deviant and unfundable, and, therefore, the individuals do not get involved.

How does the scientific establishment manage to argue that science is just a method and not an ideology? This is very tricky and circular. Science's ideology is that science has no ideology. As sociologist Stanley Aronowitz explains, both the method of knowing and the things known are considered *external* to the knower and therefore objective and uninfluenced by the knower and the larger social environment.[5] As Aronowitz puts it, "Since the 'truth' claims of science are tied to the methodological imperative, [science] insists that [it] must be held immune from the influences of social and historical situations. Science, therefore, is truth, and can, for this reason, represent itself by means of its procedures.... Hence, the self-criticism of science is conducted with-

2. Webster, 1991, p. 16.
3. Webster, 1991, pp. 143-149.
4. Mahoney, 1979.
5. Aronowitz, 1988, pp. vii-x.

in the boundaries of its own normative structures," and nonscientists are considered unqualified to criticize.

In other words, according to Aronowitz, science as an institution desiring power has managed to gain autonomy by claiming to be able to generate truth only by being immune from social influences. Since outsiders are not qualified to use and criticize the scientific method, they must leave normal science alone and accept its supposedly unbiased and unselfish authority. If we play radical sociologists and try to debunk this ideology, we must try to figure out who benefits from the authoritative or legitimate power that science has.

Science as Power

In his classic work, *The Structure of Scientific Revolutions* (1962), Thomas Kuhn discussed social influences on science, but tended to limit them to processes that were at work within the scientific community.[6] Aronowitz tries to specify larger cultural influences that Kuhn only hints at, and he does this by means of a Marxian analysis supplemented by ideas from the "critical theory" of the Frankfurt Institute, especially from Horkheimer, Adorno and Marcuse.[7] According to Aronowitz, the power of modern science (and technology) lies in its domination of nature, its separation of humans from nature, and its control over the production of capitalist goods and services. Surely someone is going to object that pure science is the best science of all, and that pure science represents a disinterested search for truth. The only science that is subject to the concerns of capitalist power is applied science. The difficulty with this idealistic picture is that although some "pure science" does get supported, a cynical explanation for this support is that pure science may someday prove useful to capitalist production and its control over nature and humans.

Increasingly, science and technology fall under the control of corporate structures and government funding, even when the laboratories are located on university campuses.[8] Those who control serious grant money control serious science. Who is going to consider UFO studies serious research when the U.S. government (publicly) denies their existence and (publicly) refuses to fund ufology?

Aronowitz, a sociologist, gives an interesting assessment of how social sciences have copied the methods of natural sciences in order to gain legitimacy (and government funding). Of course, sociology has

---

6. Kuhn, 1962.
7. Aronowitz, 1988, pp. 32-39, 127-137.
8. Aronowitz, 1988, p. 20.

become more quantitative, transforming "all experience into informa-tion."[9] If your opinions can't fit into my categories of "strongly agree, agree, disagree, strongly disagree," for example, they are less useful in my quest for a quantitative article that has a chance to be published in a mainstream sociology journal.

As Aronowitz puts it, "Like modern physics, quantitative social re-search is an *intervention* conditioned by the purposes for which the re-search is conducted. Increasingly such research is 'sponsored,' not only by political parties and their candidates, or by those who wish to sell something to consumers, but also by the state."[10] In other words, sci-ence as an institution in the modern capitalist West tends to be an in-strument of rational (profit-making) production and public policy.

Orthodoxy in Science and Religion

Seeing science primarily as a power tool for business and govern-ment is disturbing because the ideology of science has emphasized how liberating and enlightening scientific "progress" has been for the past 400 years. Academics, including me, are often inspired by the "joy of discovery" and find an emphasis on the practical concerns of money and business demeaning to the noble cause of learning.

Aronowitz points out that the revolutions in astronomy and phys-ics with the discoveries of Copernicus, Galileo and Newton were "based on the privileging of the senses, mathematical calculation, and experimental verification as sources of knowledge that were free from the mystifying power of religious belief to distort observation."[11] Mod-ern science liberated us from the ideological bias of orthodox religion and let us see things supposedly directly (objectively). If the church doctrine about the sun revolving around the Earth was wrong, maybe the church was wrong about other things, too. What the ideology of sci-ence and the myth of objectivity try to prevent us from seeing is that science has its own ideological bias.

James Redfield's New Age novel, *The Celestine Prophecy*, gives one version of this shift from orthodox religion to orthodox science.[12] The second of nine "insights" explains the cracking of Medieval church au-thority. Astronomical discoveries showed that the church was not in-fallible in terms of doctrine, and heretical groups that wanted to give their own interpretations to the Bible (aided in part by the development

---

9. Aronowitz, 1988, p. 134.
10. Aronowitz, 1988, p. 135.
11. Aronowitz, 1988, p. 149.
12. Redfield, 1993, pp. 21-29.

of printing and publication) challenged orthodoxy as well. Of course, there were other political and economic challenges to the Roman Catholic church at this time. At any rate, rational, scientific procedures, technology and capitalist production eroded the God-centered social control system of the church based on salvation and damnation.

Robert Anton Wilson says that the Church has been replaced by the "Citadel," a new elite establishment that is scientific-technological and supported by the military-industrial complex.[13] Since the Citadel is based on the science and philosophy that fought the church for legitimacy, it retains the anti-religious bias of that time. But rather than being the forum for totally open inquiry that scientific ideology claims, the scientific Citadel is really a "New Inquisition" (the title of Wilson's book) based on a dogmatic reality-tunnel (see Ch. 5 here) he calls the "New Fundamentalism," based upon certainty and absolute laws reminiscent of the Medieval church.[14]

The Citadel has a propaganda department for the harassment of heretics who challenge the New Fundamentalism: The Committee for Scientific Investigation of Claims of the Paranormal (CSICOP). Wilson contrasts Marcello Truzzi's *Zetetic Scholar* publication with CSICOP's journal the *Skeptical Inquirer*. "[Truzzi] follows the normal procedure of what is usually considered adult debate among sane people: he prints articles on both sides of every question and allows open debate, unlike the *Skeptical Inquirer*, which only prints articles on one side, since they already know the truth."[15]

As Aronowitz points out, the process of secularization of Western society led to the domination of science and technology and to the marginalization of religion and other ways of knowing. "Other discourses become poetry, religion, metaphysics, or whatever, but are zealously marginalized from what signifies science by those who constitute the scientific community."[16] Science has become "reified," i.e., an unquestioned objective reality rather than a tool or social construct.

Well, not entirely unquestioned. To a certain extent there has been an uneasy truce between science and religion. Religion has not disappeared in the modern West, and it is especially strong in the U.S. compared to most predominantly Protestant European countries, for example. But religion is supposed to deal with questions usually defined as nonscientific, like life after death. There is a boundary of sorts

13. Robert A. Wilson, 1991, pp. 20-21.
14. Robert A. Wilson, 1991, pp. 37, 45, 57.
15. Robert A. Wilson, 1991, p. 48.
16. Aronowitz, 1988, pp. 10-11, 129, 148.

between science and religion, one that is disputed at times with issues like creationism vs. evolutionism.

What makes the truce-line between science and religion even more blurred and contested is the pesky intrusion of two other cultures: parascience and New Age culture. David J. Hess discusses parapsychology (a parascience) and New Age/spiritualism, both of which are often in opposition to each other and to the normal-scientific establishment represented, of course, by CSICOP.[17] Especially parapsychology, but even New Age culture as well, incorporates scientific (CSICOP would say "pseudoscientific") perspectives into a study of the taboo subject of psychic and spiritual phenomena, topics that both establishment science and establishment religion want to see defined as religious. As we shall see again later on, ufology has a parascience (nuts-and-bolts) wing and a New Age wing that are caught in the same crossfire.

For now, the important point is that both science and religion have been social institutions with their own dogma ("fundamentalisms"), reality-tunnels and inquisitions to drive out heretics. One interesting example of how the ideology of open inquiry can be ignored both in religion and in science can be found in *The Dead Sea Scrolls Deception* (1991) by Michael Baigent and Richard Leigh.[18] Although the scrolls themselves are certainly open to interpretation, one thing that is fairly certain is that access to them was denied to scholars outside of a very small group for forty years because it was feared that controversial material in the scrolls would be embarrassing not only to the Roman Catholic Church, but to the Christian establishment in general. This was a clear violation of Merton's principle of communality or sharing of data, not to mention disinterestedness, among archaeologists (scientists) and the religious establishment.

The Antiscience Movement

The very notions of modernization and secularization as discussed by sociologists like Max Weber may have been overdone. After all, social scientists keep "uncovering" survivals of traditional culture, including magic and religion in modern society. Science, technology and bureaucracy never did convert Americans to uniform, time-clocked robots. Science and rationality, as handy as they are, have never become

---

17. Hess, 1993.
18. Baigent and Leigh, 1991.

totally dominant, although they dominate in the U.S. and in other Western countries more than elsewhere.

Having said that, let us consider to what extent the domination of science may have been "eroded." This is, after all, *the* major preoccupation of CSICOP. It is best to listen to CSICOP Fellow Gerald Holton, and CSICOP Chairman Paul Kurtz. Holton, Professor of Physics and of the History of Science at Harvard University, says that "The 'pro-science'-imbued world picture of the late twentieth century is a rather vulnerable and fragile minority position."[19] This sounds pretty serious. No wonder we need CSICOP.

According to Holton, however, some anti-science is more serious than the rest. Apparently the biggest threat lies in a scientifically illiterate populace that can be caught up in social movements, one example of which is the 19th-century British anti-technology movement of workers called the Luddites. "In a democracy," Holton says, "no matter how poorly informed the citizens are, they do properly demand a place at the table where decisions are made, even when those decisions have a large scientific/technical component. In that lies the potential for erroneous policy and eventual social instability."[20]

If scientific illiteracy can lead to less public support for science and technology, which might translate into less government spending on university science research, no wonder CSICOP is concerned about popular interest in a broad base of phenomena outside normal science, from pyramid power to natural healing to UFOs. Next, let us consider CSICOP Chairman and philosopher Paul Kurtz's analysis of the origins of the "antiscience counterculture."[21]

Most broadly, Kurtz points to C.P. Snow's "two cultures,"[22] one of which advances the perspective of science, and the other of which argues that there is truth beyond science. The latter argues for "a mystical and spiritual realm and/or aesthetic and subjective aspects of experience." Kurtz complains that the peaceful co-existence of the two cultures has degenerated into attacks on science in recent decades. By contrast, Aronowitz emphasizes the way science marginalizes or trivializes the mystical and aesthetic! I'm not sure who started it.

Next, Kurtz objects to some fellow philosophers who "have argued that there is no such thing as [objective] scientific method, that scientific knowledge is relative to sociocultural institutions, and that paradigm shifts occur for extra-rational causes."[23] Of course, this position match-

19. Holton, 1994, pp. 264-265.
20. Holton, 1994, pp. 264-265.
21. Kurtz, 1994.
22. Snow, 1991.
23. Kurtz, 1994, p. 256.

es the sociology of science critique of Aronowitz and others. Kurtz then gets into a debate with French postmodernists like Derrida, Foucault and Lyotard, who "deconstruct" scientific language (discourse) in order to take apart its supposed objectivity and reveal the underlying biases of dominant economic and political institutions.

Kurtz has "special concern" over New Age culture, including "the dramatic growth of the occult, the paranormal and pseudosciences, and particularly the promotion of the irrational and sensational...by the mass media," and, of course, "abductions by extraterrestrial beings and unidentified flying objects."[24] All of these trends are "symptomatic of a profound antiscience attitude."

Interestingly, Kurtz sees New Age beliefs in a wider context of antiscience attacks, which precisely underlines my point that the authority of science to dismiss UFO research may be declining as the overall respect for the scientific establishment declines. Kurtz gives a list of no less than ten categories of antiscience objections.

The first four on his list could be grouped together and labeled (by me) as the "Faust motif." Faust was a magician/scholar in medieval legend who sold his soul to the devil in exchange for knowledge of things that only God should mess with. The Faust motif or story line is present in many classic horror stories and films, e.g., Mary Shelley's *Frankenstein*, in which Doctor Frankenstein "goes too far" and tampers with the secret of life, something that only God should do. The monster represents the evil influence of the Devil, and scientists going mad represents possession by evil or by the Devil.

Kurtz's first antiscience attack involves opposition to nuclear weapons and nuclear energy. He considers the anti-nuclear movement to be an overreaction to real dangers, noting that "physicists [have been labeled] diabolical beings who, in tinkering with the secrets of nature, [hold] within their grasp the power to destroy all forms of life on this planet."[25] He even mentions Dr. Strangelove, and the Faustian connection is obvious.

The other three attacks in this group include environmental protest over technology that harms the ozone layer among other things, concerns about chemical additives, and "suspicion of biogenetic engineering." Kurtz refers to the fictional cloning of dinosaur DNA in *Jurassic Park* in the last of these three and makes the appropriate allusion to Dr. Frankenstein when the dinosaurs run amok.

---

24. Kurtz, 1994, p. 258.
25. Kurtz, 1994, p. 259.

Kurtz's next three categories of antiscience attack have to do with medicine and health. One is the opposition to orthodox medicine, including the "right-to-die" issue and the controversial use of animals in medical research. Another is the debate over psychiatry, the treatment of mental patients in institutions and the use of anti-psychotic drugs. The third involves "alternative health cures" through iridology, herbal medicines, etc.

There are two religious categories on Kurtz's list. One is Asian mysticism which also overlaps the health group of issues, since it includes meditation and spiritual healing. The other is "the revival of fundamentalist religion," including creationism vs. evolutionism.

Finally, Kurtz risks being politically incorrect by showing concern over "multicultural and feminist critiques of science education." These are critiques of the bias of "dead, white Anglo-Saxon males." Kurtz states, "There are, we are told, non-Western and primitive cultures that are as 'true' and 'valid' as the scientific culture of the Western world. This movement supports the complete relativization of scientific knowledge."[26] He doesn't mind recognizing multicultural and female contributions to science, but he is worried by the attack on the objectivity principle.

As if science were not in enough trouble, let me add an eleventh category of attack: fraud. One example of this can be found in Judy Sarasohn's book *Science on Trial: The Whistle-Blower, the Accused, and the Nobel Laureate* (1993),[27] the account of Margot O'Toole, a postdoctoral fellow who called attention to irregularities in AIDS-related research at MIT. Of course, there are lots of accusations of fraud in New Age practices as well, especially with certain fortune-tellers who claim the ability to remove curses for a few thousand dollars. The *Skeptical Inquirer* loves to debunk alleged frauds and hoaxes. But the point is that "objective" science is also vulnerable to fraud, because it is after all an institution like others, and where there is big grant money there are sometimes big frauds.

Defending Science

Before leaving CSICOP Chairman Paul Kurtz, I should say that one of his solutions for the antiscience problem is "to extend the critical methods of science further, especially to ethics, politics, and religion. Until those in the scientific community have the courage to extend the

26. Kurtz, 1994, p. 261.
27. Sarasohn, 1993.

methods of science and reason as far as they can to these other fields, then I feel that the growth of antiscience will continue."[28] In other words, the solution to this boundary dispute is to take over the enemy, including religion. It amounts to the secularization and "scientificization" of everything. As Kurtz says, "What is at stake in a sense is modernism itself."[29]

Before presenting another CSICOP scholar in the defense of science, let us look at a "moderate" defense of objectivity by Princeton University philosopher of science, Philip Kitcher, author of *The Advancement of Science: Science without Legend, Objectivity without Illusions* (1993).[30] Kitcher tries to construct a moderate view that lies between seeing science as evil "scientism" and seeing it as perfect. According to the perfect ideal, science is a search for objective truth; this ideal he calls "Legend,"[31] what I would call the ideology of science as an objective and therefore unbiased tool.

Kitcher does not try to pretend that Legend is alive and true, but he objects to the conclusion that "science does not advance" (approach truth) just because there are "social pressures and nonepistemic motivations" (i.e., biases having nothing to do with knowledge *per se*).[32] He advocates measuring how nearly objective science is in various instances rather than concentrating on the fallacies and condemning the whole process as hopelessly biased.

For example, it is possible to gauge how reliable or unreliable particular scientific instruments are. "Of course people make mistakes. Our observational and inferential procedures for generating belief are fallible. They are not *equally* fallible."[33]

I dare say that this is a very sensible attitude. But the reason an antiscientific polemic came about in the first place is that science was so often portrayed as infallible (as "Legend"), just as the Medieval Church claimed to be infallible. If people smelled that the church could be wrong, look out. Incredibly science fell into the same trap, claiming that all science had to do was to be "objective" in order to be correct and unbiased, as if science or any other human institution could really ever be "objective" or completely unlinked to social processes and power.

In contrast to Kitcher's moderate defense of science, there is a more rigorous defense by Milton A. Rothman, former physics professor at Trenton State College and former research physicist at Princeton's Plas-

28. Kurtz, 1994, p. 262.
29. Kurtz, 1994, p. 263.
30. Kitcher, 1993.
31. Kitcher, 1993, p. 7.
32. Kitcher, 1993, p. 388.
33. Kitcher, 1993, p. 139.

ma Physics Laboratory. In his 1992 book entitled, *The Science Gap: Dispelling the Myths and Understanding the Reality of Science*, he expands upon an article he did for the *Skeptical Inquirer* in 1989.[34]

Rothman's first "myth" about science is that "Nothing exists until it is observed."[35] This notion, he says, is a kind of idealism based upon the Heisenberg uncertainty principle and some interpretations of quantum physics. Rothman complains that his second myth, "Nothing is known for sure," results in "the danger of modesty," letting marginal views of reality seem reasonable if "all knowledge is uncertain."[36] He claims, by contrast, that some things are known by definition, and some other things have such a tiny possibility of error that we can be sure about them.

Following closely on the second myth is the third, that "Nothing is impossible."[37] Again, Rothman states that some things are impossible by definition, which cannot be argued with, assuming one works within the definition. But then he crawls out on a limb to say that UFOs suspended motionless in the air are an impossibility, since studies have shown that there is no such thing as antigravity, and magnetic fields would not be strong enough. "No physical process exists that is able to keep a UFO supported motionless in the air for an extended period of time. This is a strong conclusion." I know that Dr. Robert M. Wood would disagree, since he established in his work at McDonnell Douglas that UFOs could float on the Earth's electromagnetic field, although not with our present technology.[38]

Rothman's certainty on this matter relates to his fifth and sixth myths, that advanced civilizations of the future and in outer space will have forces unknown to us. He says that it is an inescapable conclusion of our present knowledge that there are "no strong, long-range forces" in the universe that we have not already discovered.[39] He also argues that no long-standing twentieth-century theories will be overturned.

Although Rothman's position leaves the door ajar for the discovery of some subtle energies with unanticipated potentials, his attitude comes perilously close to that of scientists and inventors in the past who claimed that certain things were impossible or that there was nothing important left to discover. I suspect that some anecdotes to this effect are mere folklore, but Dr. Beverly Rubik, a biophysicist, states for example that "Over a hundred years ago, one of the deans of Harvard

34. Rothman, 1992.
35. Rothman, 1992, pp. 19-38.
36. Rothman, 1992, pp. 39-63.
37. Rothman, 1992, pp. 65-84.
38. Wood, 1993.
39. Rothman, 1992, pp. 109, 116.

University said our science is nearly complete. He went so far as to discourage students from going into science as he felt there was nothing more to do."[40] Arthur C. Clarke (a member of CSICOP) refers to articles in physics journals in the 1930s, when Goddard was experimenting with rocketry, that claimed that it was impossible for a rocket to escape the Earth's gravitational field.[41] Clarke also supports the famous German physicist Max Planck's wry comment about science advancing every time an old (and short-sighted) scientist dies.

Of course, Rothman knows that there have been developments in physical theory, e.g., from Newton to Einstein to quantum theory, but there is some invariant knowledge involved, he says, in the sense that "the observable consequences predicted by the theory are the invariants that make up permanent knowledge."[42] Not being a physicist, I dare to suggest nonetheless that, of course, Newtonian physics, for example, is still valid within its limited perspective, but there may still be new perspectives and applications of old perspectives that we simply have not explored. This makes the so-called "invariant" knowledge incomplete.

As for the problem of there being no undiscovered "strong, long-range forces," one might still wonder about other dimensions or aspects of our existence in which other important, though poorly understood, forces might exist, even if there are no undiscovered strong forces in the currently observable dimensions.

Rothman's attitude about this sort of thing is interesting. "Is physics all there is?" he asks. "We cannot say no with total certainty...but we find no evidence for the supernatural."[43] Whenever there are claims of the paranormal or supernatural (defining and distinguishing the two is difficult), he asserts that there is no evidence, which, of course, is CSICOP's position. He claims that parapsychological experiments "invariably involve small effects producing statistical fluctuations that are just on the edge of chance."[44] There is evidence in parapsychology journals contradicting this statement, and I have even done an experiment of my own that was way beyond the chance level. Of course, CSICOP attacks these studies on methodological grounds.

Rothman dismisses studies of ghosts, which might be "supernatural," stating that "investigations by trained observers have invariably found [them] to be either natural events misunderstood by the [experiencer], or simply tricks played on the public by professional or amateur

---

40. DiCarlo, 1996, p. 54.
41. Clarke, 1973.
42. Rothman, 1992, p. 103.
43. Rothman, 1992, p. 14.
44. Rothman, 1992, p. 129.

charlatans."[45] My experience studying ghost reports[46] directly contradicts this statement as well, but Rothman has CSICOP and normal science on his side.

One other of Rothman's myths is worth examining here for its attitude of certainty. Myth number 12 (out of 16) is that "Scientists are always making false predictions."[47] He daringly and without fear of falsification predicts, "None of you is going to be reincarnated into any form no matter how good or bad you are." If there is no evidence of the supernatural, still one would think logically that it is beyond his ability to judge the truth or falsehood of reincarnation.

Surprisingly Rothman makes one attack on the myth of objectivity. His myth number 11 is that "All scientists are objective."[48] However, he uses this opportunity to cite examples of alleged errors and fraud in marginal or deviant sciences, e.g., in the debated experiments in cold fusion and in laboratory cheating in parapsychology, along with a number of other problems that could occur in any experimental research.

Although I obviously take issue with much of Rothman's dogmatic certainty, I think that his book is very well argued. It explains the perspective of normal science well. It might also serve as a set of guidelines for scholars who would explore paranormal topics or explore alternate ways of knowing, but who would also like to keep one foot grounded in skeptical science.

45. Rothman, 1992, p. 129.
46. Emmons, 1982.
47. Rothman, 1992, pp. 179, 188.
48. Rothman, 1992, pp. 161-176.

Chapter 7

The Crumbling of Certainty

Seeds of Doubt in New Physics

In the last chapter I stated that there were two reasons for doubting normal-science pronouncements about UFOs. The reason dealt with in Chapter 6 was that the authority of science and even of scientific method has been under attack. Now it is time to deal with the second reason: the new physics, or at least some interpretations of it, suggests that UFOs may be much easier to accept and to explain even within a scientific framework than previously thought.

In other words, the rebellion against science is making some people wonder whether there aren't other worthwhile ways of knowing besides science, including the use of psychic communications in altered states of consciousness. Some of these alternate ways of knowing might tell us something about UFOs and other "paranormal" subjects. But even if we must stick to scientific method as the only legitimate way of knowing, there are growing arguments that there are good scientific reasons for taking UFOs off the taboo research list and for seeing UFOs as plausible, especially when our science includes the new physics.

The new physics (including such topics as quantum physics, superstring theory and hyperspace, and wormholes) has contributed to a "crumbling of certainty" about the physical (not to mention the psychic/spiritual) world. "Certainty" is used in two senses here. In general, it means certainty about what is and is not possible in the universe. After listening to physicists talk in what sounds like science-fictional terms about 10-dimensional space, one might wonder what is so hard to believe about UFOs.

In a more specific sense, "certainty" refers to determinacy or the ability of science to discern objective properties of matter/energy and to establish causal links among phenomena. Quantum physics has opened up doubts about causation and about the nonambiguous nature of things. Once these doubts are entertained, all kinds of alternate explanations of reality, including metaphysical ones, are brought back in from the margins where they had been banished previously by authoritative science. Even without carrying new physics to its New Age horizons, however, it is easy to see how new physics has made UFOs seem more plausible.

At the 1978 MUFON conference, Dr. J. Allen Hynek asked people to remember that, barring nuclear holocaust, "There will be a 21st century science, and a 25th century science and even a millionth century science, which will know things that we can't even imagine. And even if we could imagine them, we would think them utterly silly and impossible—like UFOs for instance!"[1] This is a larger point, and one certainly well taken, but my point is simply that even 20th century science has been anticipating principles that make UFOs not so silly or impossible.

New physics is partly theoretical speculation, to be sure, as in the case of superstring theory, but it is *respectable* speculation in current physics. It is part of normal science. Parts of it, like chaos theory, were previously considered marginal, but no more.

Of course, the implications of the new physics are not seen identically by everyone. Among the nonufologist astronomers I interviewed there was general acceptance of new physics, but with different emphasis by individuals. One accepted wormholes, for example, whereas another accepted baby universes (the creation of new universes branching from this one) but not wormholes. None of them thought that living beings could travel faster than the speed of light (FTL) although some particles can. Although most saw new physics as possibly providing explanations for interstellar travel, one astronomer stressed that such applications of new physics are popular distortions.

In my sample of ufologists, there was a great deal of familiarity with new physics and enthusiasm for the insights it might give into the UFO phenomenon. Only 12% (of the 66 who gave this information) had done no reading in new physics; 52% had done a lot, and 36% had done a little. Of those who knew enough about it to make a judgment, 44% strongly felt that it would help explain the origins and operation of UFOs, and another 42% accepted new physics explanations somewhat, although considering them quite speculative.

Interestingly, it was the ufologists outside of the natural sciences who were the most involved in new physics. The only exception to this statement is that all ten of the physicists had done reading in new physics (eight of them a great deal), although the physicists were only slight-

---

1. Schuessler, 1994, pp. 174-184.

ly more accepting of new physics explanations of UFOs than other natural scientists were.

Taking all natural scientists as a group (biology, physics, chemistry, etc.), 46% of natural scientists had done a lot of reading in new physics, compared to 50% of psychologists (and therapists, etc.), 60% of social scientists (only 5 in this subsample), and 64% of those in the humanities (history, English, etc.). Only 25% of natural scientists strongly supported a new physics explanation for UFO technology compared to 40% of social scientists, 53% of psychologists, and 67% of those in humanities.

How should we interpret these differences? First of all, new physics is largely at the level of (respectable) theoretical speculation, although some things are fairly well established, e.g., the paradoxical behavior of electrons as both particles and waves. Next, the applications of new physics to other things, such as UFOs, are doubly speculative. It is not surprising that nonufologists would accept the theoretical concept of wormholes as shortcuts through the universe, but still not think that spacecraft could use them in any practical sense.

How about the irony that the natural scientists among ufologists are less enthusiastic about new physics than the ufologists in humanities and social and psychological sciences are? Some of the physicists, for example, think that the old physics is sufficient to explain extraterrestrial visitation, including the use of gravitational and electromagnetic fields at up to near-light speeds, and with a long period of colonization throughout the galaxy. And, of course, they fully appreciate how speculative the new physics is.

As we move away from the nuts-and-bolts ufologists, who tend to be grounded in physical sciences, we approach more mystical and metaphysical applications of new physics. Although these applications may be reasonable and may help explain some of the more bizarre aspects of the UFO phenomenon, they are harder for many physical scientists to follow and accept.

Two examples of mystical/metaphysical applications of new physics are the works of Fritjof Capra and Fred Alan Wolf. Although both Capra and Wolf are theoretical physicists, their books have become part of New Age culture. In *The Tao of Physics* (1976) Capra shows parallels between "modern physics" and Eastern mystical religious philosophies like Hinduism, Buddhism, Taoism and Zen.[2] Wolf, author of several books that help legitimate New Age perspectives through new physics, shows parallels between new physics (especially

---

2. Capra, 1976.

quantum theory) and the perspectives of shamans (spiritual healers) in
The Eagle's Quest (1991).[3]

Drake, Fermi, and Sagan Revisited

In Chapter 4 we considered the question of whether extraterrestrial civilizations ought to exist according to the perspective of astronomy. According to the formula of radio astronomer Frank Drake, there
ought to be about one new civilization produced elsewhere just in the
Milky Way each year.[4] Carl Sagan, another Cornell astronomer, has
popularized the quest for ETs through radio contact, but thinks that
there is no evidence for them having visited us (UFOs), although he
says it is possible that the solar system has been visited many times
over the eons.[5]

And finally there is the Fermi paradox,[6] "Where are the aliens?" If
they existed in our galaxy, the Milky Way, then they ought to have been
here by now. But, of course, they haven't been here (never mind that silly UFO evidence); therefore, they must not have existed in the first
place.

Much of the ET argument is snagged on *a priori* assumptions from
normal science. UFO evidence is dismissed out of hand partly because
of these assumptions. For one thing, it is usually assumed that reports
of aliens are invalid because the beings are too humanoid. If life
evolved independently in various parts of the universe, the chances of
them looking like us should be slim.

However, there are some arguments for biological similarity. One
is based on "panspermia" ("seeds everywhere"), the idea supported by
Nobel prize-winning biologist Francis Crick and others that simple life
forms may have been sent out by civilizations wanting to spread life to
other parts of the galaxy. Another possible mechanism that would explain similarity of life beyond a single planet is the evolution of organic
molecules in interstellar space rather than on formed planets, as Robert
Jastrow, founder of the Goddard Space Center, suggests, since such organic molecules have been found in interstellar dust clouds by radio astronomy.[7]

Even if life evolved independently on many different planets,
Michael Swords argues that there are good reasons to expect very parallel processes everywhere.[8] This is based partly on the greatly similar

3. Wolf, 1991.
4. Swords, 1986.
5. Swords, 1986, p. 38.
6. Swords, 1986, pp. 32-33.
7. White, 1989, p. 14.

elemental composition of the materials produced everywhere in the universe by fusion in stars. And, by contrast with Carl Sagan's view that earthlings ought to have more in common with petunias than with ETs, Swords presents reasons for animals everywhere to evolve into tube-shaped feeders with head and tail ends, and eventually into highly intelligent erect-standing manipulators like us.[9]

Of course, another possible reason for great similarity between humans and ETs could be a long-term connection between the two. One of the main themes in current abduction research involves reported reproductive examinations and an apparent genetic manipulation or hybridization program. Physical anthropologist Arthur David Horn writes about ET influences on Earth not only throughout human evolution, but long before that. [10]

However, there is another obstacle to looking at UFO evidence even greater than the *a priori* assumption that aliens shouldn't look so much like us. That obstacle is the assumption that the distances are just too great from there to here. Of course, those who accept the Fermi argument that they could have colonized by short leaps would not argue this. Nor would the ufologists who think that UFOs may not be extraterrestrial in the first place bother with this argument.

Nevertheless, the argument is often made that the distances are too great, assuming that no interstellar travelers could go faster than light (FTL). Einstein's speed limit (at least for living beings if not for all particles) is widely accepted even by most physical scientists who appreciate the new physics.

And finally we come to the single most important contribution, although not the only one, that new physics makes to speculation about how ET UFOs could get here more easily than previously thought: ways around the speed-of-light limit. This does not usually mean breaking the speed limit. Instead, it involves finding short-cuts through the universe and even drawing a new road-map, a map that sees the structure of the universe in ways that are almost impossible to visualize.

Hyperspace and Superstrings

Although I stated boldly above that theories of hyperspace (spatial dimensions beyond the three we can experience) and of superstrings (nine dimensions of space plus one of time) are respectable speculation

8. Swords, 1991.
9. Swords, 1991, pp. 63-73.
10. Horn, 1994.

in new physics, the respectability has emerged only with difficulty in recent decades. In his 1994 book, *Hyperspace*,[11] Michio Kaku, professor of theoretical physics at City College of New York (CUNY), relates the roots of hyperspace theory in the nineteenth century, but states that when he was a graduate student at Harvard he was told that "hyperspace…was not a suitable subject of serious study," and says that he had to come across the relevant writings in his casual reading. This is very similar to the way graduate students were advised against exploring chaos theory in physics and mathematics prior to the 1980s.

And yet Kaku reports that by now there have been over 200 international physics conferences on higher dimensions, and that the journals *Nuclear Physics* and *Physics Letters* have been flooded with articles on the theories of higher-dimensional space-time.[12] He notes that Steven Weinberg, Nobel Prize winner in physics, "commented recently that theoretical physics seems to be becoming more and more like science fiction." *Star Wars* and *Star Trek* productions rely heavily on such concepts.

Comparisons to science fiction make theoretical physicists nervous, because being labeled a "science-fiction physicist" implies that one is too "far out" for normal science. And yet the bizarre, unobservable and untestable theories of higher dimensions have great appeal in physics because they promise to yield a unified explanation of the material world. As Kaku explains, "The key step in unifying the laws of nature is to increase the number of dimensions of space-time…[so that] we have enough 'room' to unify all known forces."[13] As it turns out, according to "superstring theory," all forces can be unified if there are 10 (or 26) dimensions.

So far no one has managed to work out the mathematics to prove or solve how the electromagnetic, strong and weak nuclear forces, plus gravity can be combined in hyperspace. Nor can a human possibly visualize in any material sense more than three spatial dimensions (with time as the fourth dimension). Kaku's book explains all of this brilliantly for nonphysicists who want to understand why physicists and all other twentieth century mortals are stuck waiting for twenty-first century mathematics to clear the matter up.

Nevertheless, there are some ingenious ways of explaining our ignorance that derive from analogies to lower dimensions. Once we have looked at these, we can begin to explain what this might have to do with UFOs.

11. Kaku, 1994, pp. 7-8.
12. Kaku, 1994, p. 9.
13. Kaku, 1994, pp. 12, 152.

Since we are mere three-dimensional beings, at least so far as we can perceive on the material level, not counting time as a dimension for now, it is no wonder that we cannot imagine a fourth dimension, not to mention five more spatial dimensions required in superstring theory. And it would only confuse things to mention the just-so story from physicists who think that the Big Bang cracked the universe into two: our 3-D universe (plus time as a fourth dimension), and a dwarf twin consisting of six curled up ones that we might have to escape into when our regular one collapses again some day.[14]

Although we cannot visualize a fourth dimension, perhaps we can imagine a little bit what we are up against by visualizing the similar plight of two-dimensional beings who have trouble with the idea of a third dimension. To help us in this exercise, we have a delightful little book by a nineteenth-century clergyman, Edwin Abbot, entitled *Flatland: A Romance of Many Dimensions by a Square*.[15]

Flatlanders, of course, are beings of only two dimensions. We can visualize them as figures drawn on a piece of paper. So far so good, as long as we ignore little inconsistencies like the fact that we couldn't really see an object that had no third dimension, no thickness at all. Let's also not try to figure out how Flatlanders can see each other if they have no depth and are all staring up from the paper.

Assuming that our Flatlanders can interact on their 2-D surface, they will be unable to see us looking down upon them from a third dimension. And Abbot has the high priests of Flatland ridiculing Mr. Square when he tells about his experiences floating through Spaceland. Conversely, when Mr. Sphere visits Flatland, ask yourself, how he will look to the Flatlanders?

The answer in a moment, but first, I can't wait to tell you something about the relevance to UFOs. One reason for UFOs seemingly appearing and disappearing in and out of thin air in many reports may be that they come in and out of our 3-D space by moving in another spatial dimension, just as Mr. Sphere can come down upon and back away from the "piece of paper" that is Flatland. Hyperspace maneuvers might also explain "paranormal" phenomena like ghosts and apports (materialization of objects out of thin air), as not only psychics but even some physicists speculated in the 1870s.[16]

Have you figured out how Mr. Sphere will look to the Flatlanders? When he first penetrates their plane he will appear as a point, then as a circle growing in size, until he gets halfway through the plane, and

14. Kaku, 1994, p. 27.
15. Abbot, 1884.
16. Kaku, 1994, pp. 49-50.

then he will be a smaller and smaller circle until he becomes a point again and finally disappears after having gone all the way through. Kaku discusses monsters that might come into our 3-D space from a fourth dimension and change shapes like Mr. Sphere in Flatland by analogy.[17] Some UFOs are shapeshifters as well, changing geometric shape and size throughout a sighting, and moving through extra dimensions (hyperspace) could be the reason.

Some bizarre things can happen from the point of view of Flatlanders who cannot visualize the structure of the larger universe beyond their two dimensions. Suppose we take the piece of paper known as Flatland and curl it around in our third dimension, so that the right and left edges meet to form a tube. Flatlanders headed in one direction from right to left along the paper will eventually cross the seam of the tube and end up back on the right side of the paper again. They will be shocked, like explorers on Earth who think the world is flat and expect to fall off the edge, but circumnavigate the globe and end up back home again.

Some day some clever Flatlanders may realize that under certain conditions (namely when Flatland is held in a tubular shape), it is a shorter trip across the seam than it is to travel all the way from one side of the paper to the other across the middle. However, Flatland physicists will point out that this is possible only under extremely high energy conditions and only if an advanced civilization can figure out how to apply the energy to the universe (that is, how to hold the paper in a tube shape).

Then some really clever Flatlanders will claim that it is possible to shortcut the way around the tube by going straight through the hole in the tube. Flatland high priests will burn them at the stake. Or Flatland universities will deny them tenure.

Of course, my satire is unfair. Going through the hole in the tube is essentially the principle of the wormhole, to be explained shortly. And wormholes are (now) acceptable speculation in physics. Maybe Flatlanders who speculated about tubeholes would be tolerated in normal Flatland science. They might even write novels about beings that traveled through tubeholes. They would be ridiculed only if they claimed to see beings from the distant reaches of the Flat Universe (if the piece of paper were really big) who had actually made the journey.

Returning to the question of the relevance of hyperspace (space with more than three spatial dimensions) to UFOs, the main difficulty with the ET hypothesis for some people is the speed-of-light limit. How

17. Kaku, 1994, pp. 76-77.

could extraterrestrials get here from so many light-years distance if no living beings can travel faster than the speed of light?

For some scientists the answer is simple: they could have colonized by short leaps across the galaxy over a long period of time, as assumed in the Fermi paradox. But for those who do not accept the colonization theory (for some obscure reason), hyperspace may be the answer. When we see the universe in three spatial dimensions, certain distances seem very far, but there may be hyperspace shortcuts. Flatlanders who see a long distance from the right side of the "page" to the left have a similar problem. From their point of view (plane of view, actually), hyperspace solutions involve traveling over the seam in the tube when the page is curved to make the left and right sides meet, or tunneling straight through the hole in the tube (if Flatlanders are capable of making such a "tubehole"). More about this in the next section on wormholes.

Of course, our popular culture has contained simplistic notions of hyperspace as an interstellar shortcut for decades with *Star Trek* and the *Star Wars* films. My interviews with nonufologist astronomers revealed a variety of notions about hyperspace and whether it would actually provide a shortcut or not. As noted earlier, there was considerable familiarity with and enthusiasm for new Physics concepts like hyperspace among the ufologists I interviewed. There are also some references to hyperspace in ufology articles and books, although few authors go into much detail obviously because nobody really knows how hyperspace can be manipulated.

Some ufologists speculate on how higher-dimensional physics might allow UFO propulsion systems to beat the speed-of-light barrier.[18] Another notion, presented by French ufologist Jean-Pierre Petit, a cosmologist specializing in plasma physics, is that UFOs might travel between twin universes through hyperspace.[19] Other references mention higher dimensions with only a general idea that energies or objects may somehow appear out of these dimensions, as stated by Vladimir Ajaja of Russia[20] and Illobrand von Ludwiger of Germany.[21]

But there are also other fascinating applications of hyperspace to UFO reports. Stan Kulikowski II notes that there are several examples of UFO abductees or experiencers who claim to find the interior of a craft much larger than would seem possible judging by the exterior dimensions.[22] This phenomenon is consistent with the expectations of

18. Holt, 1986, pp. 85-87.
19. de Brosses, 1991, pp. 6-7.
20. Ajaja, 1992, p. 198.
21. von Ludwiger, 1993, p. 244.
22. Kulikowski, 1994.

hyperspace geometry. Without getting into a fourth-dimensional example, we can see the UFO cases as analogous to the astonishment of a Flatlander who managed to crawl all around on the surface of a sphere that intersected Flatland and appeared at first glance to be only as big as its intersecting circle.

Since the "face on Mars" is related to the issue of extraterrestrial intelligence and visitation, it should be noted that hyperdimensional physics is discussed in *The McDaniel Report*.[23] McDaniel explains that Hoagland and Torun have interpreted some of the mathematical relationships among objects on the Cydonian area of Mars around the face in terms of higher-dimensional geometry.

According to Richard L. Thompson, the sacred Vedic literature of ancient India contains accounts of travel to other worlds, including places in other star systems. Although there are no explicit geometric explanations involved, it is possible "to deduce from the accounts that this travel involves more than motion through three-dimensional space."[24]

Sometimes the modern UFO literature contains reports of phenomena that suggest a hyperspace interpretation (to me) even though the authors do not try to explain them that way. For example, Budd Hopkins relates an Australian case in which a family of four seem to become invisible during their abduction at a playground, based upon photographs in which members of the family should appear, but do not. "As to the physics behind such an anomaly," Hopkins states, "I will not attempt any speculation whatsoever."[25]

However, what appears to be a case of invisibility to us 3-D creatures might be a lifting of the people involved through a fourth spatial dimension during their abduction. This would be analogous to our lifting Flatlanders off their plane and setting them down again in another spot. From the 2-D perspective the abducted Flatlanders would have become invisible during their trip through the third dimension. The reason for the Australians being taken through hyperspace would appear to be to prevent them from being seen by the other people on the playground, as they almost certainly would have been if they had been lifted straight up into the UFO.

Of course, all of these hyperspace interpretations of UFO reports are lost on physicists like Kaku who do not accept ufology. Kaku states, "We do not see signs of any advanced civilization in the heavens, at least not in our solar system or even in our small sector of the galaxy."[26]

23. McDaniel, 1993, pp. 131-133.
24. Richard L. Thompson, 1993, pp. 214-217.
25. Hopkins, 1993A, p. 199.

However, he expects that "any civilization that masters the hyperspace theory will become lord of the universe," just as in Isaac Asimov's science fiction Foundation Series in which "the discovery of hyperspace travel led to the rise of a Galactic Empire."[27]

Wormholes and Time Travel

Now the most specific application of hyperspace theory to the problem of how to get around the speed-of-light limit in traveling great distances through space is found in the concept of wormholes. These wormholes, as it turns out, are not only spatial shortcuts, but potentially time machines as well.

The foremost figure in this dramatic development is theoretical physicist Kip S. Thorne of California Institute of Technology, whose book *Black Holes and Time Warps: Einstein's Outrageous Legacy* (1994) should be read by any nonphysicist who is fascinated by the subject. By a supreme irony Carl Sagan (who scoffs at ufology) was the catalyst who precipitated Thorne's involvement in the wormhole problem when he asked Thorne to check the physics in his (Sagan's) forthcoming novel *Contact* in 1985.[28] Thorne advised Sagan that the heroine, Eleanor Arroway, would not be able to shorten the 26-light-year trip from Earth to the star Vega by taking an hour's trip through a black hole because her craft would be destroyed by electromagnetic vacuum fluctuations and radiation bombardment.[29] Thorne recommended a wormhole instead.

Thorne's book can be read for a more complete explanation, but essentially a wormhole is a hyperspace linkage between two distant parts of our universe, in the Sagan case a one-kilometer linkage or shortcut route between two wormhole mouths, one near Earth and the other near Vega. Using our Flatlander analogy, it is as if Earth and Vega are flat circles on a very long piece of paper, and we bend the sheet around so that Earth and Vega are very close together in the third dimensional space between them. Instead of traveling all the way along the sheet of paper, we tunnel through the third dimension between the two bent halves.

Of course, the tricky part is making the wormhole. According to Thorne, although black holes occur naturally when dying stars implode, wormholes probably do not exist unless some advanced civili-

26. Kaku, 1994, p. 282.
27. Kaku, 1994, pp. xi, 5.
28. Sagan, 1985.
29. Thorne, 1994, pp. 483-484.

zation has managed to create them, but it could be done.[30] Sagan was happy and fixed his book.

But Thorne's speculation about wormholes continued, especially after Professor Tom Roman of Central Connecticut State University suggested to Thorne's student Mike Morris in 1986 that wormholes could be used for time travel.[31] Lest this sound too bizarre, let me point out that Michio Kaku, another theoretical physicist, states that with wormholes, "In fact, we have to make strong assumptions in order to prevent time travel from taking place."[32]

Thorne provides the hypothetical example of a short wormhole between his living room and his wife's spacecraft on the front lawn in the year 2000.[33] He in the living room and his wife in the spacecraft hold hands through the wormhole while the spacecraft zooms away at nearly the speed of light and returns in 12 hours (spacecraft time). The wormhole mouth in the craft has moved in relationship to the front lawn, but not in relationship to the other wormhole mouth. And by the laws of general relativity, the 12-hour trip for his wife would appear to take 10 years to someone on the front lawn.

Therefore, when Thorne releases his wife's hand and goes outside after 12 hours, his wife is not home yet. When the spacecraft finally returns to the front lawn in 10 years (in 2010), he will have aged ten years and she only 12 hours. Moreover, if his younger self crawls through the wormhole in 2000, he will come out onto the lawn as his younger self, but in 2010. If his older self in 2010 (or anytime thereafter) goes out on the lawn and crawls back the other way, he will end up in the living room in the year 2000.

This is all wonderful except for the horrible paradoxes created by time machines, as illustrated in the popular film, *Back to the Future*. According to the "grandfather paradox" or "matricide paradox,"[34] how can someone travel into the past and kill his/her own ancestor? Would this not prevent the traveler from being born and therefore from traveling back to kill the ancestor? Stephen Hawking, the great theoretical physicist, thinks that if time travel were possible we would be "invaded by hoards of tourists from the future."[35] This turns out to be an important question for the time-travel theory of the origin of UFOs, as we shall see shortly.

---

30. Thorne, 1994, pp. 486-490.
31. Thorne, 1994, pp. 498-499.
32. Kaku, 1994, p. 20.
33. Thorne, 1994, pp. 502-504.
34. Thorne, 1994, pp. 508-509; Kaku, 1994, p. 235.
35. Kaku, 1994, p. 235.

Meanwhile, Thorne has wrestled with a variety of technical objections in physics to the feasibility of wormholes being used as time machines. Although he has argued against most of them, as of his 1994 book he states that Stephen Hawking is probably right when he claims that quantum gravity effects would destroy a wormhole just before it was about to function as one.[36] Not enough is known about the laws of quantum gravity to know for sure.

As fascinating as the physics of wormholes is, I find the sociology of science of wormholes equally amusing. In reference to the articles by Kip Thorne and his students in *Physical Review Letters and American Journal of Physics* in 1988, Kaku states that "This marked the first time that reputable physicists, and not crackpots, were scientifically advancing a claim about changing the course of time itself."[37] However, it was not quite such a simple matter for Thorne to get this topic accepted in normal science.

In 1987 one of Thorne's colleagues, Richard Price, telephoned to say that he was worried about Thorne's work on the theory of time machines, and he was afraid that Thorne "had gone a little crazy or senile."[38] Consequently, if even his friend was concerned, Thorne decided not to publish anything until he was very sure about his work lest he and especially his students be rejected by the scientific community. He didn't want "Morris and Yurtsever's budding scientific reputations [tarnished] with a label of 'crazy science-fiction physicists.'"[39]

The article he and these two students wrote for *Physical Review Letters* in 1988 was called "Wormholes, Time Machines, and the Weak Energy Condition." As Thorne says, "Despite the 'time machines' in the title, our paper was accepted for publication without question. The two anonymous referees seemed to be sympathetic; I heaved a sigh of relief."[40] Reaction from colleagues was mixed. Richard Price was still worried, but Igor Novikov said, "I'm so happy, Kip! You have broken the barrier. If *you* can publish research on time machines, then so can *I*!"[41] And he did. What a good example for people who have trouble believing that normal science involves strong social control that sometimes inhibits inquiry. It also shows that scientific revolutions can be successful.

Nevertheless, Thorne still had to worry about sensational media coverage, as in the case of the ufologists in Chapter 4. Thorne "asked

---

36. Thorne, 1994, pp. 520-521.
37. Kaku, 1994, p. 20; Morris, Thorne, and Yurtsever, 1988; Morris and Thorne, 1988.
38. Thorne, 1994, pp. 504-505.
39. Thorne, 1994, p. 508.
40. Thorne, 1994, p. 508.
41. Thorne, 1994, p. 508.

the staff of the Caltech Public Relations Office to avoid and, indeed, try to suppress *any and all* publicity about our time machine research. A sensational splash in the press might brand our research as crazy in the eyes of many physicists."[42]

Three months after the publication of "Wormholes, Time Machines..." the press discovered it. "PHYSICISTS INVENT TIME MACHINES, read a typical headline.... I was mortified...by the totally outrageous claims.... After talking with two reporters, I abandoned all efforts to stem the tide and get the story told accurately, and went into hiding."[43]

In order to thwart the popular press, Thorne thereafter replaced the phrase "time machines" with the physicist's term "closed timelike curves." "The press, unfamiliar with physicists' jargon, was now unaware of the new time machine results I was publishing."[44] Of course, now the press will read Thorne's 1994 book and get wise. However, as stated above, Thorne now claims to agree with Hawking that time machines are not possible (probably).

In ufology, as discussed earlier, there is enthusiasm for hyperspace in general and for wormholes in particular as UFO shortcuts through space. There is little treatment of the time-machine application of wormholes, but some ufologists at least consider the possibility of time travel without specifying a wormhole mechanism. Marc Davenport's book *Visitors from Time*[45] is an excellent survey of UFO evidence of many types as seen through the perspective that at least some UFOs are from our own future. George Knapp reports the results of a Russian experiment in which watches inside UFO landing sites ran faster than watches outside.[46] This effect is consistent with Davenport's discussion of time anomalies in UFO reports.

Interestingly, ufologists have sometimes considered the time paradoxes that trouble physicists as well. Vince Johnson argues that the abduction evidence may indicate that the "Visitors" are gathering genetic material to fix a future population that has gone without the benefits of natural selection for too long (due to medical technology saving the unfit).[47] One problem with all of these abductions, Johnson realizes, is that the accumulation of interferences in people's lives could have significant, even catastrophic effects on the future. In order to reduce these ef-

42. Thorne, 1994, p. 508.
43. Thorne, 1994, p. 516.
44. Thorne, 1994, pp. 519-520.
45. Davenport, 1992B, especially pp. 62-65, 167-184.
46. Knapp, 1994, p. 300.
47. Vince Johnson, 1993, pp. 4-5.

fects, he argues, the Visitors try to program abductees to forget, and they are careful not to leave artifacts behind.

Marc Davenport presents the ingenious theory that "Men in Black" (suspicious characters reported to appear to UFO experiencers and to confiscate evidence of UFO sightings) are part of a future police force that attempts to prevent unauthorized travel into the past by UFOs and to minimize their effects on the future.[48] Of course, there might be other reasons why aliens or "visitors" would want to conceal their presence. Also one wonders why UFOs are sometimes apparently put on such obvious display, not only to select individuals but even to large groups of people.

Quantum Physics

Up to now we have seen some of the applications of the new physics to UFO questions, mainly physical questions of how nuts-and-bolts craft could travel what seem to be great distances through space as we perceive it. If the concepts of hyperspace and wormholes can shake our certainty about the impossibility of interstellar travel, quantum physics can really bring about the crumbling of certainty in a much more basic sense.

As physicist Niels Bohr put it, "Anyone who is not shocked by the quantum theory does not understand it."[49] Although it will be impossible to understand quantum physics very well from the short discussion here, we ought to be able to get at least some appreciation for why it is shocking.

First of all, "quantum" (plural = quanta) means a quantity. Specifically in the theory, a quantum is a "discrete packet of energy."[50] One example would be a photon, and there are hundreds of different kinds of quanta. All physical forces involve the exchange of quanta.

Of course, we humans can not perceive this tiny world of quanta. We are used to seeing (apparently) solid objects like rocks that obey Newtonian laws of physics, or close enough. What seems like a world of certainty to us succumbs to the Heisenberg Uncertainty Principle on the level of quanta. According to this principle, "We can never know simultaneously the velocity and position of a subatomic particle."[51]

One of the best known examples of uncertainty in quantum physics is the disturbing dual nature of electrons (and photons, etc.) as both

---

48. Davenport, 1992B, pp. 217-241.
49. Kaku, 1994, p. 111.
50. Kaku, 1994, p. 113.
51. Kaku, 1994, p. 114.

particles and waves. When observed (measured) in certain ways an electron behaves like a particle, such as when it is shot at a phosphorescent screen and leaves an observable impact point.[52] When electrons are not being observed, however, physicists have ways of determining by inference that they always act as waves. Then when one is measured, where the electron particle will show up within the wave is uncertain, but it follows a set of probabilities based on the magnitude of the wave at any place along the wave. The uncertain, probabilistic nature of electrons is not just a matter of crude instruments used by physicists, but is actually a law of nature.[53]

In the two-hole or double-slit experiments with light (photons), light shot through two holes will join up on the other side like waves coming from each hole and forming wave interference patterns when they come together on a screen.[54] If the light encounters only one hole instead of two, it will show up on the screen as if it were particles. If we open up one hole at a time, and then observe the light registered on the screen, it will amount to the accumulation of two sets of particles, not the wave interference pattern found in the simultaneous two-hole condition.

Even if we switch from a one-hole to a two-hole condition or vice versa between the time the light leaves its source and the time it arrives at the holes, the light will behave just the way it should depending on whatever the condition is as it arrives. What this suggests is that photons (and electrons and other quanta) are both particles and waves, and that bunches of them can act in unison as a coordinated system over intervening space without actual communication (without yelling, "Hey, look out, there's only one hole open, better act like particles over there, you guys!").

If photons did yell at each other, or somehow communicate over the intervening distance, it would have to be at a speed faster than light (FTL). This is another disturbing little detail. Although the physics cannot be discussed precisely here, Bell's Theorem (1964), supported especially in experiments by Aspect and others in 1982,[55] indicates that photons traveling in opposite directions remain coordinated (in angle of polarization or the way their waves are arranged) over significant distances, even though properties like polarization are not determined until measured. This suggests either that the photons are somehow

---

52. Talbot, 1991, pp. 33-34.
53. Kaku, 1994, p. 115.
54. Robert A. Wilson, 1991, pp. 176-177.
55. Wilson, 1991, pp. 108-119; Talbot, 1991, pp. 36-37, 52-53.

communicating instantaneously to bring this coordination about, or that they remain "nonlocally connected" as a system even when apart.

Bell's Theorem has been interpreted in New Age treatments of physics as evidence in support of mystical concepts of nonlocal or acausal connections in nature.[56] If photons can relate to each other at a distance, perhaps there is an actual material basis for the Taoist undifferentiated "mother of all things," or for the Buddhist "all-in-one nature of things," or for ESP sharing of thoughts and things without any apparent connections over space and time. Both parapsychologists with concepts of ESP and mystics with concepts of spirit may be dealing with "nonlocal consciousness."[57] Perhaps the universe has been nonlocally connected ever since the Big Bang.[58] And synchronicity (meaningful coincidences) may somehow represent part of the unseen connectedness or meaning in nature.

Back to the problem of quantum uncertainties or probabilities for a moment. It distresses many physicists, if they dare think about it, to contemplate the undetermined location of an electron particle. Surely it is *really* somewhere, isn't it? The absurdity of this paradox is nicely captured by the example of "Schrodinger's cat," first presented by Nobel-prize-winning physicist Erwin Schrodinger in 1935.[59] Imagine a cat inside a closed cage with a lethal-gas device set to go off at some time depending on a random-number generator inside the cage. From the outside we know only the probabilities of the cat dying at each moment, not whether it has actually died or not.

This is like the electron that can show up as a particle anyplace along its wave, but where exactly we don't know, except in terms of probabilities, until we actually measure it. And it does not really exist as a particle until we measure it this way. This would be like saying that the cat does not really die until we open up the cage and discover when it died according to our measuring device (let's say, a videotape recording). Before that, the cat's dead-or-alive state was a wave function or set of probabilities about when it might die. But surely the cat actually died at some point, didn't it? It had to be either alive or dead at each point in time. It wasn't really just a combination of dead and alive probabilities, was it? And yet this is what we are asked to believe in the case of the electron, that it really does not exist anyplace as a particle until we observe (measure) it.

---

56. Robert A. Wilson, 1991, pp. 117-121, 174-175.
57. Robert A. Wilson, 1991, p. 174.
58. Robert A. Wilson, 1991, p. 119.
59. Robert A. Wilson, 1991, pp. 21-25; Kaku, 1994, pp. 261-263.

Einstein could not tolerate this probabilistic, wave-function view of reality. He said, "Does the moon exist just because a mouse looks at it?" Of course, on the gross level of objects as big as a cat or the moon, we don't have to worry about quantum probabilities, but these examples help us to visualize the apparent absurdity of what happens on the level of quanta. The problem is that these absurdities are extremely well documented in physics and shake our notions about certainty and the basic structure of reality.

Moreover, there are macrolevel implications in the microlevel evidence for quantum physics. Physicist Stephen Hawking, who is too brilliant not to be taken seriously, says that we can treat the "universe as though it were a quantum particle."[60] This means that alternative possible events exist (like whether you say yes or no to a proposal of marriage, or whether the Enterprise does or does not make it through a wormhole), and maybe all the possibilities occur, each one in an infinite set of branching parallel universes, just like in *Star Trek*. This set of possibilities may be called "the wave function of the universe,"[61] analogous to the set of possible locations for an electron in the wave function of the electron.

If this sounds reasonable to you, like respectable theoretical speculation in physics, and not just like "crazy science-fiction physics," I have another question. What is so implausible about the idea of UFOs, or ESP, or any number of other subjects considered taboo in normal science?

The Holographic Perspective

To recap a bit, keep in mind that the new physics provides more than one reason for wondering why normal science should reject the possibility of UFOs. One reason is that wormholes and other hyperspace phenomena might help account for the mysterious appearance of ET craft even without FTL travel.

Another reason is that quantum physics shakes the foundation of certainty, not just on the level of subatomic particles like electrons and photons, but even on higher levels, as Hawking illustrates in his discussion of the quantum universe and parallel universes. All kinds of *Star Trek* possibilities exist with branching universes, connected perhaps by wormholes as Hawking suggests.

---

60. Kaku, 1994, p. 254.
61. Kaku, 1994, p. 254.

UFOs might come from many directions in such a cosmos. More-over, many other "paranormal" phenomena associated with UFOs, such as telepathy with aliens reported in close encounters, might be easier to explain in a quantum reality that involves nonlocal connec-tions.

Another outgrowth of quantum theory is the "holographic" per-spective, according to which the material world is only an "explicate order" based on a deeper, hidden "implicate order." This means that the reality we observe is analogous to the illusion of 3-D objects pro-duced on a holographic plate by a split laser beam, or like the virtual-reality scenario (VRS) on the holodeck in *Star Trek*.

Physicist David Bohm, author of the classic text *Quantum Theory*, went on to theorize, especially in his book *Wholeness and the Implicate Order*,[62] that the mysteries of quantum phenomena could be explained by a deeper level of reality or "quantum potential." According to Bo-hm, both particle and wave aspects of quanta exist in the implicate or-der, and either can be expressed in the explicate order depending on conditions. Nonlocal connections, as in Bell's Theorem, are possible be-cause the implicate order is an undivided whole, and the things we per-ceive on the explicate order are only "relatively independent subtotalities."[63]

In his book, *The Holographic Universe* (1991), Michael Talbot ex-tends the holographic model of "reality" to a broad variety of "paran-ormal" (what is real, and what is normal in this view?) phenomena in which mind participates in the creation of material phenomena.[64] In Hindu philosophy, for example, matter derives from consciousness rather than vice versa. If this sounds like too great a leap from the phys-ics, even Bohm said that the implicate order could be called spirit, al-though many physicists have trouble understanding Bohm and following him to such mystical conclusions.[65]

In UFO circles one often hears the term "hologram" used loosely as an explanation for mysterious appearances of craft and aliens, as if the UFO intelligence were presenting us with images that are some kind of illusion or magic trick. However, we can think of two kinds of hologram. One involves the laser-produced 3-D-looking images or illu-sions that can be produced today, and the other is all of material reality (explained, by Bohm and Talbot, *as if* it were a hologram).

---

62. Bohm, 1980.
63. Talbot, 1991, pp. 39-49.
64. Talbot, 1991, p. 288.
65. Talbot, 1991, pp. 53-54; Robert A. Wilson, 1991, pp. 117-120.

Karla Turner, in her book, *Taken,* gives an excellent example of what she interprets as an illusion created deceptively by aliens. One woman awoke in bed to see a helicopter over her house as if the intervening ceiling and roof had disappeared.[66] She also saw two unusual humanoid beings at the foot of the bed. Fortunately two friends were able to witness this scene, and they saw a blue sphere of light around her (as she did) with brighter lights shooting through it, but they heard no helicopter and saw no beings. Turner's interpretation is that the scene was a virtual-reality scenario (VRS), and that the only thing "real" was the blue-light mechanism for creating it.

What a fascinating case. But think of the possible interpretations. One is that the witnesses were partly switched off in their perceptions by the intelligence capable of such a high-tech performance. Another is that the perception of the beings and helicopter depended on being inside the blue light. The latter might support Turner's VRS explanation, but it might also suggest that space and time were "warped" inside the beam.

Could the beings inside the blue light have been popping in from other dimensions, i.e., traveling through hyperspace? This brings up the question of whether hyperspace and the implicate order might not be related. From the perspective of us 3-D (plus time as a fourth dimension) beings, hyperspace is a kind of implicate order in that we have no way of perceiving it. Notice that both hyperspace (higher dimensions) and Bohm's implicate order have both been suggested as places from which mystical or paranormal phenomena may emerge or be created.

Holism vs. Reductionism

In Chapter 6, I made the point that some sociologists, such as Aronowitz, see normal science as a social control system whose power is based upon using rational means of manipulating nature and humans in the production of goods and services for profit. Since the Enlightenment, science has emphasized a mechanical explanation of how reality can be analyzed and manipulated, in opposition to religious or mystical views that see reality in a larger, spiritual context. By this view, religion and mystical philosophies tend to be holistic, seeing the interconnectedness of all things; science tends to be reductionist, breaking down all that is physically evident into comprehensible component parts. Science, having successfully marginalized other ways of know-

---

66. Turner, 1994A, pp. 10-12.

ing, states that anything that cannot be analyzed this way simply doesn't exist (or that we "can't know about it").

Although many physicists would rather not think about it, much of the New Physics raises the issue of holism vs. reductionism even in a *scientific* context. One example of reductionist physics can be found in the attempt of Nobel-prize-winning physicist Leon Lederman to find *The God Particle*.[67] Lederman wants to use a superconducting super-collider to find the ultimate "a-tom," Democritus' Greek term for something that cannot be cut, although we now know that "atoms" are not the smallest unit of matter. Once this smallest subatomic particle is found, he thinks, all of physics will become one simple equation. It is by no means certain, however, that there is such a "God particle." Rothman thinks that there could be an "infinite regress" of smaller and smaller units rather than "truly elementary" particles.[68]

A more holistic search for an ultimately complete physics would be to pursue superstring theory which claims that all the forces of nature can be unified in a 10-dimensional space-time continuum. Kaku, who argues for this, does not claim that super-colliders would be worthless. In fact, they might provide evidence for superstring theory as well as particles, but he thinks that there should be more funding for "geometry" (the mathematics of superstrings).[69] Interestingly, Kaku also expects to find a single equation for the physical laws of the universe, but his search is up to hyperspace rather than down to a particle.

Nevertheless, Kaku thinks that the holism/reductionism debate is a false issue. Both sides have merit, he says. Holism and reductionism are two sides of the same geometry in superstring theory, because you can explain things from either end, from the top or from the bottom.[70] Rothman says about the same thing, "Scientists well understand the difference between particle theory and systems theory, and know how to progress from one to the other."[71]

Rothman gives a good overview of various meanings of reductionism (sometimes called linear thinking) and holism. If holism means looking at nonlinear elements like interactions and feedback loops, then scientists do understand the nonlinear.[72] The reductionism that Rothman defends is "ontological reductionism" which means that "the universe is composed of elementary particles and the forces by which they interact, and *nothing else*."[73]

67. Lederman, 1993.
68. Rothman, 1992, p. 126.
69. Kaku, 1994, pp. 15-16.
70. Kaku, 1994, pp. 320-322.
71. Rothman, 1992, p. 235.
72. Rothman, 1992, pp. 219-229.

Now we are getting someplace. The real issue that separates normal science from more radical views, in some New Age literature for example, is over the complaint that science often refuses to look at the whole as a pattern for the parts. Reductionism can involve seeing the parts as independent and as primary to all higher levels of complexity. A holistic, rather than reductionist, view of human illness/wellness, for example, involves seeing the body in a social and spiritual context rather than as a hunk of meat or as a machine.

What normal scientists like Rothman tend to dislike about holism is the inclusion of supernatural concepts like soul, something that normal science finds impossible to study.[74] As Rothman puts it, "The people who take reductionism seriously are book critics, philosophers and New Age enthusiasts."[75] James Trefil is another physicist who criticizes New Age interpretations of physics, like Capra's *The Tao of Physics*, that present a holistic, mystical view of nature.[76]

Nevertheless, Bohm's theory of "wholeness and the implicate order" is clearly a holistic interpretation of quantum physics, because it sees an undivided whole underlying specific microphenomena in the explicate (observable) order. It may be a leap to go from holism in the study of quanta like electrons and photons to holism in consciousness and the universe, a leap that most physicists would not want to make. Bohm, however, argues against the tendency to fragment reality and not see its interconnectedness, including the connectedness between consciousness and subatomic particles.[77]

Again, what is the relevance to UFOs? First of all, some physicists support a reductionist view of the universe by attempting to break it all down to an ultimate "God particle" that we can easily manipulate and understand through a simple formula. By contrast, some theories in the new physics take a more holistic view, such as in superstring theory which envisions a 10-dimensional hyperspace and thereby a bizarre new map of reality. Hyperspace is a larger reality with many windows through which UFOs and other unknowns might fly, whether physicists want to think about them or not. Among the unknowns could be things like ESP and the spirit world, both of which show up frequently in UFO reports or at least in the broader experiences of UFO experiencers. These elements are troubling not only for physicists like Rothman, but also for many nuts-and-bolts ufologists, as we shall discuss again later.

---

73. Rothman, 1992, p. 222.
74. Rothman, 1992, pp. 232-234.
75. Rothman, 1992, p. 231.
76. Trefil, 1983, p. 220.
77. Talbot, 1991, p. 49.

Perhaps the most important thing about reductionism is that it helps to make the scientific view of the world more comfortable, more manageable. How neat to have one "God particle" and one simple formula. If the world can be so easily explained, it can also be easily manipulated for profit. People who ask troubling questions about larger realities are a nuisance. Normal science is mainly about certainty, and the marginalization of other views of reality through debunking (as in CSICOP).

In contrast to the perspective of normal science, Robert Anton Wilson states, "To deny dogmatically...is to claim, tacitly, that you already know *the full spectrum of the possible*. In a century in which every decade has brought new and astonishing scientific shocks, that is a huge, brave and audacious faith indeed."[78]

---

78. Robert A. Wilson, 1991, p. 36.

Chapter 8

Physical Evidence of UFOs

In Search of Nuts and Bolts

Previous chapters have dealt with the subject of whether UFOs are plausible and reasonable as a subject of study. This is partly a sociological question involving science as an institution, and partly a scientific question about the likelihood of ET intelligence and interstellar travel. Apart from this issue of the legitimacy of ufology as a scientific endeavor, there is another related issue, namely, what kind of evidence would be useful in helping to discover whether UFOs (defined as intelligently guided craft not of current Earth-human origin, whether extraterrestrial or not) have actually been here?

Debunkers often say there is no physical evidence for UFOs. In particular, Philip J. Klass told me in an interview that there was "not a single physical artifact" that could be proven to be extraterrestrial or come from an alien craft.[1] This claim means two things for the treatment of ufology as a science. First, it implies that witness reports are insignificant as evidence, perhaps indicating a bias against social and behavioral sciences compared to natural science. Second, it suggests that even available physical evidence, short of a sizable chunk of an alien craft or an alien body, is being discounted.

What Is Hard Evidence?

Should we assume that witness memory and human testimony are unreliable, soft evidence? If so, then perhaps hard evidence is "physical." But what would constitute such physical evidence of UFOs or "aliens"? If we insist upon having a craft or body available on display for scientists to observe in a laboratory, then we will be

---

1. Philip J. Klass interview, July 7, 1994.

disappointed at least for now, perhaps because the intelligence behind the UFO phenomenon is denying us such evidence, or perhaps because the government is hiding it from us, or perhaps because all of the other evidence is somehow a grand illusion.

One problem with the grand illusion theory is that there does seem to be a lot of other physical evidence. There are physical landing traces that have been studied. And there are hair-raising cases like that of the Knowles family in Australia in 1988 when their car was lifted into the air by a bright egg-cup shaped object.[2] When the car was dropped back on the road, it blew out a rear tire and had dents in the hood and black ash on the inside and outside of the car. This event was witnessed not only by the four Knowles, but by others as well. The evidence left on the car was an obvious physical *effect*, but there was no lasting physical proof of the *cause* (the UFO, which, of course, left), except from the witnesses ("soft" evidence).

Are physical objects the only acceptable type of evidence? What if we cannot produce the UFO, but only some recorded observation or measurement of it taken by an instrument like a camera? If this is not acceptable as physical evidence, then perhaps other such physical evidence that relies on instruments of observation should not be accepted either, as in the case of astronomy. What would happen to astronomy if we insisted upon bringing the sun and planets into the lab for analysis as proof for the existence of heavenly bodies?

At least there is hard evidence for the existence of the moon, since we have rock specimens. Ah, but can we prove that the moon rocks are extraterrestrial? Even if they are, how do we know that some hoaxer didn't just chop up some meteorites? Of course, some people still think that the moon landing was a hoax. If you did not trust NASA and the community of scientists as legitimate, could you vouch for the fact that humans landed on the moon?

In fairness, although astronomy is based upon observation rather than physical artifacts, at least it involves easily repeatable physical observations, something that UFO studies cannot provide. Should we assume that ufology is therefore a waste of time, or should we press on looking for the elusive evidence on the assumption that it will be difficult, but rewarding, to collect?

---

2. Davenport, 1992B, pp. 158-159.

Crash Claims

Before going any further, it would be really convenient if we *did* have some crashed UFOs and alien bodies (preferably alive, for their sakes as well as ours). Indeed there have been claims of such, including reports of aliens who lived at least for a while. It is beyond the scope of this book to catalog these cases, but the best known is the crash (or crashes) near Roswell, New Mexico, in 1947, allegedly covered up by the U.S. Army Air Force after their initial news release that they had recovered the remains of a saucer. See especially the books and articles by Stanton Friedman and Don Berliner,[3] and by Kevin Randle and Donald Schmitt.[4] Suffice it to say that most ufologists take this case seriously, and even one rather skeptical ufologist in an interview told me, "I'm not certain that it was an alien craft, but the government is obviously covering something up there."

This does not mean that all crash claims will prove productive, except perhaps in the study of folklore. Crash stories are bound to have an appeal, since they are the most exciting potential kind of evidence, almost like a lost city of gold in archaeological lore. Separating lore from reality is bound to be difficult, especially if a high-tech intelligence is able to retrieve most of the evidence of its rare mistakes, and if the government is able to monitor and respond to crashes and seize the evidence.

At one UFO conference, Dennis Stacy took a dim view of most crash claims, noting that there had been 23 alleged UFO crashes before the one in Roswell in 1947 and that another researcher had collected 40 such reports.[5] His emphasis on hoaxes upset some members of the audience who likened his attitude to the critique of crop circles, at least some of which have been hoaxes.

Jerome Clark, Editor of the *International UFO Reporter*, published by CUFOS (Center for UFO Studies), evaluated 41 crash accounts in one issue of his journal.[6] Twelve of them were from the phantom airship era, 1862-1897, all of which he considered to be tall tales or newspaper hoaxes. In fact, the only case out of all 41 that he considered to be well documented was the Roswell case because of the statements of hundreds of informants, including seemingly reliable testimony about the humanoid remains found at one of the two sites involved.

---

3. Friedman and Berliner, 1992.
4. Randle and Schmitt, 1991, 1994.
5. Stacy, Oct. 9, 1993.
6. Clark, 1993B.

Craft Artifacts

If intact craft or recognizable pieces of crashed UFOs are hard to come by, then the next best thing would be artifacts or material deposits left behind by UFOs. A UFO experiencer might report that a UFO had left something behind, but how would a UFO investigator be able to prove that the object came from a UFO? This is analogous to proving that our moon rocks really came from the moon.

Although the ET hypothesis is by no means universally accepted, it is usually suggested that an artifact can not be proven to be from a UFO unless it can be proven to be extraterrestrial, i.e., not possible to have been made on Earth. Ufologist Stanton Friedman, a nuclear physicist, complains that astronomer Carl Sagan has suggested that a piece of wreckage from an alleged UFO could be proven to be extraterrestrial if it failed all the tests for all known elements found on Earth.[7] As Friedman points out, this is absurd because astronomers have shown by spectroscopic and other tests of light radiation from outer space that only the same elements and compounds found on Earth are found elsewhere. This follows the principle of uniformity in the universe regarding physical/chemical laws. Davenport notes that materials reportedly left behind by UFOs are typically ordinary stuff like aluminum, tin, magnesium, silicon and oil (something like transmission fluid, sometimes assumed to be part of a hoax).[8]

What one would hope to do in order to prove ET origin would be to find some unusual combination of elements or evidence of some manufacturing process beyond the present capability of Earth-humans. Boris Sokolov, a retired Russian colonel involved in UFO studies, claims that four Russian laboratories confirmed that one recovered piece of material consisted of elements that cannot be combined on Earth.[9]

According to the popular magazine *UFO*, Australian scientists determined that the ash found on the car in the 1988 Knowles case referred to above contains "potassium chloride molecules displaying...unusual velocity characteristics as if ejected from a space shuttle blast."[10] If only we could trust those witnesses just a little bit to tell us that there was no space shuttle in the area. The same article noted that

---

7. Friedman, 1993, p. 10.
8. Davenport, 1992B, pp. 192-193.
9. Gresh, 1993, p. 4.
10. *UFO*, 1989, p. 9.

potassium chloride powder was found on a police car in Pennsylvania in 1988 after the officer had a close encounter with a bright oval-shaped object 75-feet in diameter.

Some of these references are very sketchy, but the refereed *Journal of UFO Studies* published a 37-page section of three articles in 1992 dealing with the analysis of magnesium fragments allegedly dropped by an exploding UFO near Ubatuba, Brazil, in the 1950s. Essentially the material is unusual, but not clearly of ET origin. Since such material would not be used in any type of Earthly craft, this is probably either a genuine UFO case or a hoax, but not an honest misidentification. The problem is that the "pedigree" or origin of the material is somewhat dubious, and, alas, the physical evidence in itself is inconclusive.

An examination of these articles on the Ubatuba magnesium gives one an appreciation for the complexities involved in such analysis. Friedman discusses the protocol for doing analysis of artifacts.[11] There are both technical and social considerations.

It is by no means evident in all cases just what type of physical or chemical analysis should be done, or how much of the material should be risked in a destructive analysis. There are also questions about disclosure and publication rights. Some ufologists also suggest that only nonufologists should be entrusted with the analysis in order to avoid suspicion and that the lab should be given no knowledge of the material's alleged origin.

Landing Traces

Landing traces are one of the main types of physical effects that J. Allen Hynek had in mind as being left behind by UFOs in what he termed "Close Encounters of the Second Kind."[12] Ufologist Ted R. Phillips, the major researcher to investigate landing-trace cases, collected reports on over 2,000 of them by 1981.[13]

In one case investigated by the French ufology organization GEPAN in 1981, a man in Trans-en-Provence observed an egg-shaped craft land briefly near his garden.[14] Analysis of the ground impression left on that spot revealed heating to 300° to 600° centi-

---

11. Friedman, 1993.
12. Hynek, 1972, p. 126.
13. Ted R. Phillips, 1981.
14. Velasco, 1987.

grade, traces of phosphate and zinc, and 30-50% reduction in chloro-phyll pigments A and B in wild alfalfa, but no signs of radioactivity (39 days after the landing, when the investigation was done). Such landing-trace cases, when taken together with reliable witness re-ports, seem highly evidential, but for those who insist that the physi-cal evidence stand by itself, they tend to be judged as inconclusive. Another example is the 1971 Delphos, Kansas, case, in which a bright UFO 9 feet in diameter at the bottom hovered 2 feet above the ground and left a glowing circle observable in that spot by the next day.[15] Various tests were done on the ring over the next year, by which it was found that neither a simple hoax nor a fungal fairy-ring would be a good explanation. However, there was no conclusive evidence for a high-tech craft either, unless one accepts the witness report of a 16-year old boy who claimed to see the bright UFO at a distance of 75 feet when it was hovering over the circle it seemed to create.

Russian ufologist Dr. Rem Verlamov states that UFO landing sites in his country show high concentrations of lead, titanium, co-balt, barium and zinc, and that plants inside the impressions contain more phosphorous and carbon and grow at slower rates.[16] Another Russian, Dr. Yuri Simakov, found tiny glass-like balls that he jokingly referred to as "cosmic sperm" in two separate sites hundreds of miles apart.[17] George Knapp brought back a sample of these to the U.S. and had the highly respected plant pathology lab at the University of Ne-braska look at them. After 30 days, the lab found that they were not microbial (did not act like seed or open up in water), could not figure out what they were and suggested chemical analysis, which had not yet been done by the time Knapp made his report on the subject at the 1994 MUFON conference.[18]

Radiation Effects

Radiation effects on people and machines also fit into Hynek's concept of the physical traces left by UFOs in Close Encounters of the Second Kind (CE-II), just as landing traces on the ground do. In 1975 ufologist James M. McCampbell outlined six categories of UFO ef-fects that might involve electromagnetic (E-M) radiation: perfor-

15. Swords and Faruk, 1991.
16. Knapp, 1994, p. 300.
17. Knapp, 1994, pp. 302-303.
18. Knapp, 1994, pp. 302-303.

mance of the craft (levitation, extreme acceleration and deceleration, etc.), atmospheric effects (e.g., colored halos that change with acceleration), landing sites (baked earth, charred plants, etc.), electrical interference (on internal combustion engines, radio and TV, power transmission), physiological responses (paralysis, sunburn, etc.), and animal reactions (like fear).[19] It is worth noting that such a scheme provides a grand theoretical framework for comprehending UFO technology even though details are not yet understood. Contrast this patterned approach with the debunking perspective that any one case might be explained in some other way and that, therefore, the whole UFO concept is not worth pursuing.

Engineer and psychologist Richard F. Haines has analyzed 56 reports of E-M effects on aircraft that occurred during pilot-reported UFO sightings.[20] These effects include "radio interference or failure, radar contact (with and without simultaneous visual contact with the UFO), magnetic and/or gyro-compass deviations, automatic direction finder failure or interference, engine stopping or interruption, [and] dimming cabin lights." As expected by the laws of physics if the phenomenon were real, "There appears to be a reduction of the E-M energy effect with the square of increasing distance to the (UFO)."[21]

E-M effects on humans are varied and sometimes poorly understood. In many reports, the experiencer is temporarily paralyzed by a light beam or by an object held in the hand of an alien. Richard M. Neal, an M.D., hypothesizes that this effect is caused by "a selective type of microwave irradiation [unknown to us]...[that sets up] a chain reaction in the Central Nervous System to affect only certain areas and spare those that are essential to vital biological functions."[22]

In other cases the radiation effects on humans are quite injurious. In 1973 Eddie Webb was temporarily blinded and had blurred vision after being hit by a flash of light from a UFO while driving a truck in Cape Girardeau, Missouri.[23] His glasses were bubbled-out as if the wire inside the frames had been heated by microwave radiation and had caused the plastic around it to melt. In 1980 Betty Cash experienced severe burns and hair loss from her close encounter with a UFO in the road ahead of her car near Huffman, Texas, and was in intensive care and hospitalized several times thereafter.[24] UFO injuries

19. McCampbell, 1975, p. 81.
20. Haines, 1992, p. 102.
21. Haines, 1992, p. 102.
22. Neal, 1991, p. 16.
23. Schuessler and O'Herin, 1993.

from beams of light have been reported frequently in Brazil, although some of the reports seem to be mixed with rumor and folklore about "Chupacabras" (aliens creatures that drain all your blood).[25]

Ufologist Donald A. Johnson analyzed 200 UFO reports involving witnesses in motor vehicles on land between 1952 and 1978.[26] Forty percent experienced at least intermittent ignition-system interference. Interestingly, a cluster-analysis of reports based on size of the UFO, distance from the vehicle, and duration of the encounter yielded seven categories of cases. In the most awesome category, the UFOs average 10 meters in diameter, stay for about one hour, 82% of them pursue the vehicle, 36% block the road, 45% land, and 27% involve an abduction (some additional abductions might be forgotten), 45% have a light beam (often blue), 45% have a noise (usually a hum), and most of the experiencers have physiological effects and fear.[27]

Photo and Video Analysis

According to Jeffrey W. Sainio, MUFON photo and video analyst, photographs and videos are by far the most commonly studied UFO physical effects.[28] Although theoretically anything could be hoaxed on video these days ("if Stephen Spielberg is your brother-in-law," which is Jeff's joke), video is actually harder to fake than still photography, mainly because of the motion involved.[29]

In the last few years Sainio has started to get more videos than photos. Due to the popularity of camcorders, it is important to instruct potential users of the equipment in order to get more of the potentially quality evidence. He gives tips to amateurs on such things as getting foreground objects in the same shot as the UFO to help determine distance and motion, locking autofocus on infinity unless the UFO is very close, not stopping the video during the event, and keeping a running commentary on the audiotrack (which picks up not only airplane noise, etc., but also gives clues to the operator's state of mind).[30] But even what looks like a poor quality video, with annoying zoom or poor synchronization, can yield a great deal of data.

---

24. Davenport, 1992, p. 42.
25. Vallée, 1989.
26. Donald A. Johnson, 1989.
27. Donald A. Johnson, 1989, p. 139.
28. Sainio, 1992.
29. Sainio, 1993, p. 87.
30. Sainio, 1993, pp. 108-109.

As with all other types of physical-trace evidence for UFOs, photo/video evidence is typically inconclusive in the strict sense, even if it is not an evident hoax. Analysis that is directed toward eliminating hoax or misidentification of some mundane cause starts with an hypothesis, e.g., "It's really just a frisbee." Richard F. Haines gives good reasons why a UFO that appeared in a photo taken of a mountain on Vancouver Island, British Columbia, in 1981, could not be a frisbee.[31] This is fine, but, of course, it does not prove that there could be no other mundane explanation, even if we can't think of one at the moment, and even though the photographer was evidently highly credible and hardly likely to have hoaxed the photo.

Jack Kasher, physicist and astronomer, analyzed in great detail a 1991 videotape from the Space Shuttle Discovery that shows lights that float along and then change direction apparently in response to a flash in the corner of the picture.[32] He gives several quantitative proofs that the lights cannot be ice particles outside the shuttle (as suggested by four NASA scientists), and then gives a very plausible interpretation that they are space craft being fired upon by missiles from the ground. As excellent as this analysis may be, it will still not convince debunkers who refuse to accept UFOs and who imagine that there may still be some other unspecified, unknown cause.

Sometimes a mundane cause takes some time to discover. The widely exhibited 1966 photo of a UFO at Willamette Pass in Oregon was finally convincingly identified in 1993 as a road sign with snow on top, the image of which was blurred due to the picture having been taken from a moving car.[33]

In the case of real UFO photography, assuming that there is such a thing for the sake of argument, people are often dismayed when what they thought they saw just doesn't show up on film. Davenport considers such cases and suggests a possible time-warping field effect on the camera, slowing down or speeding up the shutter.[34] It has also been pointed out that infrared radiation can inhibit the formation of images on film (unless it is infrared sensitive), and that perhaps UFOs give off such radiation (whether to sabotage the photography or not), accounting for spoiled photos of UFOs at close range.[35]

---

31. Haines, 1986.
32. Kasher, 1994.
33. Wieder, 1993.
34. Davenport, 1992B, pp. 72-76.
35. Petit, 1991, p. 46.

Other Detection Devices

In addition to still and video cameras there are other, less commonly used UFO detection devices. The first one might think of is radar. As noted in Chapter 5, Philip J. Klass stated in 1985 that there had been quite a decline in radar UFO reports, a fact he attributed to improvement in radar and computer technology.[36] Although the problem of false readings or "radar ghosts" still exists and is acknowledged in some of the UFO literature, radar is still considered as a possible means of UFO detection. Petit discusses the use of radar in Belgian cases occurring in 1989.[37]

Wesley E. Ellison, a highly experienced electronics engineering technician at the Space Technology Center for Research at the University of Kansas, has put together a group of devices for tracking UFOs and for enhancing UFO photo opportunities, including laser-imaging radar, magnetometer, fluxgate compass detector (also for magnetic detection), infrared viewer (a night-vision scope), starlight intensifier and subsonic and ultrasonic sound detectors.[38] He even has a field detection device, a portable unit consisting of magnetometer, infrared viewer and target laser.

In Chapter 5, I referred to Al, a skeptical member of the Skyscan UFO study group (pseudonyms). He is a real nuts-and-bolts ufologist who likes electronic devices. On at least two different occasions, he brought his "UFO detector" to one of our regional UFO conferences. Al's detector is a simple magnetometer about 2"x3"x4" powered by a 9-volt battery that sets off an alarm when a magnetic change is detected. This reminds me of a gauss meter used to detect electromagnetic anomalies by a ghost researcher.

Of course, the E-M fluctuations picked up by the gauss meter did not always necessarily reflect the presence of a ghost as opposed to something else (like a small appliance). Nor was Al's UFO detector strictly UFO-specific, as was obvious from the way it kept going off in the room next door to mine in the motel when I was trying to sleep. Of course, I cannot prove that there was no UFO (or ghost) in Al's room, although I could hear Al speaking normally in the background.

36. Klass, 1985.
37. Petit, 1991, pp. 40-42.
38. Ellison, 1993.

Abductions: Physical or Nonphysical?

Before looking at evidence for UFO abductions, we might well ask whether this subject belongs in this chapter at all. Is there anything physical to abductions, or are they strictly psychological or psychic? Certainly it has been suggested that they share characteristics with waking dreams and sleep paralysis (part of the hypnagogic and hypnopompic near-sleep states) and are, therefore, psychological. Some think that abductions are psychic experiences, something like OBEs (out-of-body experiences).

UFO abduction researcher John Carpenter, however, points to twelve types of evidence that indicate that at least some abductions are at least partly physical.[39] Some of these twelve (collapsed) are conscious visual UFO sightings at the time of the incident, photo/video/radar confirmation of UFOs, landing traces, strange lights seen by neighbors the same night, people consciously seeing the same beings, independent accounts of the same group abduction, simultaneous amnesia by multiple persons, body marks that match memories of abductions, and documented absences and distant returns.

Notice that not all of these represent physical evidence of abduction in themselves, but they all suggest that there is some real, physical event. For example, witness corroboration in a single incident and correlation of detailed elements in a group of incidents both suggest real events, although the evidence itself is not physical.

Carpenter studied two women who were unaware of their own abduction from the same car during a period of unexplained missing time.[40] Under hypnosis, the two women independently gave details that matched each other's accounts on at least 40 points.

Researchers often claim that accounts of separate abduction events contain remarkable similarities even on matters like symbols and insignia that have been withheld from publication in order to verify such patterns. Budd Hopkins tells of abductees who are shocked or in tears when they see other abductees' drawings of UFO lettering that match what they themselves have seen in UFOs.[41]

Just what *does* qualify as physical evidence of an abduction, rather than just witness evidence that it was a physical event, is a tricky question. Leaving aside the more direct physical evidence like im-

---

39. Carpenter, 1993D, p. 16.
40. Carpenter, 1991A, p. 168.
41. Hopkins, Oct. 9, 1993.

plants for a moment, let us consider some physical phenomena observed after the event that are highly suggestive, if not evidential.

Carpenter refers to several cases of persons who seem to have been physically redeposited in the wrong locations after their abductions.[42] One truck driver on a ranch saw a bright light approaching from a pasture, lost CB contact with his wife back at the house, and was found a bit later on another ridge without intervening road or tire tracks. One woman found herself locked outside her house on several occasions, naked and minus her expensive nightgowns (one lost each time). A family of five ended up all in the wrong bedrooms without any memory of getting up in the night. "It became more interesting when they found a burned circle in the back yard and neighbors asking about the bright lights at which the dogs had been barking wildly."[43]

Budd Hopkins reports the case of a woman who found a baby on her porch.[44] The baby was that of her friend who lived three blocks away across a divided highway. As Budd puts it, these are "Out-of-the-House Experiences, not Out-of-Body Experiences" (OBEs); they are physical rather than just psychic or psychological.

Clothing mix-ups in themselves do not prove the existence of an abduction, but they are an interesting type of witness-reported physical trace, especially problematic to those who expect high-tech aliens to make no mistakes. Cynthia Hind tells of a woman in South Africa who returned from an abduction to find her track suit on backwards.[45] No one could prove that this part of the report is *not* a hoax, but it is interesting that such patterns show up cross-culturally.

New Yorker Linda Cortile, abductee in Budd Hopkins' latest book, *Witnessed*,[46] found her pajama tops on her legs, and the bottoms on the floor.[47] Budd's best clothing mix-up story involves a woman in a Victoria's Secrets nightgown and her little boy in his pajamas.[48] In the morning the woman was wearing a man's large, green t-shirt, and her son had on a larger boy's pajamas. Did the man who went to bed in the t-shirt end up in the nightgown? Did he have some explaining to do? John Carpenter gives this understanding explanation for

42. Carpenter, 1994, p. 17.
43. Carpenter, 1994, p. 17.
44. Hopkins, Oct. 9, 1993.
45. Hind, 1993, p. 23.
46. Hopkins, 1996C.
47. Hopkins, Oct. 9, 1993.
48. Carpenter, 1994, p. 17.

such bungling, "I suppose that aliens with a busy schedule and perhaps dozens of abductees aboard might confuse the proper return of one's clothes from a large assortment."[49]

Abduction Traces

By "abduction traces" I mean physical evidence of abduction left on or with abductees that might convince an investigator without necessarily relying on an accompanying witness report. Simple clothing mix-ups are not included here because anybody could hoax a backwards track suit, for example. Finding a common pattern of clothing mix-ups would be interesting, but this gets us into the analysis of witness reports. As physical evidence they are very weak.

Probably the most common type of abduction trace is observable marks on the body. Karla Turner found the typical range of these in a sample of eight women abductees, including unexplained bruises, scoop marks (apparently where skin samples had been taken), puncture marks, scratches, rashes, blood on their bodies and hair loss.[50] Other bodily effects in Turner's sample would be less observable or even unobservable by another person, including noises in their heads, "sensations of light exploding in their minds," nausea, sudden fatigue, feeling "beaten up," eye irritations and vibrating sensations.

Skeptics have typically attributed these marks to other causes or have explained the attention paid to them as selective perception on the part of UFO-obsessed people. In other words, we all have little body marks we can't account for, even nasty bruises sometimes. Often abductees try to explain their marks away like this too.

Some body marks are so symmetrical or otherwise unique that it is more difficult to imagine a mundane cause. For example, one man watching for UFOs in the vicinity of Gulf Breeze, Florida, saw a pulsating light in the sky, dozed a bit, and a bit later found a wound of seven points in a 1.5-inch-diameter circle with a point in the center on the back of his hand.[51] The investigator in this case discovered that two other people acquired similar marks "under very strange circumstances soon after this event."

Although such marks are generally better *physical* evidence than clothing mix-ups, it still helps considerably to have the accompany-

---

49. Carpenter, 1994, p. 17.
50. Turner, 1994B, p. 29.
51. Ware, 1993C, p. 19.

ing witness report (for people who are willing to listen to witness reports). Cynthia Hind reports "a small fading scar" on an abductee in one of her South African cases.[52] By itself, the scar would be slim evidence indeed, but for the abductee at least it is confirming evidence because she remembers having a needle inserted there for the taking of blood samples during the abduction.

One apparent abductee told me that she awoke one morning to find what looked like needle scars over her ovary. Her husband had a sore nose and nosebleed at the same time. She wanted to joke about this, but the fact that she had had a very close encounter with a large, bright light over her yard the night before made her take the possibility of an abduction seriously.

Probably the best hope for an abduction "smoking gun" has been the implant. However, in spite of their strangeness, implants have remained elusive and inconclusive as ET evidence, at least for hardcore skeptics. Keith Basterfield gives the history of implants from the late 1970s through 1991.[53] Speculation is that these enigmatic little devices are for locating/monitoring, communicating/controlling, and/or dispensing substances into the body. The analogy most often given is to the use of tags and implants that humans attach to wild animals.

One of the most famous implants was the little piece of metal with curly-cue anchors spotted on an X ray of Linda Cortile's nose.[54] When investigator Budd Hopkins had it X rayed again, it was gone. Skeptics were scornful of the suggestion that aliens had removed it to keep it from being recovered through surgery.

In spite of the apparent tendency for implants to disappear, perhaps because abductees are programmed to lose or destroy them, dozens have been recovered and analyzed by now. People walk up to UFO investigators at conferences and give them recovered implants. I saw one man turn over a container of little objects removed from his back with needle-nose pliers. He claimed that the cilia or hairs on them hurt when pulled out and wrapped themselves around the pliers as if alive (or magnetic).

Some of the most in-depth study of implants has been done by Derrel Sims and others in the Houston UFO Network (HUFON). Some implants are silver-colored balls about two millimeters in diameter sometimes with cilia to keep them anchored up in the nose.[55]

52. Hind, 1993, p. 22.
53. Basterfield, 1992.
54. Hopkins, July 11, 199B.

Others include a gray, flat rod about 15-20 mm long found in the nasal septum, a little oval scrotal implant, and an ocular implant about 1.5 mm long. The ocular one was suspected to be a microcamera.

All implants found so far are made of Earth elements, and their construction seems deceptively simple. There are no electrical parts. If there is a power source, it is external. Many are nonmetallic and do not show up on imaging devices. Strange, and how else would they get there, but no smoking gun from a debunker's viewpoint.

Souvenirs are another hope for physical evidence. Oh, to bring back the captain's log from a UFO! Good luck. But abductees often report asking for a souvenir to help prove to others that the experience was real. Or they try to sneak something. Of course, they are seldom if ever successful.

One of Karla Turner's informants reported that she brought back a "green healer rock" from a UFO encounter when she was eleven.[56] Unfortunately, some military personnel investigating the incident later on confiscated it. One six-year-old boy handed Budd Hopkins a beautiful set of rosary beads he said he had picked up on a UFO when a nun left them behind after being examined.[57] But Earthly rosary beads are hardly physical evidence of contact with the Visitors.

Just like implants, souvenirs are often illusive, mislaid, stolen or strayed. Two abductees told Cynthia Hind in South Africa that an alien had written down on a yellow piece of paper a number representing the elevation of the craft at the moment.[58] When they got home they absentmindedly put the piece of paper in a drawer, and later on they could not produce it for Hind because it had been packed somewhere in a box when they moved.

Victoria Alexander thinks that there is no excuse for such poor collection of physical evidence.[59] Seeing most abduction accounts as apparent crimes (involving breaking and entering, kidnapping, assault and rape), she asks why not use criminal detection methods. Although some methods would be too expensive, they could be adapted in a less costly form, including a simplified rape kit, masking tape to lift fingerprints, and flour as a cheap thief- detection powder. Anytime objects or beings come in contact they may leave physical

55. Sims and Florey, Sept. 17, 1994.
56. Turner, 1994B, pp. 18, 24.
57. Carpenter, 1991B, p. 166.
58. Hind, 1993, pp. 22-23.
59. Alexander, 1993.

traces, but seldom is there any attempt to collect hair (from hybrid babies and the few aliens who seem to have hair), pollen, dust, etc.

Videotaping in bedrooms has been suggested by David Jacobs and others, but so far this has only delayed abductions apparently, until people get tired of setting up the camera, or until the abductee sleeps somewhere else. One wonders if someday there will not be a unique accidental videotaping of an abduction that eludes the detection of the Visitors. Would this convince any debunkers? Or would it more likely be interpreted as clever computer graphics or someone in a latex costume?

The Missing Embryo/Fetus Syndrome

One important physical effect reported in abduction cases that deserves special attention is missing pregnancies, allegedly part of an alien genetic program to create alien/human hybrids. Dr. Richard M. Neal refers to this as the "missing embryo/fetus syndrome" (the arbitrary dividing line between embryo and fetus being eight weeks).[60] Dr. Neal, who is not out to debunk every UFO claim, as can be seen from his analysis of microwave injuries,[61] has stated that he has been unable to confirm with medical evidence a single case of a pregnancy taken through abduction.

Before a 1992 presentation on the subject, Dr. Neal corresponded with Dr. Eddie Bullard and Dr. R. Leo Sprinkle, both of whom had studied sizeable numbers of abduction cases covering many years.[62] Neither of them had encountered this syndrome, although Leo had received some mail from women who thought that their sexual encounters with aliens had resulted in babies with big eyes and great psychic ability. Neal wondered why so many cases had appeared recently then, beginning with the 1987 publication of Budd Hopkins' book *Intruders* in which Kathie Davis (pseudonym) had a pregnancy that disappeared in 1978 without any miscarriage.[63]

According to Dr. Neal, there are five mundane medical phenomena that might lead nonhoaxing abductees to believe that they had lost a pregnancy to aliens: imaginary pregnancy (pseudocyesis), blighted ovum (due to early absorption of amniotic fluid), missed

---

60. Neal, 1992.
61. Neal, 1991.
62. Neal, 1992, pp. 216-217.
63. Hopkins, 1987.

abortion (retention of dead products of conception), spontaneous abortion, and secondary amenorrhea (cessation of menstrual cycle).[64] He also explains that if a real pregnancy *were* removed from the uterus, it would leave obvious marks, since the procedure would require "intervention/invasion."[65] And, finally, he calls for careful documentation through medical records to allow any alleged cases of missing embryo-fetus syndrome to be tested properly.[66]

More cases keep surfacing, such as one mentioned by Budd Hopkins at a UFO conference in October 1993, in which a pregnancy disappeared in almost the seventh month, leaving behind only a placenta.[67] Dr. Jean Mundy, a psychotherapist, stated that a partial analysis of cases submitted to *Omni* indicated that "around nine percent of women with alien contact report medically confirmed pregnancies which disappeared, usually in the fourth month."[68]

In a personal communication with Dr. Neal in 1993, I pointed out another missing pregnancy claim I had heard at a UFO conference. Dr. Neal replied that he still had cases to check, including some unresolved ones from Dr. David Jacobs, author of *Secret Life*.[69] In an interview with me, Dr. Jacobs said that one major problem in this issue is that medical science has no concept into which this type of missing pregnancy can fit. Doctors will usually assume spontaneous abortion, or, in a fall-back position, attribute it to absorption.

I would add that medical science has a particular reality tunnel, as Robert Anton Wilson would say, through which to observe missing pregnancies. Although Dr. Neal's research is excellent and holds forth exciting possibilities for discovering more about what is really happening in abduction cases, it may well be that there is an alien technology involved that exceeds our current capability for understanding how pregnancies could vanish without evidence of "intervention/invasion."

---

64. Neal, 1992, pp. 221-225.
65. Neal, 1992, pp. 226-228.
66. Neal, 1992, pp. 228-229.
67. Hopkins, Oct. 9, 1993.
68. Mundy, 1991, p. 23.
69. Dr. Richard M. Neal, personal communication, July 2, 1993.

Other Physical Evidence: Animal Mutilations, Crop Circles, and the Face on Mars

In addition to all of the above types of physical evidence that have been considered in UFO reports, there are other physical phenomena allegedly related to UFOs. Perhaps the strongest connection in these tangential areas lies between UFOs and animal mutilations, thanks mainly to the research of Linda Moulton Howe.

Ms. Howe (see page 227) has accumulated considerable evidence of animal mutilations (mostly cattle) that cannot be explained as the work of predators or cultists.[70] She has found incisions made by precise instruments and under conditions of high heat. Fluids have been drained, and sometimes internal organs have been removed without external incisions.[71] There have been UFO sightings closely associated with some of these mutilations, and in a few cases humanoids seen directly in contact with the animals.[72]

In the past it has been difficult to get veterinary medicine to pay attention to this phenomenon, partly because of normal science, and partly because ranchers have not wanted to spend the money to have their dead animals examined. Recently, however, Ms. Howe has managed to acquire research funding to have necropsies performed by veterinarians, and she has documented their startled reactions on video.[73]

Linda Moulton Howe, among others, has also participated in having physical evidence analyzed from crop circles, especially recently to try to determine the differences between hoaxed and genuine ones.[74] Some analysis has been very high-tech, as in the work of the Project Argus team, involving such techniques as scanning electron microscopy, electrophoresis (DNA analysis), and various types of electromagnetic field detection.[75] Of course, it is by no means certain that nonhoaxed crop circles are a UFO phenomenon, but George Wingfield, for example, argues for the connection.[76]

Another type of physical evidence can be found in the debate over the "Face on Mars." As discussed in Chapter 5, *The McDaniel Re-*

---

70. Howe, Sept. 16, 1994; 1993A, 1993B, 1992, 1991.
71. Howe, Sept. 16, 1994.
72. Howe, 1993B, p. 196.
73. Howe, Sept. 16, 1994.
74. Howe, 1993B, pp. 4-93.
75. Chorost, 1993.
76. Wingfield, 1994.

port reveals a normal-science struggle over whether to frame the face as a natural phenomenon or as an artificial one.[77] If it is seen as artificial, this raises important questions about extraterrestrial intelligent life. The face may not be as good evidence as a crashed UFO, but if it should become accepted as a humanoid artifact, it will surely undermine the legitimacy of the normal-science position that there is no hard, physical evidence of visitation from elsewhere.

Elusive and Inconclusive?

In the strictest sense, Philip J. Klass and his fellow debunkers are right. There is no single piece of physical evidence, like a crashed saucer (at least not one that is available to the public and to the community of scholars), that conclusively proves the existence of UFOs (in the sense of intelligently guided craft not produced by Earth-humans existing here and now). Does this mean that all the other physical evidence for UFOs is worthless?

As Harvard psychiatrist John E. Mack puts it, "Debunkers will even say that there *is* no physical evidence. There is actually a great deal of physical evidence, but it is largely corroborative."[78] In other words, it helps to verify that an abduction was physical and not just psychological if an abduction report coincides with an apparent UFO landing trace in the back yard. However, unless a sizeable chunk of a UFO is produced, something the aliens and/or the U.S. government may be able to prevent for some time, ufologists are not going to get very far relying strictly on physical evidence as proof for the phenomenon. They have to utilize witness reports as well, which brings us to the next chapter.

As Richard L. Thompson explains, Ed Walters' video of a UFO in Gulf Breeze needed to be considered in connection with Bruce Maccabee's investigation into the whole context of the situation, including other witnesses who saw Ed taping the UFO.[79] People reading about the case need to trust Maccabee's report. Thompson says, "The only alternative would be to go to Gulf Breeze and conduct one's own investigation."[80]

---

77. McDaniel, 1993.
78. Mack, 1993A, p. 209.
79. Richard L. Thompson, 1993, p. 6.
80. Richard L. Thompson, 1993, p. 6.

Of course, the problem here is that ufology to many people, and especially to the funding agencies, is not a legitimate discipline governed by a legitimate community of scholars. If it were, then there would be a greater tendency to trust UFO reports and less need for people to do their own investigations (or to need to have their own UFO close encounters before they accept the phenomenon as real).

On the other hand, about 10% of Americans think they have seen a UFO, and these 10% have a lot of friends and relatives. Public opinion, led in part by popular TV shows and films, is making an end-run around normal science. CSICOP is trying to tackle this maneuver, or at least to prevent the popular movement from affecting normal science and its funding agencies.

But let's get back to the "real world" of science where UFOs are perceived through the reality tunnel that insists on physical evidence in the form of a single conclusive ET artifact or being. Philip Klass's $10,000 offer illustrates this perspective nicely. He offered to enter into agreements by which he would pay the money if any of the following three occurred: a crashed spacecraft or major piece thereof were found that the U.S. National Academy of Sciences (NAS) considered clearly extraterrestrial, or the NAS found other evidence that Earth has been visited by ETs in the twentieth century, or an ET visitor appeared live at the U.N. or on national TV.[81]

Certainly such evidence would convince a lot of people, but sticking to the demands of this debunker reality tunnel obstructs progress in ufology, assuming that the subject is important though difficult to study. This is not to say that researchers, including Philip Klass, should stop looking for hoaxes and mundane explanations. However, if all investigators were to follow debunker methods and logic, there is a chance that important information would be lost.

In the absence of conclusive evidence, the elusive UFO phenomenon requires a game of "what if." "What if" there *is* something to all these reports? Since no single piece of physical evidence is conclusive, and since physical evidence is often dubious without the context of witness reports, and since witness reports (especially abductions) seem more plausible when accompanied by physical evidence, it makes sense to combine both physical and witness reports and to look for patterns in the data. This approach advances science more than an obsessive concentration on single pieces of evidence.

---

81. Klass, 1976, pp. 421-423.

Chapter 9

Witness Reports of UFOs

Are Witnesses Believable?

It has already been established earlier in this book that many UFO reports are honest misidentifications of mundane phenomena (See "Nocturnal Lights" on page 2.). Hoaxing is also a possibility when fame, fortune or fun are at stake (see page 87), although I seriously doubt that there is very much hoaxing because fear of ridicule is a strong disincentive against making a public claim of a UFO sighting.

However, should UFO reports from apparently reliable witnesses be considered valid with or without corroborating physical evidence? (see Chapter 8) Ufologists often point out that such testimony would be accepted in a court of law, especially with multiple independent witnesses. As Budd Hopkins noted in the introduction to Raymond E. Fowler's book, *The Allagash Abductions*, "If these four men were giving similar testimony in a trial of Earthly abductors, conviction would be a foregone conclusion."[1] The problem, of course, is that the alleged abductors are aliens/visitors from somewhere or "somewhen" else and have not been apprehended. Debunkers emphasize alternate psychosocial explanations for such strange experiences.

In Chapter 1, I pointed out that distant sightings of nocturnal lights and daylight disks are usually not considered to be very important in ufology these days because they usually do not provide much information and because they are so often explained as misidentifications of planets, airplanes, etc. Close encounters are more interesting, but especially CE-III (with humanoid occupants) and CE-IV (abductions) are likely to contain bizarre details and to put the witnesses under suspicion. People suspect either a hoax or some type of psychological anomaly, if not abnormality.

Multiple witness cases are harder to explain away than reports from single witnesses. Although many UFO sightings seem to be pri-

---

1. Fowler, 1993, p. 3.

vate single-person experiences, perhaps by design of the UFO intelligence, there have also been some remarkable cases in which UFOs have seemed to be on display to large numbers of people. One of these, the "Williamsport wave," is presented on page 3.[2]

One of the classic UFO flaps was the Hudson Valley sightings involving lighted boomerang shapes seen by over 5,000 total witnesses from 1982-1987, sometimes hundreds of witnesses on a single night.[3] Triangular craft were seen by about 10,000 people in Belgium from 1989-1991, with over 300 witnesses on one night.[4] Over one million Chinese saw a spiral-shaped UFO over central and northwestern China on July 24, 1981, and over 1,000 sighting reports were filed.[5]

UFO Types

UFOs have been categorized in terms of several characteristics, including lights, sound, size and shape. Lights have frequently been observed on, around, or emitted as beams from UFOs, and it appears that light is associated with essential aspects of propulsion and with a variety of other electromagnetic operations, possibly including space-time manipulation.[6] Sound is less frequently heard and seems to be less important for hovering and propulsion, according to Willy Smith who found that 61% of 573 reported UFOs (for which information on sound was available) were silent.[7]

In spite of the cartoon popularity of small, domed saucer-shaped UFOs, there has been a very wide range of sizes and shapes observed for several decades. Size estimates range from a foot or so in diameter (which may be "probes" or even something unrelated to UFOs) to several football fields long.

As pointed out in Chapter 1, Kenneth Arnold reported crescent-shaped craft that were labeled "flying saucers" in press headlines. Contrary to the theory that the saucer shape in popular culture has determined the nature of subsequent UFO reports, there have been other shapes reported frequently for decades.

According to Jerome Clark, boomerang shapes have been reported in 1947, 1951 and, of course, in the early 1980s in the Hudson Valley, as well as in the early 1990s.[8] Torpedo shapes were seen in northern Eu-

---

2. Greco and Gordon, 1992.
3. Hynek, and others, 1987.
4. Ferryn, 1992.
5. Chiang, 1993, p. 43.
6. Davenport, 1992B, pp. 63-68.
7. Smith, 1993, p. 20.
8. Clark, 1993A, p. 3.

rope in 1946, when they were labeled "ghost rockets," but they were categorized as "flying saucers" a year later, he says. Similar torpedo-shaped UFOs were also seen in 1948 and 1992. Triangles go back at least to the 1970s.

Even in first-hand reports given to me by people whom I know well enough to consider reliable witnesses, there are several nonsaucer shapes. These include one that was a large rectangle (as large as a ten-story building) and another that was a blend of a sphere with one triangular side. Nevertheless symmetrical shapes, especially circles and spheres or ovoids, tend to predominate.

In one interesting study by Linda Kerth and Richard Haines, 347 UFO drawings by Swiss children aged 7-15 were analyzed to look for stereotypical elements.[9] Circular/oval/cigar shapes predominated (44%), followed by domed shapes of various types (35%). Much less frequent were irregular rectangles (4%), rockets/cylinders (4%) and triangles (3%). In particular, the researchers noticed that complex disc types (domed top-and-bottom, and flat-bottomed domes) appeared much more frequently in the drawings of children above age 11, which could be due either to psychological development or to increased awareness of UFO stereotypes.[10] Kerth and Haines note that complex discs are more commonly part of the UFO concepts of nonwitnesses than of witnesses, according to earlier research by Haines, although they do show up in some UFO sighting reports.

There are several methodological problems involved in getting a valid measure of the frequency of different craft shapes. One is that UFOs can apparently change shape during a sighting, partly due to rotation of a disc until it shows a circular surface. Shapes may also appear different at different distances, especially if they are luminescent.

Not all classification systems used by ufologists are the same either. In one sample of 31 cases from the MUFON Abduction Transcription Project, Dan Wright found the most common vehicle shape to be discoid (47%), followed by spherical (17%), cylindrical (13%), rectangular (6%), triangular (6%), oblong (6%), asymmetrical (2%) and conical (2%).[11] If abduction cases are correlated with a particular type of craft, then this set of percentages might differ greatly from ones derived from close encounters with no abductions involved.

Of course, only abduction cases can provide witness evidence about the interiors of UFOs. Wright, in a sample of 150 reports, found tables mentioned in 39%, computer/TV screens in 13%, computers in

---

9. Kerth and Haines, 1992, pp. 55-56.
10. Kerth and Haines, 1992, pp. 56, 72-73.
11. Wright, 1994A, p. 4.

12%, chairs in 8%, counters or shelves in 7%, cabinets in 7% and benches in 4%.[12]

Close Encounters of the Third Kind (CE-III)

Although it might not seem so surprising to find beings inside apparently artificial, high-tech craft like UFOs, CE-III reports (involving humanoids) were treated gingerly in the 1960s. As David M. Jacobs put it, "Eventually the number of cases grew too large to ignore, and NICAP (National Investigations Committee on Aerial Phenomena) accepted these reports as genuine."[13]

Richard Hall, one of the first to investigate such reports for NICAP, explains that they "shied away from *publicity* and *controversy* about them while quietly investigating them," because humanoid reports were "not exactly the topic to focus discussion on if you were trying to gain attention for UFOs among scientists, government officials and other important people."[14] In other words, the level of strangeness involved in CE-III was especially difficult for normal science to tolerate.

Entity Types

Although a great variety of humanoids or entities (some not very human-like) have been reported in UFO cases, two general types prevail: a shorter, less human-looking type, and a taller, more human-looking type. Coral and Jim Lorenzen, separating short from tall humanoids at 40 inches, found 81 of the former and 60 of the latter (and a small scattering of monsters and robots) in a study of 164 humanoid reports published in 1976.[15]

Due in part to popular media representations, such as on the cover of Whitley Strieber's book *Communion*, the short "greys" are best known, especially in the United States. These are generally portrayed as large-headed (in comparison to the rest of the body) with large, dark eyes; with rudimentary nostrils and mouth slit; thin body and long, thin appendages; usually with no obvious sexual differences or genitalia.

Jenny Randles, whose British cases involve more tall than short humanoids, was impressed with the fact that an American woman had reported to John Carpenter her experience with a tall blond whose

12. Wright, 1994A, p. 4.
13. Jacobs, 1992A, p. 15.
14. Richard Hall, 1992A, p. 17.
15. Lorenzen and Lorenzen, 1976, pp. 406-415.

characteristics closely matched those in the British cases.[16] This "tall blonde or Nordic" type includes the following features: 6 to 8 feet tall; built like muscular humans; shoulder-length blonde hair; perfect, handsome facial features; kind blue eyes; warm and pleasant expression; telepathic communication; human-style jumpsuit or uniform.

Although it probably embarrasses some ufologists to have to think about it, there are also a few other bizarre types of beings reported. John Carpenter says that he has collected several reports of lizard or reptilian beings from abductees, none of whom had ever heard of such a thing before.[17] His composite description of the "reptilians" includes the following characteristics: 6 to 8 feet tall; smooth, lizard-like scales; green to brown body; four-fingered claw with brown webbing; human-snake face; cat-like eyes with vertical slit; repulsive and aggressive; never communicate.

From Dan Wright's preliminary analysis of cases from the MU-FON Abduction Transcription Project mentioned earlier, it is evident that short, gray beings predominate. Out of 66 cases in which height is mentioned, 57 involved at least one short entity, 47 had at least one that was taller than the other beings present or as tall as a human, and 10 cases involved a super-tall being over six feet and usually over seven feet.[18]

Although Wright's preliminary article does not separate skin tone by height of the entity, the gray associated especially with small beings is the most commonly reported (28%), followed by white (14%), "dark" (13%), "aura/glow" (10%), pale (7%), blue (6%), green or gray-green (5%), tan (4%), mottled (4%) and a few others.[19] By far most eyes were large, almond-shaped and solid black, but a few reported a pupil and an iris of green, blue, brown or gold. Out of 44 cases with a description of garments, Wright found 24 mentions of a robe or cape, nearly always worn by an on-board leader, 23 mentions of a loose jump suit or tight wet suit, and 14 in which an entity appeared to be naked (some of which might be tight suits).[20]

As seen by the witnesses, two-thirds of Wright's cases involved "verbalized" communication, nearly always telepathic. Witnesses perceived mostly positive, but also some negative, emotions: caring (23%), friendliness (21%), anger (11%), detachment (no emotion) (9%), humor (7%), fear (6%), surprise (5%), pleasure (5%) and a variety of others.[21]

---

16. Carpenter, 1993B, p. 10.
17. Carpenter, 1993B, p. 11.
18. Wright, 1994A, p. 6.
19. Wright, 1994A, p. 5.
20. Wright, 1994A, pp. 6-7.
21. Wright, 1994A, pp. 4-5.

One major issue regarding reports of alien entities, of course, has been whether the witnesses are not expanding, intentionally or unintentionally, upon stereotypical images of aliens in popular culture or folklore. In the study of drawings by Swiss children mentioned earlier, Kerth and Haines noted that they contained much of the LGM (little green man) stereotype, rather than the "black-eyed, noseless, slit-lipped, three-foot-high 'gray.'"[22] In the Swiss drawings, 34% of the entities had green skin[23] compared to only 5% who were green or gray-green in the Wright study. Since the Swiss drawings were done in 1981, it is possible that a decade or so later Swiss children would have seen enough of the grey type in popular media to make them dominant in their drawings. The important thing to remember is that the color descriptions in the Wright sample are from abductees and supposedly based on real experiences, whereas the Swiss children were not a sample of experiencers. And the abductees did not emphasize the LGM stereotype which is still common in cartoons and other media representations.

Folklorist Thomas E. Bullard states that the presence of a tradition about how UFOs and ETs are supposed to look does not necessarily mean that there is no real phenomenon behind the tradition. Moreover, "the contrast between the fluidity of complex folk narratives and the stability of abduction reports points to [the origin of the latter] in some kind of experience."[24]

Close Encounters of the Fourth Kind (CE-IV)

CE-IV involve humanoids or entities of some kind just as CE-III do, but in addition there is an "abduction" of the human witness. Some so-called abductions may not actually involve being taken into a craft, but at least there is some kind of examination or treatment of the individual, possibly right in bed, for example. Abductions are considered different from the classic contactee cases in the 1950s, for example George Adamski's (see page 89), which were generally friendly interactions sometimes with an invitation to take a ride in a UFO.

Here is an ideal-type or generalized description of the abduction experience found in recent UFO literature. You are usually in some private or isolated place, such as your own bed or in your car on a country road or camping in a tent, typically at night. You may see a UFO or have seen one a bit earlier. If you are asleep, you may wake up and see un-

---

22. Kerth and Haines, 1992, pp. 72-73.
23. Kerth and Haines, 1992, p. 64.
24. Bullard, 1991, p. 1.

explained lights around you (those who don't wake up may not re-member anything at all). You may feel your body start to go numb, and you see one or more entities close to you, probably short, but possibly tall ones. If you try to scream to wake up a person near you, either you can't make any noise or he/she seems to be out cold. However, some-times the other person perceives some of what happens, or even goes with you.

You may float or be led, quite possible through a closed window or a wall, outside and into a craft or into a beam of light (white or blue) that draws you into a craft. Maybe you are transferred to a larger UFO. Then you sit around alone or with others, or proceed directly to be shown things and/or to be examined on a table. If you are examined, samples may be taken, and implants set into or taken out of your body. Communication with the beings is telepathic. They may do a "mind scan" and show you realistic scenes of such things as global problems either to test your emotions or to teach you lessons.

Back in bed or in your car or tent, you wake up or continue driving almost as if nothing happened. But perhaps your clothes are on back-wards, or your drive takes you an hour more than it should, or your head is outside the tent instead of your feet. And where did those bruis-es and scars come from? You will probably remember only part of this, if anything, until you have dreams later on or waking flashes of recall that get you to investigate and perhaps undergo hypnotic regression.

Such a composite description may be useful in coming to under-stand the abduction phenomenon, but how uniform and consistent are abduction experiences? Budd Hopkins points out that there are inter-esting odd consistencies that point to the physical reality of the phe-nomenon. For example, he said in 1993, the ETs never show any interest in the human heart, which is odd because this is a regular part of examinations by human doctors.[25] If abductees are imagining or dreaming up their abductions based on the commonly known pattern of the ET physical exam, why don't they ever include such a basic ele-ment? How would they have known to leave it out?

On the other hand, Karla Turner argues that the literature pub-lished by abduction researchers tends to gravitate toward a standard stereotypical abduction scenario, ignoring some of the bizarre varia-tions that often occur. Her best illustration of this comes from a conver-sation she had with a prominent abduction researcher in 1989. This man claimed to be able to test the validity of abduction reports based upon the existence of certain scars. When Dr. Turner asked about an-

---

25. Hopkins, July 4, 1993.

other type of scar that she had come across several times in her research, he denied ever having collected any such cases. When she persisted, he admitted knowing of "a couple of instances.... But they're so rare that I have to ignore them."[26]

In defense of the methodology that excludes the more unusual cases, David M. Jacobs states in his book, *Secret Life*, "I have not included one-of-a-kind accounts—no matter how dramatic—because no reliable inferences can be drawn from them without confirming testimony from other abductees."[27] In a private interview, Dr. Jacobs told me that he does not take chances with unusual cases because they may involve false memory or envisioning. Therefore, he puts them on the back burner and keeps them out of the data base.

This is certainly an important scientific issue. One hopes that the overall patterns and full degree of variability will become more evident as computer data files are developed like the MUFON Abduction Transcription project mentioned above. If there is selective data gathering or reporting by different researchers, perhaps some of these biases will be corrected in a file that contains contributions from a wide variety of researchers. At the same time, one hopes that a high percentage of the data will be valid.

Comparisons should be useful not only within the United States, but also cross-culturally. European ufology used to be considered a bit strange by American ufologists because of the bizarre CE-III cases that were reported there in earlier decades. Now the situation is reversed, and European ufologists seem reluctant to give as much credence to abductions (CE-IV) because they are so bizarre.[28] In Australia, ufologists have collected abduction cases very similar to those in the U.S.[29] And in South Africa, Cynthia Hind has also found essentially the same kinds of experiences, but often with a different cultural interpretation.[30] The Visitors may be interpreted as ghosts, especially ancestors, rather than extraterrestrials, who are something of a white-man's demon.

In contrast to the comparative perspective, there is another approach: looking for the one undeniable case that will prove that abductions (not to mention UFOs) exist as real, physical phenomena. One candidate is Budd Hopkins' "Case of the Century" involving multiple independent witnesses to Linda Cortile's (pseudonym) abduction as she floated through a closed window in her twelfth-story apartment in New York and was drawn up in a column of light with three small

---

26. Turner, 1993, p. 26.
27. Jacobs, 1992B, p. 15.
28. Huneeus, 1992.
29. Basterfield, 1994.
30. Hind, 1993.

aliens into a UFO.[31] A major political figure was allegedly one of the witnesses, and if he comes forward when the full report is published, his authority could help legitimize ufology (see page 92).

Having more than one abductee is the next best thing to having nonabductee witnesses, if the abductees are given hypnotic regression independently and show great similarities in their sessions, which helps reduce the possibility of confabulation or false memory. John Carpenter has such a case involving two women abducted from their car in western Kansas in 1989.[32]

One of the richest and best documented multiple abductee cases is *The Allagash Abductions* book by Raymond E. Fowler.[33] In this case, four men with hidden memories give very similar accounts of their group abduction from a canoe thirteen years after the fact, and as artists are able to give an excellent graphic record.

Of course, the demand for the one undeniable case is a hurdle set up by normal science in general and by debunkers in particular. If it were not for this need to legitimize the subject, abduction research would probably concentrate more on comparisons. But due to the high strangeness of abduction reports, a great deal of concern is directed toward "proving" that abductions are real. This results both in the search for an iron-tight case and in the debate over methods and interpretations of reports.

Witness Memory

One basic methodological question, of course, is whether the memory of an alleged abductee can be trusted. Witness memory is even an issue without the use of hypnosis, as was evident in a series of articles in the *International UFO Reporter*, starting with "The Invention of a Gulf Breeze UFO" by Barbara Becker.[34] Becker emphasized the importance of memory loss between an alleged UFO observation and the reporting of it and stated that post-event information, such as hearing about other people's sightings, can distort memory. Linda Kerth, in an opposing view, discussed the various conditions that affect the reliability of memory and said that UFO experiences might be personally significant enough to trigger an accurate "flashbulb memory."[35]

When hypnosis is used to trigger repressed memory, questions of validity are intensified. Philip J. Klass is a pioneer in this regard, having

31. Hopkins, July 11, 1992.
32. Carpenter, 1991A.
33. Fowler, 1993.
34. Becker, 1992.
35. Kerth, 1992.

suggested in 1981 that hypnosis, such as that used since the mid-1960s by Dr. R. Leo Sprinkle, might be implanting "pseudo-memories" in UFO experiencers.[36] By the March/April 1995 issue of *Skeptical Inquirer*, false-memory syndrome (FMS) was a major issue as discussed in the lead article by psychologist and memory expert Elizabeth Loftus.[37]

Ufologist and psychotherapist David Gotlib, warned in 1993 that legal accusations might be leveled at abduction researchers for generating FMS, just as they had been leveled against therapists who had dug too deep for repressed memories of childhood sexual abuse.[38] He encouraged researchers to take seriously the concerns of the FMS Foundation, an organization led by some prominent behavioral scientists. And, as of this writing, the Mutual UFO Network was working on a code of ethics for abduction researchers and therapists.

One example of an accusation of FMS came in a review by David Boras of Leah Haley's book, *Lost Was the Key*.[39] Boras said that "she fails to provide any convincing evidence that something extraordinary happened to her," and that the book "illustrates how one's perception of reality can be subtly influenced [by various factors leading to] false memories."[40] John S. Carpenter, hypnotherapist and abduction researcher, defended Haley in the foreword of her book, saying that "despite having no knowledge...[of] UFO abduction reports...she produced countless details under hypnosis with strong correlational ties to both published and unpublished data despite leading questions and paradoxical suggestions deliberately designed [to create confabulation]."[41]

In other words, Carpenter was saying that Haley's case is an example of hypnotic regression done correctly, using leading questions deliberately to see if the witness is highly suggestible and is confabulating to please the hypnotist. Also, he claims that detailed matches between abductee accounts on unpublished factors strengthen claims of validity, and that minor (undetected) confabulation will not invalidate the entire process.[42] Moreover, Carpenter points out, similar details are reported by the approximately one-fourth of abductees who undergo *no* hypnosis.[43]

In an excellent empirical study testing the reliability of hypnosis in abduction research, folklorist Thomas E. Bullard found that "The form

36. Klass, 1981.
37. Loftus, 1995.
38. Gotlib, 1993.
39. Haley, 1993.
40. Boras, 1993.
41. Haley, 1993, p. 4.
42. Carpenter, 1993D, p. 15.
43. Carpenter, 1991B, p. 156.

and content of abduction stories seems independent of [whether] hypnosis [was used or not]. The same key traits appear with similar frequency among hypnotic and non-hypnotic reports, [and] the beliefs and personalities of investigating hypnotists show little influence on these frequencies."[44] This final point is very important because perhaps the most serious potential methodological problem is the creation of false memories by hypnotists leading their subjects.

Of course, the reason for using hypnosis in the first place is that a high percentage of suspected abductees have at best only partial memories of the alleged events. This loss of memory could either be induced externally by hypnotic suggestion on the part of the aliens/visitors or be caused by internal psychological processes like Post-Traumatic Stress Disorder (PTSD) or Dissociative Disorder (more on these later).[45] To what degree external vs. internal causes are involved is unclear. One point seldom discussed in the abduction literature, however, is that high-tech visitors might be able to switch off most abductees so effectively that very few have anything to remember (or forget) at all. If abduction reports represent extremely rare events, the ones in which the abductors make a mistake, it is conceivable that UFO abduction is far more common than anyone suspects.

Dr. John Mack points out that "Virtually every abductee...will report that the aliens told them not to remember or forbade them to tell about their experiences," and, therefore, hypnosis is an ideal tool for "undoing the repression and bringing back into consciousness the forgotten experiences."[46] He also emphasizes that "the accuracy of memory tends to increase according to how salient the matter in question is for the person."[47] And, of course, an abduction experience is more salient or important for the individual than some situations that people are asked to recall under hypnosis as trial witnesses, for example.

Mack realizes that the hypnotist must be careful not to lead the subject into confabulation or "false memories." However, he also says that abduction memories recovered under hypnosis are often more valid than those consciously recalled, because some uncomfortable or embarrassing things tend to be hidden from consciousness. One example of this is the case of a man who told Dr. Mack that he had had sex with an attractive alien hybrid woman. Under hypnosis, the story changed to a humiliating account of a mechanical taking of a sperm sample, an account very similar to what has been reported in other such cases.[48]

---

44. Bullard, 1989, p. 3.
45. Meyer, 1992.
46. Mack, 1993A, p. 206.
47. Mack, 1993A, p. 205.
48. Mack, 1993A, p. 206.

Although many abduction researchers have made statements supporting the validity of hypnosis for studying abduction accounts, many have also laid down safeguards for avoiding such potential problems as confabulation. As noted above, John Carpenter asks deliberately leading questions to see if the subject is highly suggestible. If the hypnotist asks, "What color was the alien's hair?" but the subject insists there was no hair, this suggests resistance to being led. Jacobs and Hopkins warn about three areas of confabulation to watch out for: physical description of aliens (especially at first when the subject is nervous), the recounting of alien conversation (since telepathic impressions are hard to distinguish from the subject's own mental impressions), and the interpretation of alien motivations or intentions (subjects may project their own ideas onto what is difficult to fathom).[49]

Jacobs and Hopkins, both highly suspicious of New Age interpretations of abductions as spiritual transformation, are especially against "guiding a subject into a dissociative state in which 'channeled' messages come out."[50] In other words, the subject may be encouraged to go into an altered state of consciousness ("dissociative state" in psychological terms) in order to communicate telepathically with the aliens, almost like a spirit medium, right during the hypnosis session. Adding to this problem, from Jacobs' point of view, is the possibility that the subject "was also in an altered state of consciousness during the abduction itself."[51] During this altered state, the aliens may have deliberately created misperceptions and pseudo-memories (see Karla Turner on alien disinformation, page 136).

Another example of a very careful abduction researcher is Dr. Richard F. Haines, a psychologist, who uses among other procedures a "three stage technique."[52] In the first stage, the subject describes everything seen, felt and heard. In the second stage, the subject adds verbalizations and thoughts. Finally, in the third stage, the subject imagines the hypnotist going through the experience with him/her, and they discuss it together. This is designed to minimize bias and influence on the part of the hypnotist.

Are Abductions Physical or Psychosocial?

In Chapter 8, we looked at arguments for the physical reality of the abduction experience. But even in those cases that seem to have a defi-

---

49. Jacobs and Hopkins, 1992, p. 148.
50. Jacobs and Hopkins, 1992, p. 147.
51. Jacobs, 1992B, p. 323.
52. Haines, 1989.

nite physical basis, there still might be some psychological component to the experience. Aside from the issue of false memory syndrome and the validity of recall under hypnosis, there are other psychological possibilities, including psychopathology and fantasy-prone personality (FPP), the latter occurring in healthy individuals.

FPP involves a rich imagination, ease in being hypnotized, and a tendency to experience apparitions and other psychic phenomena. As Budd Hopkins points out, waking memories are no more reliable than "hypnotically-refreshed recall" in fantasy-prone individuals, as he discovered with one such person who gave him three different descriptions of an object that had terrified him, one description evidently derived from a scene in a movie.[53] Hopkins has techniques for screening out these cases that come to him "occasionally."

Related to the idea of fantasy in individuals is the folklore process in groups. As pointed out in the discussion of entity types above, however, Bullard discovered that abduction reports as a group tend to have more stability than is typical of the variation found in folklore.[54]

In one very important study, especially important because it appeared in a mainstream academic journal, the *Journal of Abnormal Psychology*, Nicholas P. Spanos and others found that UFO experiencers "did not score as more psychopathological, less intelligent, or more fantasy prone and hypnotizable than a community comparison group or a student comparison group."[55] This was great news for ufologists who wanted to emphasize that UFO experiencers, including abductees, are not crazy or hallucinating as they are so often labeled under a deviance perspective. Ufologist Mark Rodeghier and others also found that a sample of abductees were not as a group high on fantasy-proneness, hypnotic responsiveness or psychological pathology, although there were 2 individuals out of 27 whose cases might be explained by fantasy-proneness.[56]

However, the more complete story on the Spanos study is that the authors found that "intensity of UFO experiences correlated significantly with...proneness toward fantasy and unusual sensory experiences."[57] In other words, although the overall UFO experiencer group did not differ psychologically from nonexperiencers, there was a difference between non-intense (mere lights in the sky) and intense (close encounters) experiencers. Not only were the intense experiencers more fantasy prone, but they also had higher belief in UFOs and in paranor-

---

53. Hopkins, 1989, p. 30.
54. Bullard, 1991, p. 3.
55. Spanos and others, 1993, p. 624.
56. Rodeghier and others, 1991.
57. Spanos and others, 1993, pp. 624, 631.

mal phenomena in general. The authors concluded that "beliefs in alien visitation and flying saucers serve as templates against which people shape ambiguous external information, diffuse physical sensations, and vivid imaginings into alien encounters that are experienced as real events."[58]

This suggests that UFO belief serves as a "reality tunnel" within which "ambiguous external information" (an apparent sighting or alien visitation) is interpreted as a UFO experience. I might say that this could be interpreted either as being open to or as being biased in favor of acknowledging a UFO experience (rather than denying it). There is also the question of just how *much* correlation there is between belief and experience, or how big of an impact belief has on the interpretation of the experience. Moreover, the Spanos study cannot tell us the direction of cause and effect. It is possible that the experience came before and caused the greater belief in both UFOs and in other paranormal phenomena, since the transformation people experience after a UFO encounter sometimes brings about psychic and other strange experiences later on.

Altered States and Psychic Phenomena

Aside from FMS and FPP, then, there is an additional possible non-physical explanation for UFO abductions, and that is a psychical/spiritual one. Kenneth Ring states that both UFO experiencers and people who have had near-death experiences (NDEs) may have an EPP, or "encounter-prone personality."[59] This EPP is conducive to entering an imaginal realm through altered states of consciousness. Imaginal vision accesses other "realities" and is, therefore, not the same as sheer fantasy (in FPP).

Other researchers are not so sure. Psychologist Robert A. Baker, an abduction debunker, thinks that EPP and imaginality are no different from FPP.[60] Bartholomew and Basterfield criticize Ring and Rosing for not testing for FPP with a complete enough battery of questions.[61] In response, Ring states that previous measures of FPP were a "heterogeneous hodgepodge" that picked up everything from FPP to "the kitchen sink," and, therefore, he designed his own measure.[62]

---

58. Spanos and others, 1993, p. 631.
59. Ring, 1992; Ring and Rosing, 1990.
60. Baker, 1991.
61. Bartholomew and Basterfield, 1990.
62. Ring, 1990.

In contrast to critics of Ring's *The Omega Project* (1992), [63] who prefer to see abductions as a strictly mundane trick of the mind (psychopathology, FMS, or FPP), David Jacobs objects to Ring's EPP concept on the grounds that it sees abductions as part of some kind of alternate reality rather than as real physical events. Jacobs particularly complains that Ring ignores evidence for abductees being missing, something that does not occur in NDEs.[64]

Nevertheless, Ring's ideas about UFO experiences being associated with altered states of consciousness resonate with other suspicions that at least some abduction reports contain elements similar to altered-state experiences like out-of-body experiences (OBEs)[65] and hypnagogic/hypnopompic sleep paralysis, although there may be some obvious differences as well, as pointed out by Jacobs in the case of NDEs as mentioned above. The most commonly cited source in this area is David J. Hufford's 1982 book, *The Terror That Comes in the Night,* [66] which interprets experiences of bedroom ghosts and feelings of paralysis or pressure on the body as part of the hypnagogic state (falling asleep) or hypnopompic state (waking up). My book, *Chinese Ghosts and ESP,* [67] published the same year came to the same conclusions independently in regard to Chinese *"bei guai chaak"* ("being pressed by a ghost") cases. Walter Webb, among others, has applied the Hufford perspective to some UFO abduction cases.[68]

Overall the abduction literature is not a strong fit with the phenomenon of hallucinations during sleep paralysis, for various reasons, including the evidence for physical absence and for medical exam procedures during abductions. However, some of the indicators of possible abductions used in the 1992 Roper poll on "unusual personal experiences" seem to be characteristic of sleep paralysis hallucinations and other altered-state phenomena like OBEs. One such question was "How often has this happened to you: Waking up paralyzed with a sense of a strange person or presence or something else in the room?"[69] Ufologist and sociologist Robert L. Hall and others argue convincingly that the estimate of perhaps 2% of the population being abductees, based upon a positive response to 4 of 5 items on the Roper poll, is on very shaky grounds because the indicator items are of dubious validity in identifying abductees.[70] Of course, one of the problems is that even

63. Ring, 1992.
64. Jacobs, 1991, p. 163.
65. Spataford, 1993.
66. David J. Hufford, 1982.
67. Emmons, 1982, pp. 144-156.
68. Webb, 1993.
69. Dawes and Mulford, 1993, p. 51.
70. Robert L. Hall and others, 1992.

if a known group of abductees had been tested and found to give a high percentage of positive responses on the indicator items, it would be hard to contrast them with a group of nonabductees, since it is impossible to prove that someone has not been abducted secretly with no memory of the event.

"Please Tell Me I'm Crazy Instead!"

I pointed out earlier that studies by Parnell and Sprinkle[71] and by Spanos and others[72] found abductees and other UFO experiencers not to be more psychopathological than the general population. However, many abductees/experiencers find it difficult to process what seems to have happened to them. Some expect to be told that they are "crazy" and are shocked to find evidence that their experiences may be real.

John Wilson[73] among others has applied the concept of Post-Traumatic Stress Disorder (PTSD) to the condition of UFO experiencers. As in the cases of war or rape victims, some abductees allegedly experience disturbing intrusive recollections of the event, avoid situations that will trigger the recall, and have difficulty sleeping or being calm.

Whether PTSD is the appropriate designation for most post-abduction mental states or not, many researchers have noted similar conditions among their subjects. David Jacobs prefers to use the concept Post-Abduction Syndrome (PAS), presented by Ron Westrum in 1986.[74] As Jacobs points out, abductees may actually want to remember their repressed memories, unlike the situation with PTSD, and many of the repressed episodes are nontraumatic.[75] Nevertheless, many abductees/experiencers have sleep disorders and various fears and anxieties.[76] Another significant problem for abductees is what John Carpenter calls "second trauma,"[77] the social rejection from family, friends and community at large who label them deviant.

Following Westrum and Jacobs and going even farther away from PTSD, Richard and Lee Boylan prefer to use the term Close Extraterrestrial Encounter Syndrome (CEES).[78] They say that CEES would be classified as an adjustment disorder, but it is certainly less serious than PTSD, mainly because two elements of PTSD are often missing: "un-

---

71. Parnell and Sprinkle, 1990.
72. Spanos and others, 1993.
73. John P. Wilson, 1990.
74. Westrum, 1986.
75. Jacobs, 1992B, p. 246.
76. Jacobs, 1992B, pp. 247-251.
77. Carpenter, 1993A, p. 7.
78. Boylan and Boylan, 1994, p. 51.

usual intentional harm or disastrous incident" and "psychic numbing."[79]

How should professionals deal with people who come to them with apparent abduction experiences? One perspective is that investigative and therapist roles can be combined. Such is the case with psychiatrist John E. Mack who also states, "I do not regard abductees as patients in the usual sense. Rather, they are, with some exceptions, normal and healthy persons who have undergone disturbing and mysterious experiences."[80]

Jacobs and Hopkins describe what could be called a quasi-therapeutic technique, not so different from what is used by other UFO investigator/therapists. In the process of gathering data about the case, it is often necessary to overcome "threshold anxiety" in the initial stages of hypnosis through relaxation and to get around blocks in the subject's memory.[81] Two functions are served at the same time: ufological investigation and therapeutic processing of the event for the subject.

Even those who combine the roles of investigator and therapist recognize that abductees may need further help, especially when "second trauma" occurs and disturbs relationships with spouses and other family members.[82] David Jacobs states, "If a person is suffering emotionally from the effects of abductions and needs more help than I can give, it is important for them to have professional counseling from a sympathetic psychologist or psychiatrist."[83]

"Sympathetic" is a key word, since many therapists are highly skeptical about the abduction phenomenon. Many investigators may be more sympathetic than many available therapists, although the investigators may not be very skilled in the therapy role. On the other hand, Dr. David Gotlib emphasizes that the use of hypnosis strictly for data gathering on the part of a therapist "diminishes his effectiveness as a caregiver and is unfair to the patient."[84] These difficulties may indicate a need for specialized roles and the inclusion of both an investigator and a mental health professional, as John Carpenter argues, with patient well-being taking ethical priority over data-gathering.[85]

One other mechanism to help experiencers deal with their memories and with second trauma is the support group.[86] This is extremely important because of the tendency for outsiders to doubt the physical

79. Boylan and Boylan, 1994, p. 49.
80. Mack, 1992, p. 11.
81. Jacobs and Hopkins, 1992, pp. 139-141.
82. Jacobs and Hopkins, 1992, pp. 149-150.
83. Jacobs, 1992B, p. 326.
84. Gotlib, 1990, pp. 27-28.
85. Carpenter, 1993C, p. 18.
86. Jacobs, 1992B, p. 326.

reality of the abduction phenomenon. Most ufologists seem to recognize the need for abductees to share experiences with each other in groups, although a few complain that support groups sometimes degenerate into "cults" with bizarre theories about UFOs and abductions.

Resisting Abductions

If witness reports of abductions are taken seriously, and if abductees are considered important as individuals rather than just for the information they provide, it is logical to ask not only what therapy they might need, but also whether some action should be taken to prevent the reoccurrence of their abductions. Of course, those who see abduction or visitation experiences as positive will not want to stop them.

In Chapter 8, I referred to Victoria Alexander's call for crime-detection methods in abduction research in order to get evidence of these "crimes against humanity."[87] Although she did not discuss techniques of physical resistance in her 1993 article, she did take the perspective of reacting in an active, rather than in a passive, way to abductions.

Ufologist Ann Druffel also takes an active rather than passive orientation and recommends resistance techniques for people who feel violated by the experience. She identifies an escalating order of tactics from simple mental struggle to righteous anger ("Go away and leave me alone.") to protective rage (even stronger language in order to provide a protective shield over the household).[88]

Although there is not a great deal of evidence about the effectiveness of these techniques, it is interesting that they parallel the attempts of ghost experiencers to protect themselves in hauntings. They might be effective at least psychologically if there are some mental or psychic aspects in abduction experiences. Although people involved in New Age or metaphysical thought tend not to believe strongly in evil, or in a negative view of abductions, they may use one of Druffel's techniques for protection, which is "wrapping oneself with white light."[89]

Ufologist and clinical hypnotherapist Virginia M. Tilly is not a proponent of resistance. Nevertheless, she lists techniques that she knows abductees have used including "taping messages to their abductors on their bedroom windows or walls, or on their own legs...setting up video cameras...using prayer, meditation, the Bible, crosses, crucifixes, rosaries and the Sacred Heart."[90]

---

87. Alexander, 1993, p. 7.
88. Druffel, 1992, pp. 4-6.
89. Druffel, 1992, p. 5.
90. Tilly, 1992, p. 12.

Samuel P. Faile, Ph.D. in Solid State Science, has devised a passive "anti-UFO abduction device." It is constructed of "double-ply insulating wire in 'harmonic' single knot in passive mode."[91] Faile bases his invention upon the theory of Mobius fields. Instructions for use include the following: "Hand carry this passive and totally safe item...wherever protection is required.... No external power is needed or desired for it.... It is believed that...the device is activated by UFO fields. The antenna knot structure collects scalar electrical radiation given off by a UFO, transforms it, then radiates back a disrupter field with time distortion features to break up UFO fields designed for abduction purposes."[92] Dr. Faile has given his devices away at no charge, is in the early stages of testing their effectiveness, and has no plans to take out a patent. He may be contacted at Cold Fusion Products; 4002 Sharon Park Lane, Suite 13; Cincinnati, Ohio 45241.

Trauma or Transformation?

Close encounters, especially abductions, can be awesome experiences. But are these awesome events positive or negative for the experiencers? Should they be seen as trauma or transformation? It is amazing how varied the opinions are on this subject. Although their samples are not exactly comparable, which is part of the problem, some researchers say that nearly all experiencers are traumatized, and some say that very few are.

Veteran and respected ufologist Richard Hall in speaking of abductees he had worked with over a period of four or five years said, "A good 95 percent of those who have confided in me feel victimized; only a few feel that there *must* be something good or positive about the experience."[93] Prominent abduction researcher David Jacobs refers to abductions as "terrifying experiences."[94] When asked how he would react if he found that all abductions were strictly imaginary, he responded, "If that were true, I would weep with joy. I want to be wrong."[95] In his introduction to Raymond Fowler's book, *The Allagash Abductions*, Budd Hopkins, who of course is another prominent abduction researcher, uses words like "negative" and "traumas" although he notes that Fowler does not draw such evaluative conclusions.[96]

---

91. Faile, 1994.
92. Faile, 1994.
93. Richard H. Hall, 1993A, p. 12.
94. Jacobs, 1992B, p. 317.
95. Jacobs, 1992B, p. 318.
96. Fowler, 1993, pp. 3-4.

Some well-publicized abductees have also made negative statements about their experiences. Linda Cortile, subject of the book *Witnessed* by Budd Hopkins[97], speaks against the notion that she might have had a positive, spiritual transformation. Some people have suggested to her, "'Linda, perhaps you're spiritually underdeveloped.' Well, it's true that I'm no Shirley MacLaine," she says. "However, getting mugged in Central Park in New York City would seem more enlightening to me."[98]

Ed Walters, central figure in the sightings in Gulf Breeze, Florida, describes many abduction events that terrified him and makes the negative comment, "I propose that the alien interaction in my life is not the exception but, rather, a common experience suffered by many."[99] Travis Walton, who was abducted and missing for five days in Arizona in 1975, subject of the movie "Fire in the Sky" and of his book by the same title, is primarily negative about his experience, although not as much as he used to be.[100] He still says he would rather it had never happened.

By contrast, ufologist James Harder says that in a sample of 28 people with a conscious memory of a close encounter "two-thirds did not even report a scary feeling during their experience, and only one of that group checked the line, 'Do you have a good feeling about the experience?' with a no."[101] In a sample of 44 experiencers (abductees), Dr. Richard Boylan found 59% with a positive attitude toward their CE-IVs, 32% ambivalent, and only 9% negative.[102]

As pointed out previously, Dr. Boylan does not think that CE-IVs ("abductions," although he would not use this negative term) generally cause PTSD, although some experience the less severe adjustment disorder he calls Close Extraterrestrial Encounter Syndrome (CEES).[103] Boylan supports the "expanded consciousness school," which emphasizes the transformation that often occurs with experiencers. This transformed consciousness includes the following traits: broadened cosmic perspective, global humanitarian concern, Earth ecology focus, decreased materialistic focus and increased spiritual orientation.[104]

Of course, Dr. Boylan is a transformed experiencer himself, as are many other ufologists as discussed in Chapter 4. Alice Bryant and Linda Seebach also fit into this category, although they understand that

---

97. Hopkins, 1996C.
98. Cortile, 1994, p. 244.
99. Ed Walters and Frances Walters, 1994, p. 174.
100. Walton and Rogers, Oct. 10, 1993.
101. Harder, 1994, p. 236.
102. Boylan and Boylan, 1994, p. 61.
103. Boylan and Boylan, 1994, p. 51.
104. Boylan and Boylan, 1994, pp. 48-49.

some trauma can be involved, as they point out in their book *Healing Shattered Reality*.[105] Linda Seebach has spoken at UFO conferences against the negative "abductionist" view of CE-IVs promoted by Jacobs and Hopkins among others.

Part of the New Age or New Thought philosophy behind the positive view of CE-IVs is that souls agree before an incarnation to be taken by aliens while on Earth, and that, therefore, a CE-IV is not a violation of rights. This subject is often debated hotly pro and con in question-and-answer sessions at UFO conferences. One skeptic on this point said, "I could say that you agreed in a past life to give me your car, so let's have the keys."

Some experiencers and researchers recognize a combination of perspectives. Betty Andreasson Luca, subject of books by Raymond Fowler, states, "My own personal encounters have been benevolent. The reason it is not possible to claim or classify every UFO abduction as such is because, although there are good beings, there are also fallen ones interacting with mankind."[106]

Dr. John Mack recognizes both trauma and transformation, but he emphasizes that "Virtually *all* the abductees with whom I have worked closely have demonstrated a commitment to changing their relationship to the Earth, of living more gently on it or in greater harmony with the other creatures that live here.... Consciousness expansion and personal transformation is a basic aspect of the abduction phenomenon."[107] Karla Turner, with a mostly negative view of CE-IVs like her own, nevertheless sees that some abductees experience positive growth, something she attributes not to alien good will but to "a new resilience" under stress on the part of the abductees.[108]

Although it is seldom stated in public or in print, there is suspicion among ufologists, including abduction researchers themselves, that the great differences in interpretation of CE-IVs as traumatic or transformative rest in large part upon bias in the researcher. However, it should be recalled that Thomas Bullard found that there is not much difference by researcher in the important elements reported in hypnotic-regression abduction accounts.[109]

I think that self-selection has a great deal to do with the difference in interpretation by researcher. That is, experiencers who have a rather positive attitude about their close encounters are much more likely to go to researchers like Leo Sprinkle, known for his transformative per-

105. Bryant and Seebach, 1991.
106. Casteel, 1991B, p. 23.
107. Mack, 1994A, pp. 398-399.
108. Turner, 1994A, pp. 268-269.
109. Bullard, 1989.

spective on UFO experiences, and to attend his Rocky Mountain UFO Conferences each June in Laramie, Wyoming.

And even if researchers emphasize one value interpretation or another, it is interesting that the experiences upon which such interpretations are based do *not* vary that much. One excellent example of this occurred at a UFO conference when an abductee was asked if she wasn't traumatized by the alleged loss of not one but two fetuses taken by aliens. She replied, "No. I know they're being well taken care of. And besides, I've got lots more genetic material." The same experience might have been evaluated as a tragedy by a different experiencer or researcher. One could also conclude that the similarity of experiences in spite of differences in interpretation, argues for the objective reality of the phenomenon.

"Ask the Aliens"

With all of the doubt about the nature of the UFO abduction experience, UFO researchers Forest Crawford, John Carpenter and Tom Stults decided to give a list of questions to experiencers who seemed to get the opportunity to communicate with aliens, and then to have the experiencers ask these questions of the aliens.[110] One subject was the location of the visitors' galaxy. Answers to this varied, but two references were made to the area called M13 or the "near" vicinity, and two mentioned the specific star Tau Ceti.[111] Four different experiencers received a similar answer to the question, "How do you eat and/or drink?" It was absorption, rather than eating and swallowing.[112]

Budd Hopkins objected to Crawford's article on this on methodological grounds, saying that it was unstated how the aliens were questioned: through channeling, intuition, in dreams or during abductions.[113] He also suspected disinformation and wrote, "Never believe a thing you are told by either an alien or a government source," since both have the capacity and motivation for deception. [114]

Karla Turner is especially dubious about information, emotional impressions and visual appearances communicated during abductions. She accounts for such misleading content in terms of virtual-reality scenarios (VRS, like holograms on the *Star Trek* holodeck) when the abductee is in an altered state of consciousness, and telepathic emotional messages that are insincerely designed to control the abductee.[115]

---

110. Crawford, 1991.
111. Crawford, 1991, p. 12.
112. Crawford, 1991, pp. 13-14.
113. Hopkins, 1992A.
114. Hopkins, 1992A, p. 18.

Sometimes experiencers see through the deception, she thinks, and sometimes they don't.

As George W. Earley points out, people like Betty Andreasson Luca, who see alien abductors as angelic figures seeking to protect humanity and the Earth, are somewhat reminiscent of the contactees like George Adamski in the 1950s who received messages from benevolent "Space Brothers."[116] Although the contactees have been generally dismissed, he says, perhaps they deserve a second look.

As noted earlier, Jacobs and Hopkins have warned about possible confabulation when abductees are asked to report on alien communication, since the telepathic mode used is hard to distinguish from the internal imagination of the abductees.[117] In their same article, paralleling Hopkins objection to the "ask the aliens" project by Crawford, Carpenter and Stults, they (Jacobs and Hopkins) write, "A few researchers are in the habit of requiring the abductee, during an hypnotic session, to ask the aliens a question even though the abduction event was obviously in the past and no such question was asked at the time."[118] This, they complain, is like asking the abductee to "channel," a technique which they obviously consider scientifically useless.

Channeling

A channel is a person who serves as a medium through which entities or spirits can allegedly communicate. The term "trance channel" emphasizes that the channel or medium goes into an altered state of consciousness in order to be able to receive messages. Barbara Marciniak, well-known author of *Bringers of the Dawn*, in which she channels entities from the Pleiades, says that the trick is to relinquish control and to "get out of your own way," as the Pleiadians told her.[119] People who "serve spirit" in Spiritualist churches say the same thing about giving messages or readings, that is that one should get one's ego out of the way and clear one's mind in order to become a clear channel for spirit guides to come through.

Some UFO experiencers say that they began to receive messages from ETs after having a close encounter. One such person told me that she watched a large UFO by the side of the road with her father and many other bystanders when she was eight years old. Although she had been quite psychic even at age three, at that very moment she re-

---

115. Turner, 1994B, pp. 25-26; Turner, 1994A, p. 267.
116. Earley, 1990.
117. Jacobs and Hopkins, 1992, p. 148.
118. Jacobs and Hopkins, 1992, p. 147.
119. Marciniak, 1992, p. xvii.

ceived information from inside the craft and was even more psychic after that. Sometimes there is a delay in awareness, as in the case of Ida
M. Kannenberg, who began to "hear interior voices" in 1968 after having had a close encounter in 1940.[120]

Although the content of ET channeling could be almost anything,
one popular topic is the state of the Earth and impending "Earth changes." For example, at one conference a channel communicated to the audience from the Ashtar Command that 1995 would be a big year for ET
messages about saving the Earth.

One popular book of channeled material is *The Starseed Transmissions: An Extraterrestrial Report*, the author of which is listed as Raphael.
This is a book by Ken Carey, who explains that it is channeled from
creatures that he sometimes "considered...extraterrestrial, at other
times, angelic, occasionally...as information cells within a Galactic or-
ganism of some sort."[121] The content ranges from philosophy of personal development to statements about the planet and the universe.

One magazine consisting largely of channeled articles is *Connecting Link*.[122] In addition to articles by the Pleiadians (channeled by Barbara Marciniak), there have been pieces from a variety of other entities.
For example, Lyssa Royal channels Germane who "is from a realm of
integration that does not have a clear-cut density/dimensional level."
Darryl Anka channels Bashar, "an extraterrestrial consciousness from a
planet called Essasani. He has his own body, his own world, in an altered dimension. He is from a telepathic society." Steven Otero channels Sanaka, "the third son of the Kumara who came from Venus to
start the White Brotherhood. Among his past lives were Aaron, Elijah
and John the Baptist."

The magazine *Sedona*, a reference to the place in Arizona that is a
center of New Age interest, also has a wide variety of channeled articles. Of special interest are the pieces channeled about UFO cases from
Zoosh through Robert Shapiro. Following one article by Travis Walton
about his 1975 abduction experience, for example, Zoosh explains the
technology used by the aliens and the meaning of the encounter for
Walton and for beings involved who are referred to by Zoosh (or Shapiro) as ET police from Andromeda.[123]

Of course, such channeled material is extremely frustrating to
nuts-and-bolts ufologists who would like to truth-test UFO claims vig-
orously. One of my informants who is sympathetic to channeling said

---

120. Kannenberg, 1992, p. 7.
121. Raphael, 1982, p. 2.
122. *Connecting Link*, 1992, pp. 30-33, 36-38, 55-56, 6-8.
123. *Sedona*, 1994, pp. 20-30.

that you have to decide whether the material "rings true" or not, which carries us closer to intuition (a respected concept in New Age culture) than to normal scientific method.

Part of the problem involves our very concepts of truth and reality. In a holographic universe (See "The Holographic Perspective" on page 134.) there can be multiple perceived realities emerging from an implicate order of many possibilities. Uncertainty in quantum physics roughly parallels New Age ideas about "creating one's own reality." Barbara Marciniak's Pleiadians warn, "We refuse to be your answer. Just when you think you have us pinned down, we'll tell you something else. No one belief system can encompass all of reality in a complex universe."[124] Is this the "truth," or more of what Karla Turner would consider alien deception, or merely a product of Barbara Marciniak's altered consciousness?

---

124. Marciniak, Aug. 19, 1994.

Chapter 10

Ufology's Great Debate

Three Cultures

In Chapters 4 and 6, I discussed the attack on ufology and ufologists from normal science. In Chapters 6 and 7, I considered the attack from various quarters on normal science and on its claims to objectivity and certainty. In particular I argued that even new physics, which is respectable in mainstream normal science, contains speculations that support ideas of extraterrestrial civilization and interstellar travel, thereby undercutting the normal science claim that ufology should be considered a deviant science.

Now it is time to consider ufology itself more closely both in terms of how it relates to normal science and in terms of how it deals internally with issues of scientific legitimacy in ufological research. This turns out to be more complex than just a confrontation between normal science and ufology. It is very useful to see it as a contrast among three cultures, as David J. Hess does in his book, *Science in the New Age.*[1]

Hess explains that psychic/spiritual phenomena are seen differently by New Agers, parapsychologists, and scientific debunkers represented by CSICOP (Committee for Scientific Investigation of Claims of the Paranormal). Each of these three perspectives or cultures is skeptical of the other two and represents a kind of claim to orthodox truth.[2]

Historically, the schism between science and religion (including magic and mysticism) came about more gradually than it might seem. Although the Copernican revolution was a threat to the infallibility of religious authority, the sixteenth-century Polish astronomer Copernicus himself actually appealed in part to Hermetic (mystical) doctrine about the "spiritual exaltation of the sun" and saw divine order in the cosmos.[3] By the end of the nineteenth century, however, Darwinian evolutionary theory and geological perspectives on the great age of the

---

1. Hess, 1993.
2. Hess, 1993, pp. 11, 14-15.
3. Richard Tarnas in DiCarlo, 1996, p. 22.

Earth had put religion in a clearly marginal position. Scientists who studied psychic phenomena associated with Spiritualism in the late nineteenth century, thereby creating parapsychology, threatened both normal science and normal religion by bridging the uneasy truce-line between the two.

Debunkers in normal science often lump New Agers and parapsychologists together as both pseudo-scientific. New Agers, representing a combination of spiritualist, Eastern mystical religious and environmentalist beliefs, are interestingly both skeptical of normal science and yet also anxious to include a "new" scientific approach to phenomena that are generally considered paranormal. Parapsychologists are willing to examine psychic phenomena that are denied by normal science, but they want to distance themselves from New Agers by de-emphasizing spiritual explanations and by using strict scientific methodology.

An examination of UFO studies reveals a close parallel to the situation described by Hess for psychic/spiritual studies. Of course, CSICOP and other debunkers represent the normal science position in both areas (see Chapter 5). New Agers are also present in both. And finally there are "nuts-and bolts" scientific ufologists who are parallel to the parapsychologists and who "play the science game" (a phrase used by Mahlon W. Wagner in a comparison of ufology and parapsychology).[4]

The main difference between the two situations lies in the fact that ufology has somewhat less clear or less strict boundaries than parapsychology does, and there is a distinct "infiltration" of New Age ideas and topics into ufology. This means that there are New Age and nuts-and-bolts wings within ufology itself, with gradations and blends of perspectives in the middle. Consequently, ufology does not just debate with an external New Age community, as parapsychology might, but it has its own internal great debate about topics and methods, especially when it deals with highly strange phenomena like UFO abductions.

Seeking Legitimacy

As discussed in Chapters 2 and 4, the definition of ufology as deviant, a situation created mainly by governmental and academic authority, has made it extremely difficult for UFO researchers to legitimate their work. This means that there are no publicly acknowledged federal funds for UFO research, no college or university departments or positions allocated to UFO studies, and very few college courses that deal with ufology. Most problematic is the rejection of

4. Wagner, 1991, p. 18.

UFO topics in mainstream academic journals, as illustrated in detail by Bruce Maccabee.[5] One interesting and significant exception is the article by Spanos and others, "Close Encounters: An Examination of UFO Experiences," that appeared in *Journal of Abnormal Psychology* in 1993.[6]

A consequence of this lack of academic legitimacy has been that ufology has been presented to an interested public through the press, making a kind of end run around the scientific establishment that may engage everyone, including academics, on a popular level. One problem with this for ufology, of course, is that superficial, and especially sensationalistic treatments of UFOs tend to contribute to the ridicule of academics who risk becoming enmeshed in such coverage (see Ch. 3).

Budd Hopkins, however, follows George Bernard Shaw, pointing out that "bad publicity is a contradiction in terms."[7] In general he sees increased press coverage in the 1980s and 1990s, as well as improvement in the level of seriousness and acceptance. This includes newspaper reviews of UFO books produced by major publishers like Random House, articles in magazines like *Omni*, and television programs like *20/20*. By contrast Barry Greenwood complains that "with virtually no real connections with the scientific establishment, ufologists have taken to the media…[where] the public court of opinion has always been easier to deal with than science's…[and] the most astounding absurdities regularly get showcased to audiences of millions."[8]

At any rate, until there are greater breakthroughs in the treatment of the UFO subject in normal science, the only significant avenues of communication and debate outside of the circle of ufologists themselves lie in popular media. Consequently, the Mutual UFO Network puts forth great effort to communicate through media channels, as for example with its press conference held at the beginning of each year's international symposium.

One attempt to influence both public opinion and government through press coverage is Operation Right to Know, an organized group protest held periodically in Washington, D.C., with a call to "end the UFO cover-up." It is an issue within the UFO community whether such protest is effective, given the rather diffuse goal and lack of large numbers of protesters who attend, compared to other tactics like letter-writing campaigns and lobbying efforts directed toward particular officials on the part of UFO organizations.[9]

---

5. Maccabee, 1986, pp. 149-155.
6. Spanos and others, 1993.
7. Hopkins, 1994A, p. 10.
8. Greenwood, 1991, p. 19.
9. Whiting, 1992.

Creating Alternative Institutions

As pointed out in Chapter 2 (see section "The Effects of Delegitimation"), a lack of recognition of UFO studies by the government and by academe led to the creation of alternative institutions within which ufologists could do their work. This means especially UFO investigatory organizations and journals.

APRO (Aerial Phenomena Research Organization), under the leadership of Jim and Coral Lorenzen, existed from 1952 to 1988 and published the *APRO Bulletin*.[10] NICAP (National Investigations Committee on Aerial Phenomena) "was formed in 1956, flourished through about 1970, and declined gradually thereafter."[11] Most significant in more recent years has been MUFON (Mutual UFO Network), which began in 1969 as the Midwest UFO Network, under the leadership of Walter H. Andrus, Jr., and which publishes the *MUFON UFO Journal* for its approximately 5,000 members worldwide.[12] Other important organizations are CUFOS (Center for UFO Studies), which publishes *International UFO Reporter*, and the Society for Scientific Exploration, which publishes the *Journal of Scientific Exploration* on a variety of unexplained topics, including UFOs. There is also a variety of broader organizations, such as the International Association for New Science, that include UFOs as a topic of interest.

Since publicly acknowledged governmental funding of UFO studies is nonexistent, and there are virtually no mainstream private granting foundations that support ufology, there has been little grant money available at least until recently. FUFOR (Fund for UFO Research) has helped, and recently a coalition council of representatives from FUFOR, MUFON and CUFOS has been formed to administer significant funds provided (at least for a while) by the Bigelow Foundation.

To a great extent ufology and ufologists have depended on voluntary labors of love by dedicated, curious researchers: academics, educated professionals and amateurs, using spare time, retirement time and semi-professional, quasi-work time on the ufology circuit.

Very much like psychics and healers in the spiritual/New Age community who sell their wares and services at "expos" or fairs, some ufologists try to support their research through talks at UFO conferences (making at most a few hundred dollars per lecture or workshop) and by selling their often self-published books, tapes, and other materials. One ufologist has a 900 telephone number for UFO information.

---

10. Harder, 1994.
11. Richard Hall, 1994, p. 186.
12. Schuessler, 1994; Andrus, 1992.

Playing the Science Game

Throughout the brief history of organized ufology there have been calls for professional standards in the discipline to improve UFO studies and to bring them legitimacy in mainstream science. In 1981, Dr. J. Allen Hynek, the recognized father of ufology, put out a call "to set up a code of professional standards, a code of ethics for investigators, researchers, and writers on the subject.... Support for serious research will come if we can but present Ufology to the world in a dignified and professional manner."[13]

More serious ufologists are still complaining, both in the U.S. and in other countries like Brazil and Russia, that scientific standards are too low in the discipline. For example, Dr. Stuart Appelle, a psychologist and MUFON consultant, recommends stricter editorial policy in the *MUFON UFO Journal* to improve writing style and to reduce "unfettered speculation, and the use of innuendo or gratuitous *ad hominem* argument."[14] Michael Swords, a historian of science, points out that the lack of a sanctioned, disciplined community of UFO scholars within mainstream science has led to the involvement of amateur researchers, some of whom "do good, thoughtful work, but most do not. Rogue research...ravages the data, unchecked by any higher court of discussion and analysis."[15]

There is no doubt that establishing scientific standards and boundaries is difficult in a discipline like ufology that is so interdisciplinary, eclectic and dependent for support upon a grass-roots community of amateurs who buy the books and attend the conferences. I recall two MUFON members telling me one time just to collect data on a case that had come to my attention and to never mind the fact that I had not taken a test on the *MUFON Field Investigator's Manual*. They made it clear that some investigators are casual about methodology.

The other perspective one could take on the situation is that ufology would never have progressed as far as it has without volunteers. As Marc Davenport puts it, "With very few exceptions, ufologists are amateurs.... Using their own resources for support and their curiosity for incentive, they have compiled and painstakingly documented an immense—and impressive—amount of valuable raw data over the last 40 years."[16] Although I am in favor of improving methodology and scholarship in UFO studies, I cannot help but be skeptical of the attitude that

13. Christensen, 1988, p. 13.
14. Appelle, 1994, p. 17.
15. Swords, 1992A, p. 203.
16. Davenport, 1992B, p. 46.

normal science will graciously invite ufologists into the club just as soon as they clean up their scientific act.

When I heard Dr. Richard F. Haines, one of the model scholars in ufology, appeal to the large audience at the 1994 MUFON International UFO Symposium in Austin, Texas, to get involved in their own research, I was surprised. Was this encouraging more sloppy amateur involvement, or just a nice gesture to make MUFON appear less elitist? After all, MUFON would be fortunate if all of their consultants did UFO research, but should all MUFON members or conference attendees be encouraged to start their own projects? His article in the September 1994 issue of the *MUFON UFO Journal* showed that he was serious.[17] As one might expect, in this article he laid out an excellent list of specific research questions and suggested sources of data. But then he added to his methodological rigor a democratic inclusion of amateurs by saying, "Don't let anyone tell you that you aren't qualified. You probably are!"[18]

One scientific tool for UFO researchers that is being developed is the centrally available data base. This is especially important in the controversial area of abduction research, in which complaints have been made that some researchers hoard cases they might write about and trim off the cases that don't fit their theories. One such data base is the MUFON Abduction Transcription Project coordinated by Dan Wright beginning in 1993. Progress is also being made with files on possibly related phenomena like crop circles.

Of course, computer technology that provides ready access to data does not necessarily combine with expertise on statistical analysis and scholarly interpretation. However, there has been a grand proliferation of data along the information superhighway. There are already dozens of computer bulletin boards available on the MufoNet Bulletin Board Systems Network with names like Space Link, Crystal Cave, The Encounter and Astral.[19] These systems provide all sorts of recent sighting news, research queries and idea sharing. There are also Internet news groups such as "alt.alien.visitors".

Another aspect of professionalism that a scholarly discipline must address is ethics. Both MUFON and CUFOS have approved the Ethics Code for Abduction Experience Investigation and Treatment written by Mark Rodeghier and others that developed out of the work done at a 1992 abduction conference at MIT and was completed by 1994. Such

---

17. Haines, 1994B.
18. Haines, 1994B, p. 15.
19. Komar and Theer, 1992, p. 11.

codes are designed to protect subjects from mistreatment and to protect researchers and therapists from charges of malpractice.

One more important institution of scholarly activity is the conference. As I have already pointed out, conferences are an important source of financial support for the UFO community. Unlike most academic conferences, where there are many sessions going on simultaneously, attended by fellow academics, UFO conferences usually have only one speaker presenting at a time, and most of the audience consists of amateur ufologists and some people who have little knowledge of UFOs, but come to be enlightened and entertained. Vendors sell books (including ones written by the presenters), t-shirts, tapes and other items, providing table rent to help support the UFO organization or entrepreneur.

Since UFO conference attendees and even some of the presenters are not always highly "professional" ufologists, there is sometimes an inclination to hold preconference meetings or even entire conferences that are limited to a small circle of more serious or prominent researchers. Of course, this tends to give rise to complaints of elitism from those who are excluded. One such by-invitation-only conference was the TREAT (Treatment and Research of Experienced Anomalous Trauma) conference held at Virginia Polytechnic Institute and State University, February 1-4, 1990. This was an abduction conference, as was the Abduction Study Conference held at MIT June 13-17, 1992.

Chair of the MIT conference committee David E. Pritchard explained that the conference was closed in order to be able to select attendees for their rational contributions and for their honor in keeping discussions confidential.[20] He argued that experiencers and researchers both needed to be protected from irresponsible media coverage, and said that only written contributions, not oral presentations, would be included in the published proceedings.

When conferences are open, sometimes there is at least some social control applied to keep activities in line with standards of professionalism in the organization. For example, the yearly MUFON International UFO Symposium is announced in the journal with the comment that "New Age paraphernalia is not permitted" at vendors' tables.

I also observed one person in the audience making a mini-speech rather than merely asking a question of the speakers; this person was asked to curb his behavior. The same individual was permitted by the hotel to put up a table in the lobby area where he had literature expressing his very unorthodox views on UFOs, and a representative of MU-

---

20. David E. Pritchard, 1994, p. 20-21.

FON announced to the audience that this table was not part of the conference.

Also speakers are chosen by MUFON leadership, and this leads to some individuals complaining about not being included. One person was included, but was asked not to discuss a prominent case of an experiencer who allegedly channeled aliens because of the New Age emphasis in the material.

Of course, some other conferences are more New-Age oriented, such as the Rocky Mountain UFO Conference held annually at Laramie, Wyoming, and organized by Dr. Leo Sprinkle. Vendors are more likely to sell "New Age paraphernalia" like crystals, and many of the presenters make references to the products and services that they are there selling as vendors as well. Speakers are not afraid to present channeled information and may even channel right in front of the audience. And yet some of the sessions are "closed" in the sense that no one is allowed to take notes or make audio or video recordings. This protects the privacy of experiencers for whom the conference is designed, a similar theme to that referred to by David Pritchard at the MIT conference.

Boundary Maintenance

One thing that makes it so difficult to play the science game in ufology, as should be obvious from material in Chapters 4 and 9, is the persistence of apparently psychic and other paranormal elements associated with UFO reports, elements considered by some to be dangerously New Age, and, therefore, not scientifically respectable to study. As philosopher Michael Grosso puts it, UFOs reportedly "affect radar, cause burns, leave traces in the ground and at the same time pass through walls, appear and disappear like ghosts, defy gravity, assume variable and symbolic shapes, and strike deep chords of psychic, mystic, or prophetic sentiment."[21]

Perhaps some of the more "paranormal" aspects can be seen as an extension of an advanced technology, one that might even be capable of telepathy. Nevertheless, many ufologists are concerned that the stranger or "flakier" aspects under consideration go too far beyond the boundary of respectable nuts-and-bolts, scientific ufology.

As Chris Rutkowski points out, mainstream "North American ufology seems to have a definite slant towards nuts-and-bolts theories..." in contrast to "the 'preternatural' bias of European ufolo-

---

21. Grosso, 1988, p. 10.

gists."[22] Richard Hall is clearly engaging in an attempt at boundary maintenance, trying to keep (American) scientific ufology respectable, when he writes, "The biggest problem in ufology is the unscientific, mystical, muddleheaded New Age element that tends to make a shambles of the enterprise with completely uncritical and illogical outpourings. As long as we passively embrace them rather than openly disown them, we deserve as a field not to be taken seriously."[23] James Harder spoke in a similar fashion about "new-age prophets and channelers...having a field day with little constraint from scientific logic or reasoning."[24]

Jerome Clark emphasizes that there is plenty of evidence that UFOs are "the product of an extraordinary technology," and that therefore "the scientific method remains our best hope for dealing with the UFO phenomenon in rational fashion."[25] If UFOs are really some paranormal phenomenon beyond science, he says, then science ought to ignore them. This draws the issue nicely. Can there be a science of the truly "paranormal?" More on this a bit later. To Clark, ufologists like John Mack who focus on high-strangeness abduction cases (and minimize the importance of physical evidence), make ufology vulnerable to the criticism that it is a religious quest instead of a scientific enterprise.[26]

Bruce Maccabee is another ufologist who stresses the importance of nuts-and-bolts methodology. In praising the Gulf Breeze Research Team, he stated that "their approach...is not that of the UFO cultist or contactee. There are no rituals, no prayers to higher powers, no messages from the space brothers, no guru explaining the occult.... Instead there are cameras...video recorders...angle measurements and triangulations, [etc.]."[27]

Of course, the issue of nuts-and-bolts vs. New Age in ufology is more complex than just a contrast between observers using photographic equipment and gurus channeling aliens. There are questions of methodology, especially involving the difference between physical evidence and witness reports (see Chapters 8 and 9); New Age interpretations are more likely to come from the latter than from the former. And there are different interpretations of the abduction phenomenon (see Ch. 9), some more positive and spiritual (New Age) than others.

22. Rutkowski, 1990, p. 166.
23. Richard Hall, 1993B, p. 7.
24. Harder, 1994, p. 234.
25. Clark, 1993C, p. 3.
26. Clark, 1994A, 1994B.
27. Maccabee, 1991D, p. 16.

If the mainstream of ufology is more nuts-and-bolts than New Age, then what New Age beliefs or activities provoke enough reaction to have them labeled as deviant? One example can be found in the removal of Donald M. Ware from the MUFON Board of Directors effective June 1, 1993. According to Walter Andrus, Director of MUFON, "This action stemmed from continued advisory statements by members of the Executive Committee to Don that he refrain from mailing books to Board members and Eastern Regional State Directors espousing 'channeling' philosophies and techniques over a two-year period."[28]

Walter Andrus (see biography) explained to me in a personal interview that MUFON does not try to control people's thoughts, and indeed some of the material presented in MUFON conferences and publications does not exactly fit the MUFON perspective. Nevertheless the goal of the organization is scientific investigation, and the job of the board is not to proselytize for New Age techniques like channeling that he sees as having no scientific merit.

Conflict can also arise in the context of local group meetings. Roberta Puhalski complained in 1994 that in her previous year of working with UFO abductee groups, "Instead of the usual group therapy atmosphere of caring and sharing, New Age material slowly filtered its way into these meetings.... Within months people were aligning with one alien group or another, and arguing with each other!"[29]

Although the situation is complex, it is evident that issues of methodology (such as the analysis of landing traces, use of witness reports and channeling) are intertwined with issues of interpretation and ideology. And, finally, there are competing groups with differing scientific, therapeutic and even religious orientations.

For ufologists acting in the role of scientist it is impossible to ignore all questions of the ultimate religious or philosophical significance of the UFO phenomenon. However, they do try to adhere to standards of appropriate scientific method and attitude. It is amusing to listen to ufologists when they present high-strangeness material. They often say something like, "I'm no New-Ager, but..." as if they were in danger of crossing some border between science and religion merely by considering evidence that sounds absurd or paranormal.

John Mack, Harvard psychiatrist and author of *Abduction*, is not afraid to consider high-strangeness reports. On many occasions at UFO conferences, he has stated that he doesn't know where to draw the line

28. Andrus, 1993, p. 23.
29. Puhalski, 1994, p. 15.

when collecting accounts from abductees. Past lives, people who claim to *be* aliens? Why are these things any harder to believe than the rest of the abduction scenario, including floating through walls, telepathic communication with aliens and the on-board examinations? It's all absurd from our Western rational, scientific point of view, he says, partly because of the "core belief in our culture...[in] the total separation of the spirit and the physical world."[30]

MUFON State Director for Louisiana, W. L. Garner, in an article appropriately entitled "MUFON Versus the New Age," states clearly that the core issue is one of methodology: "UFOs, extraterrestrial aliens, abductions, telepathy, out-of-body experiences, etc., are all valid areas for scientific investigation, but scientific investigation demands the protocols of specific research objectives, techniques, and proofs."[31] These protocols, Garner says, "are well established in the *MUFON Field Investigator's Manual*," and are in contrast to "grandiose tales...of otherworldly experiences presented as unquestionable, factual events." Emphasis on the latter "turns your organization into a cult."

This is precisely the problem that Clark has with Mack, whom Clark considers to be on more of a religious than a scientific quest for the truth about abductions. "Mack," he says, "shows only modest interest in investigative efforts...[that would indicate] that something is going on beyond hypnotically induced fantasy."[32] Recall that other researchers like John Carpenter *have* gathered physical evidence and multiple-witness corroboration of abductions (see Chapters 8 and 9) in a manner that would answer Clark's objections.

Although it is to be expected that many nuts-and-bolts ufologists would have the same reaction to Mack's *Abduction* as Clark, Timothy H. Heaton, a professor of Earth sciences, takes an interesting, more sympathetic view. First, he recognizes that Mack is in trouble for dragging in "all the shady New Age phenomena...from shamanism to reincarnation...with little critical analysis or justification."[33] Heaton says, "It took someone with Mack's genius to realize that the abduction phenomenon is bound to change our whole epistemology as well as our world view, and therefore a 'scientific' study did not seem appropriate."[34] Mack broke the rules of science and just let the experiencers tell their tales of spiritual growth. Heaton thinks that this "severs the UFO phenomenon from scientific rationalism, and it may be that we can no longer see UFOs in isolation from other psychic phenomena."[35]

---

30. Mack, 1994A, p. 418.
31. Garner, 1993, p. 13.
32. Clark, 1994B, p. 8.
33. Heaton, 1994, p. 13.
34. Heaton, 1994, p. 14.

It seems to me that the fundamental question here should be one of methodology, rather than ideology, although unfortunately the latter often clouds the former. If we take Garner literally, remember that any topic should be open for investigation, no matter how absurd it sounds. The question seems to be whether the accounts of people like Mack's subjects under hypnosis should be taken seriously, even when they start getting into past lives and other "New Age" topics.

Once these accounts are collected, we still have a problem of interpretation of evidence. Clark would not give the more fantastic accounts a great deal of credence without corroborating physical or multiple-witness evidence, or at least some waking rather than hypnotic accounts. Mack, on the other hand, lets the accounts speak for themselves and heads toward an explanation involving spiritual transformation of our species and the rescuing of the Earth environment. At this point we have arrived at a debate over ideology (New Age vs. nuts-and-bolts) through the process of arguing over the *interpretation* of evidence. Oh, well.

Perhaps it is really the ideology at the end of the road that motivates researchers more than they would like to admit in their decisions about what types of evidence and interpretations of evidence to accept. Leo Sprinkle says, "Over the years I have become less excited about physical evidence, because I believe that we shall never accumulate enough physical evidence to 'convince' ourselves of what we know is happening: gradual awareness of ET/ED [extradimensional] interaction."[36] He goes on to discuss the insufficiency of biological, psychological and social evidence, and then notes, "Today I seek 'spiritual' evidence." Although he, "like many UFO contactees," is tolerant of other types of data gathering. "We believe that someday it will be okay to focus on channeling activities and interaction with ET/ED and humankind."[37]

A nuts-and-bolts ufologist might criticize Dr. Sprinkle for letting his New Age bias determine his approach to research, and might consider Leo's claimed UFO experiences to make him less "objective." On the other hand, would anyone with a CE-III or CE-IV experience need physical evidence to "convince himself/herself of what he/she knows is happening," to paraphrase Dr. Sprinkle? Are these personal experiences not evidence? All of this should remind us of the basic paradigms and "reality tunnels" of normal science (see Ch. 6) that "bias" our judgment of what is acceptable evidence. See also Chapter 4 on how ufolo-

35. Heaton, 1994, p. 15.
36. Sprinkle, 1992.
37. Sprinkle, 1992.

gists come to question this bias largely due to their own UFO experiences.

Although it is perfectly understandable that some researchers would prefer to focus on certain methods over others due to their own ideological preferences, one might hope that a spirit of open scientific inquiry would allow the coexistence of several approaches without premature closure. A quotation from Richard Hall, whose comment about the "muddleheaded New Age element" I referred to earlier, would seem appropriate here: "Despite having the reputation of being a 'nuts and bolts' advocate [believing in extraterrestrial intelligence (ETI), or spaceships from another planet], I do not by any means rule out alternative explanations...[including] denizens of a 'parallel universe,' time travellers, or 'others'.... Science has to do with suspended judgment...not the 'rush to judgment' that all too often prevails in the UFO research community."[38]

New Science: Methodologies for the Mysterious

By now it should be clear that ufologists need to come to grips with the issue of nuts-and-bolts vs. New Age. I am not saying that ufology should "settle" the matter collectively, because that would imply some disciplinary decree, and I much prefer open inquiry and controversial tension to dogmatism. All I am saying is that ufologists who are interested in increasing their understanding of the UFO phenomenon should contemplate what this all means in terms of the sociology of knowledge (or philosophy of science).

Essentially, what is going on is a pull in two directions. One pull is toward standard science (playing the science game), and the other is toward the more apparently paranormal, or high-strangeness aspects of UFO reports. In order to maximize legitimacy in mainstream, normal science, ufologists should just forget about people who claim to channel aliens, to be married to aliens, or to remember past lives as aliens. In order to maximize learning about UFOs, however, ufologists may have to follow John Mack into the never-never land of altered states of consciousness and bizarre personal experiences.

As Mack says, how do we know where to draw the line? It's all absurd, really. Even a sighting that follows the old joke about the type of report acceptable to NICAP, "Engineer sees light in sky," becomes silly when you get down to imagining the UFO behind the light and the alien driving the UFO. And yet, when new physicists talk about a ten-

---

38. Richard Hall, 1992A.

dimensional universe in superstring theory, can anything be considered absurd?

Starting from the perspective of methodology, ufologists can focus on physical scientific instrumentation with cameras, radar, chemical analysis, etc. Or they can move one step from nuts-and-bolts into psychological and sociological testing of UFO witnesses. Or they can move another step into spiritual interpretations of channeled messages from aliens. This does not really exhaust all the possibilities, but the point is that each step departs farther from "hard" science, but gets closer to the ultimate reality (or fantasy if you prefer) behind the phenomenon. Each step is a risk. One option is to take minimal risk and just to wait for a UFO crash or an alien visit to the U.N. Of course, *any* study of UFOs is a risk in one sense, since even the nuts-and-bolts perspective is usually sneered at by debunkers.

Is there any way to move in the direction of studying the more paranormal aspects without walking off the pier and drowning in a sea of unconfirmable, imaginary realities? Is there any way to do a science of the paranormal? Jerome Clark, as noted earlier, would seem to be saying no: UFOs represent a high technology and not something "paranormal"; if they are really paranormal, then science should ignore them.[39]

However, there is another answer. It is to extend science beyond its normal boundaries and to call it "new science," as in the International Association for New Science (IANS) with its headquarters in Fort Collins, Colorado. IANS declares in its statement of purpose that its "goal is to unite individuals of a New Science philosophy and initiate a paradigm shift in science and health care…[to] help the evolvement of mankind in a manner that will complement and preserve the natural order of the universe." The new paradigm includes an acceptance of "the reality of [a variety of] anomalous phenomena" such as alternative medicine, spiritual and psychic phenomena, "new" energy, new physics and mind/matter interaction.

Having attended two IANS conferences, I have been curious as to what is actually new or not "normal" in "New Science." After all, new physics is by now normal or legitimate in physics, as, for example, in regard to quantum physics or speculation about hyperspace and wormholes (see Ch. 5), although some New Age interpretations of new physics principles to account for spiritual/psychic phenomena are not.

Generally the answer I have gotten to my question is that part of new science is merely an application of standard scientific methods and

39. Clark, 1993C.

measurements to topics considered too flaky in normal science. Parapsychological studies of ESP and psychokinesis using laboratory methods and statistical analysis would illustrate this. However, some new science involves a search for new methods of knowing (dare we call them scientific?), recognizing that meditative techniques, altered states of consciousness and channeling may have to serve in the absence of other ways of measuring forces or frequencies that escape present-day instruments.

An examination of the literature in New Age book stores would show that "New Age" is largely a reframing of folk and nonWestern culture (on health, spirituality and the environment) for the consumption of Westerners with liberal doses of science to legitimate it, and a reframing of science (especially new physics) in terms of a more holistic/mystical view of humans and the universe that is more satisfying. This is not much different from what new science is all about.

Is there ultimately a continuity between the normal and the paranormal, one that we fail to see at this point because of the limitation of current scientific measurements? Dr. Brian O'Leary, an astronomer/physicist who is one of the founders of IANS, recognizes that some scholars consider the new physics a map for the paranormal. He himself is uncertain about this; but he emphasizes that "inner and outer space are constantly interacting."[40] In other words, humans and their outer, physical world, seem to interact with their inner or mental/spiritual states.

It strikes me that even without using "paranormal" methodologies, like channeling *per se*, we can develop some "methodologies for the mysterious" that are extensions of normal physical and behavioral science. My overall strategy is to use a multi-disciplinary approach in order to test a variety of "normal" explanations for "paranormal" phenomena. What escapes through the filter of normal explanations is a residue of possibly paranormal or at least nonordinary phenomena.

This is what I did in my study of *Chinese Ghosts and ESP*.[41] It became clear that Chinese culture was not sufficient to explain the firsthand apparition reports I collected in Hong Kong. In spite of the Chinese expectations that ghosts would produce often dire physical effects, such as injuring humans, only one of my 176 cases involved an evidently physical effect. Therefore, I was able to discount a cultural explanation and to find support for what appears to be a culture-free theory of ghosts that comes from Western parapsychology, based upon

40. O'Leary, 1989, pp. 44, 52-53.
41. Emmons, 1982.

ghost reports in Europe and America, namely that apparitions are a
form of ESP (almost always) without any physical component. I also
collected ghost rumors and ghost stories in Hong Kong, showing how
folklore and literary processes produce something very different from
the first-hand reports of actual experiences.

Likewise, folklorist Thomas E. Bullard has done studies of UFO abduction accounts and found that first-hand abduction reports do not fit
the usual patterns found in folklore.[42] He and others have also compared reports gathered by different hypnotists and compared reports
under hypnosis with ones derived from conscious recall, finding no
consistent pattern of differences.[43] In other words, abduction accounts
have essentially escaped through the filters testing for these explanations: folklore, hypnotic fantasy or false memory syndrome (FMS), and
bias of the researcher (also linked to FMS). Other checks of the validity
of abduction accounts have involved looking for corroborating physical evidence, related UFO sightings and multiple witnesses, although
these do not necessarily validate the entire account.

There are still other normal methodologies for the mysterious that
we might consider, including comparative content analysis of UFO/
alien material produced by several channelers. If common threads develop that seem not to be merely a shared New Age culture among
channelers, then we may be able to give some verification for the unseen. See Chapter 9, however, for a discussion of how difficult this
might be, especially if the Pleiadians are trying to play games with us.

And, of course, there may be elements of the paranormal that really do escape scientific verification of any kind, especially if there are
multiple, independent realities, or if mind and ideas are all there is and
the physical is just an illusion. If we are all creating our own holograms,
then no wonder there are so many synchronicities in our lives, and
maybe we should stop trying to explain them in terms of one physical
reality. What is so disturbing about this paragraph from a scientific perspective is that it suggests that we may have to be satisfied with ambiguity and never get to some single ultimate Truth. From a more New
Age perspective maybe we should laugh at this "knowledge addiction," lighten up a little and, as Leo Sprinkle put it as early as 1975, learn
how to "play" instead of "working" so hard at the job of UFO research.[44]

_____

42. Bullard, 1991.
43. Bullard, 1989.
44. Sprinkle, 1975, pp. 42-43.

Chapter 11

At the Threshold

The Quest and the Question

Is the scientific quest for understanding of the UFO phenomenon nearly complete? Are we at the threshold of solving the enigma?

Sometimes ufologists have made premature claims that something big will happen soon, some "case of the century" or "October surprise" (government revelation) that will "blow the lid off the UFO phenomenon." It almost sounds like millennial religious prophecy. The usually cautious and reasonably skeptical Jerome Clark wrote in 1988, "We soon, I think, will know what UFOs are.... Our long quest is almost over."[1]

By contrast to the anticipation of an impending solution, there have also been premature reports of the demise of the phenomenon and of interest in it. Keith Thompson wrote in 1991 that "some longtime observers have concluded that, other than as mythology, the UFO phenomenon is for the most part over—for good,"[2] based on a decline in both sightings and media coverage.

It seems hard to believe that nowadays either of these two predictions could be embraced with certainty. J. Allen Hynek expected in the late 1940s that he could explain UFOs away by meteorological or other known causes, and that interest in UFOs would go away in several months. But the phenomenon has proved to be far more mysterious, complex and enduring.

Part of the problem is that UFOs have often been seen as a manageable mystery susceptible to being cracked by good sleuthing.[3] In 1994, I heard side comments by speakers at the MUFON International UFO Symposium to the effect that MUFON would put itself out of business if and when it "solved" the UFO enigma, as if it were a simple question

---

1. Clark, 1988, p. 72.
2. Keith Thompson, 1991, p. 245.
3. Theresa M. Barclay in Barclay and Barclay (Eds.), 1993, pp. 127-128.

rather than a complex one requiring ongoing study as in other academic disciplines.

In fact, not only is the UFO question complex, but the boundaries of the issue are not even clear. What exactly qualifies as a UFO? Anything unknown in the sky? What about a strange object on the ground? Does it have to be extraterrestrial? How about small flying balls of light? Should we consider crop circles, animal mutilations and religious vision cases, like the one at Fatima in 1917, as part of the phenomenon? It is difficult to expect answers when we are still unsure of the question.

"Why Am I Confused?"

I often tell my students at Gettysburg College, "If you are not confused by this material, then you don't really understand it." Just because an intellectual puzzle is problematic, this is no reason to discard it. The important thing is to try to understand why it is so confusing.

It turns out that there are some very good reasons for frustration in ufology. The more data or information one gets, the more questions arise. When you open one door, you see a room full of bizarre, otherworldly evidence, and five more doors leading to other rooms full of even stranger stuff.

Many ufologists suspect that disinformation is a cause of much of the confusion. As Vince Johnson puts it, "The visitors could be deliberately adding so much 'noise' that the 'signal' is lost.... The bogus platitudes, prophecies, purposes, and places of origin that they reportedly communicate to contactees hinder any attempt to correlate the data."[4] Recall in Chapter 9 Budd Hopkins' critique of the "Ask the Aliens" project, in which he said that neither aliens nor government sources can be relied on to tell the truth about anything regarding UFOs. Karla Turner also considers aliens to be untrustworthy, as she makes clear in her book, *Taken*.[5]

If some ufologists mistrust aliens/Visitors, even if they trust the humans who carry their alleged messages, then they mistrust the U.S. government even more. Although I have deliberately sidestepped most of the controversy over alleged government cover-ups in this book, I must say that I consider it very likely that there is at least a little fire under all of the smoke.

I don't know if the government has crashed saucers or alien bodies, or if it has secret agreements with ETs, or if it hires ufologists to create

---

4. Vince Johnson, 1993, p. 5.
5. Turner, 1994A.

false UFO data. However, I think that it is very likely that some of the endless black-marked lines of text released under the Freedom of Information Act to ufologists like Stanton Friedman contain important information on government involvement in UFO matters. I also tend to believe some of the insiders who have told me of their own observations of UFOs and of UFO data when they were associated with the military.

One other source of noise is cultural elaboration of UFO experiences and evidence on the part of human beings. Even without any intention to distort, experiencers are bound to be influenced to some degree by what they remember about UFOs and aliens in popular culture. And anything they see they have to process within their own cultural categories and with the use of their human senses and mental powers.

There is no clear or consistent pattern we can detect from this elaboration. On the one hand, a person who sees an unusual light in the sky sometimes honestly jumps to the erroneous conclusion that it is a UFO (alien craft), when in fact it is the planet Venus or just an airplane light. On the other hand, some UFO experiencers are so baffled by what they see that they have great difficulty describing it in human terms. One example of this is the way people struggle to describe the color and texture of lights on a UFO. "It was alive like no other light I have ever seen" would be such a response.

In spite of all these difficulties, the UFO phenomenon is still well worth investigating. Of course, it takes dedication to persist under the ridicule of normal science, but there is good reason to believe that the difficulty in reaching solutions is due to the toughness of the problem (with perhaps some deliberately deceptive road signs twisted around by alien pranksters or devious humans), rather than merely due to the absurdity of the question or to the delusions of the researchers.

Some Attempted Answers

As noted above, I do not think that the UFO phenomenon is a simple question with a simple answer. If I did, it would be analogous to claiming that psychology will put itself out of business once it answers the simple question of how the brain works. However, there have been some attempts on the part of ufologists to create theoretical frameworks that may help to make sense of the subject even if they don't "solve" the mystery.

On one level it may seem that we already have the general answers, and that the main question is simply, "Do you believe in them or not?" Basically people want to know who they are, where they are from, and what they are up to. Well, they seem to be high-tech human-oid visitors from outer space who want to check us out, but not reveal themselves too much. How's that for an answer?

Well, perhaps, but this statement already claims too much for some and says too little for almost everybody. And, yes, it is still hard to swallow, even if it is correct, because of its enormous implications.

Chapters 4 and 7 contain discussions of the Drake equation and of the assumption on the part of most astronomers that there are plenty of high-tech civilizations even in our galaxy. Although there have been objections to the idea that we may have been visited by ETs, due to the great distances involved and due to the speed-of-light limit, respectable speculations in new physics about such things as wormholes seem to negate these arguments.

It may well be that future physicists and astronomers will discover that faster-than-light travel is possible or that there can be visitors even from many other galaxies beyond our own, or that the Drake equation was too conservative in other ways. My point is merely that even with our current state of knowledge (or "normal" speculation), it does not seem reasonable to argue that ETs could not get here. Nevertheless, the extraterrestrial hypothesis (ETH) for the origin of UFOs and their occupants has some opposition even in ufology.

Michael D. Swords, the most prominent proponent and explicator of the ETH in ufology, has taken on the various objections to it, including the distance argument.[6] One objection is that the reported humanoids look too much like us. Contrary to the evolutionary dissimilarity argument upon which this idea is based, Swords' evolutionary convergence (or parallelism) perspective argues that there are good functional reasons to expect similar evolutionary paths anywhere in the universe.[7]

Other barriers to accepting the ETH in ufology are the doubts that any distant society would go to all that trouble to get here (for what purpose?) and the observations of so many UFOs that visit repeatedly and that would seem therefore not to be coming from such a great distance. Swords creates an ingenious scenario in which ET intelligence wants to explore for nonmaterial reasons, including mental curiosity and growth, and does so not directly, but indirectly through robotics and nano-technology (microminiature machines that can reproduce and build at the end of the trip), keeping track of things through some advanced type of telepresence (mind-to-machine connection).[8]

6. Swords, 1992C, p. 6.
7. Swords, 1991.
8. Swords, 1992C, pp. 7-8.

One reader of this manuscript suggested to me that these craft may be able to dematerialize and rematerialize at great distances, just as some mystics in India, Sai Baba for example, seem to be able to materialize beads out of nothing (or out of spirit). I wanted to object that this had no known scientific foundation, but then I remembered ideas of nonlocal connections in the new physics and threw up my hands. There may indeed be a great many things in this universe that escape our current imagination.

Another major theoretical perspective on UFOs is that they are from our own future, as explained by Marc Davenport in his book, *Visitors from Time: The Secret of the UFOs*.[9] It is fascinating how many aspects of UFO reports fit nicely into this model: strange electromagnetic effects distorted by space-time manipulations, ET fascination with time and our conceptions of time, anachronisms in dress and in material objects linked to "Men in Black" (MIBs), etc. Vince Johnson sees the "Visitors" as members of a future population coming back to gather genetic material to fix itself after a long period of doing without natural selection.[10]

Both Davenport and Johnson recognize that there are troublesome paradoxes associated with the idea of time travel (see Ch. 7), including the risk of wrecking one's own present by altering the past upon which it is based (as in the popular film, *Back to the Future*). Davenport sees Men in Black as a future police force attempting to restrict unauthorized UFO trips back to our time and to minimize their effects on the future by covering up the UFO evidence.[11] Johnson also interprets the Visitors' attempts to make abductees forget their experiences as a safeguard against undue influence on abductee lives and against subsequent changes in the future.[12] "Alien" disinformation, he thinks, may be deliberate noise to keep us confused, which is the next best thing to ignorant.

Although the time-travel hypothesis (TTH), if correct, could mean that no UFOs come from long *distances*, it is possible that both the ETH and the TTH are true. Davenport pointed this out to me when he said that some people mistakenly took his book to mean that *no* UFOs were extraterrestrial (from other star systems).[13]

Perhaps the most prominent theory about UFOs in the 1990s has been the abduction genetic/hybrid theory (AGT) of which the main proponents are Budd Hopkins and David M. Jacobs.[14] Although an

---

9. Davenport, 1992B.
10. Vince Johnson, 1993.
11. Davenport, 1992B, pp. 217-241.
12. Vince Johnson, 1993.
13. Davenport, personal communication, Oct. 11, 1994.

ETH is generally assumed under this theory, the main focus is on what they are up to rather than on where they are from. Of course, many objections have been leveled against the AGT, especially in terms of the interpretation of witness reports (see Ch. 9).

Some ufologists also think it absurd that so many visitations would occur for experimentation purposes, when it would be simple to take a few DNA samples and work with those. Hopkins' perspective is that the genetic manipulation involves the altering of individuals and the creation of hybrids, rather than a simple experiment for purposes of acquiring scientific knowledge.

Be that as it may, the AGT is highly significant in its implications for alien/human interaction. Linda Moulton Howe adds to this "alien harvest" of human genetic material the phenomenon of animal mutilations and the collection especially of tissue from cattle, allegedly, according to one of her informants, in a program necessary for alien survival.[15]

Jerome Clark has stated that abduction reports suggest "that we are at the mercy of utterly alien beings who...do not especially care about us and apparently regard us as a lesser form of life."[16] This unsettling perspective contrasts, of course, with the view of ufologists like John Mack who says that "consciousness expansion and personal transformation is a basic aspect of the abduction phenomenon."[17]

Transformation of consciousness and spirit (TCS) could be the label for another major theory of UFOs then. TCS contrasts especially with the trauma perspective (see Ch. 9) that is emphasized in the AGT, but it does not necessarily contradict any other theories, like ETH or TTH. We could also call TCS the NAH (New Age Hypothesis). Its emphasis is less on material questions of where the Visitors are from and how they got here, and more on what all of these delicious mysteries mean for the development of self, species and the universe.

In addition to these major theories or perspectives in ufology, there are other views that emphasize the noise or deception itself as an answer, rather than merely as something to be penetrated to get to the answer. Of course, there are many conspiracy theories, all of which I have declared to be largely outside the framework of this book, including theories of government/alien connections. However, it is at least worth mentioning Jacques Vallée, the ufologist who has written several books

---

14. Hopkins, 1987; Jacobs, 1992B.
15. Howe, 1991, pp. 145-146.
16. Clark, 1988, p. 71.
17. Mack, 1994A, pp. 398-399.

relevant to deception hypotheses, including *Messengers of Deception* (1980) and *Revelations: Alien Contact and Human Deception* (1991).[18]

In a 1990 interview with Keith Thompson, Vallée explained his view of the absurd and mysterious body of UFO information and disinformation available to ufologists. "I have been led to conclude that there is a spiritual control system for human consciousness and that paranormal phenomena like UFOs are one of its manifestations."[19] Vallée's unorthodox, eclectic ufology consists of high suspicion of the ETH, the thought that a combination of worldly and other-worldly forces may be duping us for good or ill, and a willingness to widen his view of UFOs to pick up possibly related phenomena like fairies and other "little folk" in world folklore.

Another UFO theory involving deception is the idea that the whole phenomenon may be a game. David Barclay thinks that we may be caught up in a virtual-reality scenario, but unlike Karla Turner, who thinks that ETs put on displays to prevent us from knowing their real intent (see Ch. 5 and 7), he dares to speculate that we may be holograms (see Ch. 7 on the holographic perspective) in their computer game, thereby challenging our basic views on the nature of what is physically real.[20] Swords presents something very similar in his suggestion that ETs may be playing games with us through telepresence and restricted displays in front of humans in order to manipulate us without destroying our viability as a species.[21]

Limiting Assumptions and Leaps of Logic

I respect the various attempts at UFO theorizing, learn from them, and would like to see all the contributors get medals. Having said that, I agree with David Barclay that ufology contains "too many unwarranted anthropocentric assumptions masquerading as indisputable inferences."[22] This doesn't mean that Barclay himself, debunkers or I am free of such assumptions either.

If our assumptions are really "anthropocentric" (human-centered), then good luck on any of us eliminating them all. Some of them, however, are probably more institutionally created, by the collective wisdom either of normal science or of ufology or both.

Some of these assumptions were seen in the previous section, for example the idea that ETs are just too far away ever to get here. This

18. Vallée, 1980, 1991.
19. Keith Thompson, 1991, p. 194.
20. David Barclay in Barclay and Barclay (Eds.), 1993, pp. 182-189.
21. Swords, 1992C, pp. 7-8.
22. David Barclay in Barclay and Barclay (Eds.), 1993, p. 176.

was based on the axiom that no object can go faster than the speed of light. Although the FTL limit is sound, at least within the limiting assumptions of Einsteinian physics, this does not mean that ETs could not colonize over great distances in a few million years rather than dropping by from Zeta Reticuli over the weekend. Exactly how long it might take is probably irrelevant, because such a process might have started hundreds of millions of years ago.

And, of course, the "too-far" argument never considered the possibility of shortcutting through hyperspace via wormholes, not to mention reappearing somewhere else after returning to the implicate order (in David Bohm's version of quantum physics, for example). Who knows what other bizarre-sounding possibilities might sound plausible in twenty-fifth century science.

Other such (largely normal-science) assumptions that supposedly invalidated the ETH were that ETs would probably have evolved so differently from us that the reports of humanoid ETs must be fallacious, and that no ETs in their right minds would finance a boondoggle designed just to visit our backward planet. "It can't be, therefore it isn't." Of course, Michael Swords has argued interestingly against all of these assumptions in his defense of the ETH.

There are more of these, including the idea that the "Visitors" *must* be extraterrestrial, which is just as limiting as the idea that they *can't* be. Although it is useful to argue one way or the other (with the aid of supporting data), surely nobody can be so sure of the evidence to date as to rule out either possibility.

What fascinates me is the fervor with which limiting assumptions are sometimes embraced, and the implication that we can be so sure about them that anybody who goes beyond them to look for contrary data must be either stupid or crazy. Why, everybody knows that if there were really any UFOs, surely there would be a crashed one and the government would show it to us. I heard a new one (to me) when a caller on a talk radio show on which I appeared in Erie, Pennsylvania, in May 1995, told me that any ETs who had figured out how to escape gravity would never want to be planet-bound again. So, obviously, they wouldn't want to visit us either since we're stuck on earth.

And why don't they just land on the White House lawn? Or break into a hospital at 3:00 A.M. and swipe all the DNA they want once and for all, instead of engaging in all these silly abductions if they're really interested in our genes? Or program us to love each other and to recycle all our containers if they're really interested in transforming us and saving the earth?

I don't know. Why doesn't God just make everybody happy if She's so perfect? All I really know for certain is that I don't know anything for certain, and I'm certain that I don't know everything. If ETs/Visitors/"whatever-they-are" are different from us in significant ways, and if they have very high technological capacity, then I would not be surprised to discover that our assumptions about them are sometimes far from the mark.

Another problem related to the premature acceptance of limiting assumptions is the tendency to make leaps of logic from shallow bases of knowledge or from superficial resemblances among little understood phenomena. The similarity between limiting assumptions and leaps of logic lies in the way they both tend to restrict thought before there are enough data to warrant such restrictions. Even worse, they both are reality tunnels used in normal science as excuses for not even looking at the data in the first place. "Deviant science" or "pseudo-science"; case closed.

One example of a leap of logic would be to notice the similarities between abduction experiences and hypnogogic/hypnopompic hallucinations (sleep paralysis) and on this basis to declare that abductions are strictly a mental phenomenon (see Ch. 9). In this case, the leap of logic is directed toward eliminating abductions from consideration as genuine UFO experiences.

When it works the other way and brings more allegedly UFO-related phenomena into ufology, especially psychic phenomena, it fits what Richard Hall refers to negatively as "mixology."[23] Following Hall, Jerome Clark criticizes "the tired and foolish analogy between modern CE3 reports and fairy beliefs,"[24] noting that fairy traditions, unlike reports of alien beings, vary widely around the world.

This is a very interesting theoretical issue. Of course, it is invalid to assume that two phenomena are identical in every way just because they have some features in common (this is the leap of logic fallacy). Fairy folk and other "little people" like leprechauns might be similar to UFO-linked humanoids who are short, put you to sleep or into some other altered state, and kidnap you. However, who ever heard of aliens washing the dishes or doing other chores for humans as brownies are supposed to do (see the story of "The Elves and the Shoemaker")? Of course there could still be some spark of UFO contact in the distant past that has entered as an element in some of this folklore.

---

23. Clark, 1988, p. 65.
24. Clark, 1988, p. 70.

On the other hand, perhaps noting the similarities and correlations in time and place among UFO experiences and other "paranormal" phenomena like telepathy, sightings of Bigfoot and visions of the Blessed Virgin Mary may help us to understand more about the processes involved in all of them. Opening the inquiry to an investigation of possible connections is not in itself a "leap of logic." Nor does it serve to reject topics from legitimate study just because they sound "too New Age," for example.

In general, it should be remembered that reality is always more complex than our theories. ("The map is not the territory.") We should expect theories to be partial and hope that we can come closer to understanding the universe by testing or exploring competing theories for whatever insights they may offer. This is always a frustrating process, especially for people who insist on quick, unambiguous answers. It is even more difficult when trying to explain a mysterious, shape-shifting, possibly even paranormal, topic like UFOs (see "new science" in Ch. 10).

A Hierarchy of Uncertainties

Nothing is completely certain, except for some logical propositions within a given set of axioms (although see the defense of certainty by Rothman in Ch. 7). Given our numerical system, for example, we can be "certain" that $2+2=4$.

In the acquisition of new knowledge (or new ideas about what might be), however, there are always degrees of uncertainty. Sociologically, of course, we would need to add that some groups and institutions (like normal science, see Ch. 4 and 6) have more power than others to decide how "certain" or acceptable ideas are.

If all academic or scientific assertions or conclusions are uncertain to one degree or another, should we never decide to give more weight to some lines of inquiry and to de-emphasize or shut off others? Such decisions could lead to the limiting assumptions and leaps of logic discussed in the previous section of this chapter. On the other hand, wouldn't it be useful to concentrate more on the more promising leads?

Well, yes it would. But let's promise, while we're at it, not to condemn other people who want to explore notions that we think are not as promising as our bright ideas. This is the spirit of open inquiry. Then when we write our academic journal articles presenting our findings, we would like to think that other scholars will make their own judgments about them based on fair and logical criteria (rather than on the influence and reputation of the authors). So much for an expression of the scientific ideal. Now it is time to assert a few general claims about what we may have learned about the UFO phenomenon and to what degree of certainty. I am doing this as much to illustrate the process of deciding about relative certainty as I am to actually look for answers to the UFO question.

First of all, it seems to me that the vast collection of UFO reports tells us one thing above all: once the misidentified mundane phenomena (and hoaxes) are cleared away, the core of "true UFOs" indicates technological capacity far above that found in contemporary human societies on earth. It is tempting to draw a corollary from this that high intelligence is behind the technology. However, we may be seeing a lot of robots and imitation of humans in the entities that seem to be the operators of the craft.

Perhaps something else drives the phenomenon from a distance. Whether it is conceivable that something other than "intelligence" (living *or* machine) could be doing this, I haven't a clue. I hesitate only because I suspect that my anthropocentric perspective is incapable of seeing other possibilities.

Something additional can be said about UFO technology. There is a great deal of evidence gathered by Richard Haines and others on the use by UFOs of energies throughout the electromagnetic spectrum (see Ch. 8). Light is used not only for illumination and communication, but apparently for manipulating objects as well, as in cases of people being dragged through hollow tubes of light into a craft.

Human brains also seem to be affected at a distance, whether electromagnetic forces are involved or not. There may well be other "subtle energies" operating. As George Leonard says, let's not be "electromagnetic chauvinists.... There's got to be more to the world than the electromagnetic spectrum."[25] From our limited perspective at least, this appears to be mental telepathy. Also, some mental disturbances on the part of UFO experiencers may be the aftermath of hypnotic suggestion or the effects of implants, rather than ongoing manipulation from an external source.

By now I am becoming less certain about my claims. Nevertheless, it does seem that the Visitors are interacting with humans physically and not just through their brains or consciousness, although some of these interactions may involve altered mind states. As pointed out in Ch. 8 and 9, there is a significant accumulation of evidence for the physical nature of at least many abductions.

---

25. DiCarlo, 1996, p. 165.

Finally, I am willing to assert that the Visitors are deliberately elusive in their contact with humans, and yet they want to be seen on a limited basis. Some people are either targeted as frequent experiencers or have "encounter-prone personalities." And sometimes they even show themselves to large numbers of people in one or several related sightings (see Chapter 9).

Even less certain is the proposition that the Visitors are extraterrestrial. Some certainly may be, but there are other strong possibilities. As discussed earlier, some may be from our own future, or some may have arrived through hyperspace from a very short distance away along some other dimension or dimensions that we are normally incapable of experiencing. Just because the Visitors often allegedly tell experiencers that they are from outer space, and even from somewhere in particular like the Pleiades or Zeta Reticuli, this doesn't necessarily mean that they are telling the truth. In fact, there is a fairly good suspicion that they often lie to humans.

Perhaps the most vague and uncertain of the issues that we are highly interested in is the question of their purposes in being here and in interacting with humans. Earlier in this chapter, the most commonly mentioned reasons were presented: a genetic/hybrid program, saving the planet and transforming human consciousness, and their curiosity about us perhaps to the point of wanting to play games with us.

One of the reasons for the great uncertainty about their purposes is that they may be highly motivated to deceive us about their purposes. Or elements in the U.S. government (or in some shadowy "control group") are trying to spread disinformation. Another reason may be that the UFO phenomenon is very complex, involving forces from several sources, all of which (of whom) have different sets of purposes or agendas. After all, if the historical cases of possible UFO reports going back thousands of years are valid, this may be a very large and diverse phenomenon.

Combinations of Possibilities

After arranging a hierarchy of uncertainties (probabilities), the next bit of speculation we might engage in would be to work out combinations of elements with emphasis on what we consider to be the highest probability items. This is essentially what Michael Swords did in his 1992 article about the ETH referred to earlier in this chapter,[26] in which he reasoned that ETs would explore our world from a distance

---

26. Swords, 1992C.

with nano-technology and telepresence, and play games with us for their own curiosity and development of consciousness.

I must say that Swords' scenario sounds as good as any. I doubt that we have much chance of testing its validity at this point given the amount of noise in our data (due in part to disinformation perhaps), and given the multiplied uncertainties that occur every time we try to combine more than one element in a more complete explanation of the phenomenon.

Nevertheless, I would like to try my hand at an explanation. I do this with humility, without saying that anybody else is necessarily crazy who has a different idea, and remembering that our anthropocentric perspective makes it very difficult to comprehend some (but not all) of the phenomenon.

First of all, I think that they are other-worldly in origin, from somewhere/"somewhen" else. As far as we are concerned, this could be from distant stars in the universe we can see with our telescopes, from different places and times along dimensions we are incapable of understanding, or from combinations of these. I think that they are from several origins, not just one.

Second, they have interacted with Earth and its inhabitants for at least thousands of years. Their technology is so advanced that we are bound to misunderstand much of what they are doing. However, none of them have really tried to conquer us or kill us off. If they had, they would have succeeded already. They do monitor us and especially our dangerous nuclear toys. But they are also not trying to fix *all* of what we consider to be our problems. It *is* possible that some of them have been working in part to modify us genetically as a species and to alter our consciousness collectively and individually. Some people and their families get a lot of attention both mentally and physically.

Some of the Visitors want to be seen (or at least don't care if they are) at least part of the time by large numbers of people and quite often by certain selected individuals who are meant to have the experience consciously. None of the Visitors or groups of Visitors wants to leave enough evidence for hard-core nonbelievers and debunkers to be forced to accept the UFO phenomenon. This "probably" (as if I knew anything that strongly) means that there are some tricky lessons to be learned in the process, and that some of the changes are easier to effect if levels of awareness are lower among parts of the population. I suspect that this is a profound insight, but I cannot explain why.

I doubt that the partial secrecy is related to not wanting to alter the future (see discussion of Davenport and Johnson above), because the amount of impact already seems to have exceeded a level that could change the future a great deal; it doesn't take much to change a system drastically, as we know from chaos theory. It is possible that there is some kind of "prime directive" as in *Star Trek*, according to which we are not to be interfered with excessively, although how much is too much is hard to figure.

Here I must admit that I do not see much evidence of active "evil" intent on the part of the Visitors. Sometimes, however, they seem not to care much about human rights or autonomy. And some human groups (governments especially) are probably deceiving the public about what they know (see Ch. 2 and 5), which could be a violation of public trust, but this doesn't necessarily involve any conspiracy between government and aliens/Visitors.

The Larger Reality

I have already stated that I suspect that the UFO phenomenon is complex rather than a single mystery capable of solution. In other words, the "answer" will not be as simple as, "They're a renegade group of Pleiadians here on a mission to create a hybrid species with themselves and humans." Something like that might be part of what is going on, but I suspect that the origins and purposes of the Visitors are many.

But this is only part of the story. What makes the UFO subject so baffling is that there are so many persistently reported phenomena associated with it that stretch our credulity. It is hard enough for normal scientists (or anybody for that matter) to accept reports of nuts-and-bolts UFOs and their humanoid occupants. What are they to make of people who get intuitive impulses to go to a window and see UFOs (and they're there), of UFOs that shape-shift into apparent birds or angels in the sky, of abductees floating through walls, of hybrid babies in vats of liquid, of experiencers who encounter beings made only of light, or of telepathic powers and poltergeist activity linked to people's UFO experiences?

It is certainly possible to deny the plausibility of any of these bizarre elements, but my reading of the reports, including reports from people I know well, leads me to think that there is something highly significant going on in most if not all of them, something that ought to get us to rethink our understanding not only of UFOs, but of the entire universe.

Although I recognize the nuts-and-bolts physical basis of many or of most UFO reports, I agree with Leo Sprinkle that UFOs involve both physical and psychical/spiritual phenomena. It is these latter "paranormal" aspects that are especially disconcerting to ufologists when they try to play the science game (see Ch. 10). Essentially the problem is that the deeper we look, the more we find connections between the physical and the psychic, as in the case of experiencers who have UFO sightings involving physical effects, but who also have a rash of telepathic communications not only during but after their UFO encounters.

UFOs seem to pull us into a "Larger Reality," a place that operates on more than the standard physical principles we understand scientifically. They beckon from beyond a smudged window where there are more than the three spatial dimensions plus time. What is so frustrating is that the smudges seem to be mostly on the other side of the window, and we are in a basement sealed off from the Larger Reality so full of wonders on the other side.

There are many analogies and metaphors that have been used to portray our isolation from the mysteries beyond the basement window. Ufologists frequently refer to humans as "lab rats" in some alien experiment.

John Mack tells the Tibetan folk tale about the ocean frog and the well frog.[27] When the frog who has lived in the well all his life cannot believe the ocean frog's statement that the ocean is so much larger than his well, the two frogs leap off to the ocean together to have a look. When they arrive, the well frog is so amazed that his head explodes. Mack implies that discovering the UFO reality could be mind-blowing for us, especially for those of us who follow the restricted belief system of normal science.

Another animal analogy is presented by Michio Kaku, theoretical physicist and author of the book, *Hyperspace*, although he draws no connection to UFOs, only to our lack of understanding of other dimensions. He imagines what would happen to carp who leap out of the water to see the world of air-dwellers like us, and who then return to the water and try to explain what they have seen to other carp.[28]

Of course, the point of all these comparisons is to try to convey how limited the world view may be of humans stuck in a four-dimensional basement (including time, which we really don't understand) when, according to superstring theory in physics, there may actually be a total of ten dimensions in the Larger Reality. As discussed in Chapter 7, however, we may derive some insights into other dimensions (hyperspace) by projecting higher-dimensional patterns onto lower-di-

27. Mack, 1994A, p. 387.
28. Kaku, 1994, pp. 3-5.

mensional spaces or areas, just as we did for the fictional Flatlanders who live on a two-dimensional space.

If UFOs move through more than four dimensions, they may be coming in and out of our space like Mr. Sphere when he came through Flatland and appeared first as a point, then as an increasingly large circle, a decreasing circle, then a dot again before disappearing. This would be like somebody entering our basement, even though we cannot see through the window adequately.

In the case of UFOs, the intelligence involved with them seems to be able not only to enter our basement periodically, but also to drag in a number of other exotic phenomena like telepathy and religious experiences. Also, however, there are some humans (Ring might say they have encounter-prone personalities) who can see more than others can through the smudged window and who are visited frequently by the "UFOlks" (Leo Sprinkle's witty designation).

What all of this means is that there is hope for us to learn something about the mysteries outside our basement in spite of our limited perspective. We are not completely cut off from the Larger Reality. At the very least, we ought to get a greater appreciation for why things are so confusing. The first step is humility, through which we recognize our anthropocentrism and comprehend how limited we are with the help of the animal analogies (lab rats, Tibetan frogs and carp).

Second, we can try to study what we see through the smudged window. This can be done to at least some degree through science and "new science" (see Ch. 10), using some "methodologies for the mysterious." We might even be willing to go partly "New Age" and use our own or other people's intuition (or psychic or spiritual powers).

As an aside, some of us might even decide that a scientific explanation of the material world we thought we knew is largely an illusion and that intuitive, symbolic ways of knowing, including astrology, finding guidance in synchronicities, and channeling communications from aliens and spirits are more valid. Others might opt for feeling rather than knowing when it comes to topics that seem to be too mysterious for science. These are issues for the sociology of knowledge.

Third, although this may overlap with the first two, we can reason by analogy, like figuring out how a sphere (Mr. Sphere) or a cube might look to Flatlanders, in order to imagine how an object in four or more spatial dimensions might look to us when projected onto our 3-D space.

Fourth, if there really are UFOs (and if you are *sure* there *aren't*, you can stop reading), we can pay attention when they actually enter our 3-D space. And they just might bring some interesting baggage with them that will give us clues to other wonders out there in the Larger Reality. We may discover that some of the humans who are especially good at perceiving the world outside the window are stimulated in their abilities by these UFO experiences.

Through these various means, and possibly others, we can expect to learn more about the Larger Reality. If and when we do, many things that we currently think of as paranormal may become defined as normal when seen as part of the ten-dimensional universe postulated in superstring theory in physics. Psychic and spiritual phenomena like ESP, ghosts, near-death experiences, out-of-body experiences and angels may all inhabit the Larger Reality along with UFOs.

Perhaps Michael Talbot was right, that all of these phenomena are part of a "holographic universe,"[29] in which minds co-create reality. And Carl Jung may have been right on some level in saying that UFOs are in part a creation of an evolving human collective unconscious, while still having a "physical" aspect.[30] If UFOs help open us up to these other phenomena simply because they are all occupants of the same space, the same Larger Reality, then no wonder the UFO phenomenon seems so bizarre.

Consequently, if there is any validity to this discussion, what we conceive of as the UFO phenomenon may be a conglomeration of wonders from the Larger Reality with many links among them. When they intersect our limited basement world, they confuse us profoundly. No wonder we get confused about "UFO cases" that have characteristics of Marian visions, angel sightings, telepathy or apparitions. No, I do not think that there will be a simple answer to the UFO question. On the other hand, what we do learn may be profound, if indeed the Visitors are high-tech travelers from the Larger Reality.

Tolerance for Ambiguity

Are we at the threshold of comprehending the UFO phenomenon? I don't know. If we are, it may depend more on the Visitors than on our own scientific efforts. After all, even if we are highly intelligent lab rats, we probably need a lot of help from the alien psychologists to understand the experiment. I doubt that we can predict when some of the Visitors might decide to make themselves clearly and publicly known.

In the meantime, I have some significant hope that at least we are at the threshold of open and serious *inquiry* into the UFO phenomenon. There are already some encouraging signs. First, there are many good

---

29. Talbot, 1991.
30. Jung, 1970.

and serious ufologists at work, some of them of high profile in the academic community, like Dr. John Mack. Second, there have even been some ufology articles in mainstream academic journals, like the *Journal of Abnormal Psychology* when it published Spanos and others' skeptical, but fair analysis of UFO experiencers.[31]

Third, there is some worthwhile treatment of UFOs in print journalism (the *Washington Post*, the *Atlantic*), and on television (*Sightings, Unsolved Mysteries, Encounters* and *The Paranormal Borderline*). Although standards of entertainment and profit drive most popular media treatments, with some sacrifice of scientific rigor, at least the UFO question is raised in a fairly serious way (excluding the tabloids, of course), creating an end run around normal science and engaging the consciousness of large numbers of people.

At the threshold of open inquiry, we have to be prepared to tolerate high levels of ambiguity. As we approach the Larger Reality, the data become more bizarre and confusing. Ufologists typically experience frustration as they look at the data. It is like opening one door behind which there is one answer, but in that room there are also five more questions with a door for each. And so it goes: the more we find out, the more we discover we don't know.

There is no single static answer to a simple question, "What are UFOs?" There is only an evolution of understanding. As Barbara Marciniak said when allegedly channeling the Pleiadians, "Once you think you have us figured out, we will tell you something else."[32]

Returning from the New Age to a nuts-and-bolts ufologist, Richard Hall states that abductee "reports are at once compellingly credible and totally inexplicable in terms of conventional scientific knowledge.... So, if you are scientific in spirit and refuse to let imagination substitute for evidence, you *suspend judgment*."[33] Who could ask for anything more from a scientist operating under the true spirit of open inquiry that is supposedly part of the scientific ideology or ethic?

Part of the Western scientific version of the anthropocentric perspective is the notion that we humans are capable of mastering the universe at least intellectually by means of scientific method and theory, even though we may take centuries to unlock some of the universe's mysteries. From another point of view, more consistent with Eastern mysticism and New Age thought, this scientific perspective could be seen as an arrogant addiction to knowing. A more humble approach

---

31. Spanos and others, 1993.
32. Marciniak, Aug. 19, 1994.
33. Richard Hall, 1993A, pp. 12-13.

would be to realize that we are not very smart or in-the-know, as we peer out of our smudged window at the Larger Reality.

It would be more liberating and enlightening, however, to change metaphors at this point and to imagine ourselves staring up in wonder at a crystal-clear night sky. Although they are far away, from our point of view, the stars are right there for us to appreciate and perhaps to discover eventually by means of science and through other ways of knowing as well. And though they are light-years away in terms of the three spatial dimensions we can perceive through "normal" means, some of the stars may be very near via wormholes in hyperspace. There may also be other worlds and beings mere inches away from us through other dimensions that we are unfamiliar with, but which are just at the threshold of our awareness.

Appendix

Ufologist Case Studies/ Biographies

Most of the following case studies/biographies of ufologists are based upon personal interviews supplemented by material gathered at UFO conferences or available in print. They follow no standard format, but emphasize information for each individual that seemed to me to be the most interesting or significant for this particular study. Length of entry is not necessarily an indication of how important the person is to the field, nor does the absence of anyone from the list mean that he/she is unimportant. It is merely an indication of the incompleteness of my work. For an excellent collection of biographical sketches of ufologists, as well as other entries about the field of ufology in various countries, see Jerome Clark's book, *UFOs in the 1980s: The UFO Encyclopedia, Vol. I.*[1] Clark includes 7 of the 18 people on this list plus about 18 others, and still there are others who deserve recognition, many of whom at least appear in the footnotes and bibliography of this book.

Andrus, Walter H., Jr. is the International Director of the Mutual UFO Network (MUFON) which he helped found in 1969, a member of the Board of the USA/CIS Aerial Anomaly Federation and a member of the Board of the UFO Research Coalition.

Having graduated from the Central Technical Institute in Kansas City, Missouri, in 1940, he acquired further training in U.S. Navy electronics and taught technicians during World War II. After serving in managerial roles at the Quincy, Illinois plant of Motorola, Inc., he transferred in 1975 to their plant in Seguin, Texas, where he retired in 1982.

Mr. Andrus first became interested in UFOs in 1948 in Phoenix, Arizona, when he and his wife and son saw "four round aluminum-colored objects...drifting across the sky...in a definite formation."[2] Seeming to disappear (he suspected they were discs tilting their flat surfaces away), three of the four discs later reappeared farther west evidently having tilted back enough to be seen again.

---

1. Clark, 1990.
2. Schuessler, 1994, pp. 174-184.

While with Motorola, he was a contributor of articles on UFOs, including one on his own experience, to *The Voice of Motorola* and was generally supported at the company not only for this, but for his appearance on the 1974 full-hour NBC documentary, *UFOs: Do You Believe?* Although one vice-president gave him a hard time and temporarily impeded his advancement on the grounds that his UFO involvement detracted from a person in a position of authority, this problem ended after a statement of support from the personnel director.

Ironically, there was one other person in management who wrote even more UFO articles for *The Voice of Motorola* than Walt did, and he got himself fired, not for his ufology, but for his astrology. This individual let it interfere with his job, not wanting to take a road trip when the astrological signs were wrong, for example. Walt thinks that astrology is not valid, as illustrated by the fact that both he and this other gentleman were born on the very same day and year, but the only thing they had in common was an interest in UFOs.

Mr. Andrus has worked tirelessly for MUFON, as evidenced by how much time he spends in the office. Nevertheless, he is sometimes criticized for being too scientific or "nuts-and-bolts" and not sympathizing with perspectives that lean toward the New Age (like astrology?). He explained to me that any aspect of the UFO phenomenon is okay that "can be observed, studied, or researched." We should not have blinders and ignore phenomena that may be connected to UFOs, he says, e.g., animal mutilations, crop circles and bigfoot. Although he has a vision for MUFON as scientific, he does not expect to "dictate to people what they believe."

Boylan, Richard J. is a clinical psychologist from Sacramento, California. He is the author and co-editor with his wife Lee K. Boylan of *Close Extraterrestrial Encounters: Positive Experiences with Mysterious Visitors.*[3]

His Ph.D. is in Anthropological Psychology from the University of California, Davis. This specially designed interdisciplinary degree has helped prepare him not only for an understanding of world cultural effects in human psychology, but for possible extraterrestrial cultural interactions (exoanthropology). His most recent interests in ufology lie in helping the world get ready for such contact.

Although Dr. Boylan has followed the UFO phenomenon since the Kenneth Arnold and Roswell cases in 1947, his first involvement in close encounters (CE-IV) began in 1989 when four clients told him about their experiences. By 1991 and 1992 he had been doing formal re-

---

3. Boylan and Boylan, 1994.

search on such cases for four months when he had his own encounter (see Ch. 13, "Dr. Rich's Account" in their book). He considers these encounters essentially "positive," as in the subtitle of the book referred to above.

As discussed in Chapter 4 here, Dr. Boylan considers himself to have a sense of mission, having been influenced to do compulsive reading in sciences and math, to write about close encounter experiences, and to help the world prepare for contact. He thinks that it is not surprising that investigators should find themselves visited. Many contacts come in the form of personalized UFO flybys with telepathic communication and altering of consciousness, "whether they lift the blankets off you or not."

Davenport, Marc is Vice President of Greenleaf Publications, and author of *Visitors From Time: The Secret of the UFOs,*[4] and a founding editor of *Contact Forum: The Roundtable of Universal Communication.*

Mr. Davenport studied chemical engineering at the University of Missouri at Rolla and worked as a manufacturing engineer before doing free-lance writing full time since 1985. Although his first UFO experience came at the age of ten when he saw a distant daylight cigar-shaped craft, this was not what first got him interested in the subject. Marc cut his reading teeth on *Fate* magazine, and UFOs were a frequent topic of conversation at home.

In his book, *Visitors From Time*, he gives an extensive review of UFO literature with emphasis on how a great number of investigated sightings seem to fit the theory that UFOs warp space-time, whether they are extraterrestrial or from our own future or both. Issues of science and hypothesis testing are also prominent throughout the book.

One of the ufologists mentioned in Chapter 4 as having a sense of mission, Mr. Davenport is now most interested in the abduction experience as it relates to expectations of coming global disasters. In fact, he is also author of *Dear Mr. President: 100 Earth-Saving Letters.*[5]

Downing, Barry H. is pastor of Northminster Presbyterian Church in Endwell, New York; author of *The Bible and Flying Saucers,*[6] and on the board of the Fund for UFO Research (FUFOR).

Dr. Downing has a Ph.D. in the Philosophy of Religion from the Divinity School at the University of Edinburgh, Scotland. Having majored in physics as an undergraduate, and having completed a degree

4. Davenport, 1992B.
5. Davenport, 1992A.
6. Downing, 1968.

from Princeton Theological Seminary, he wrote a doctoral dissertation on the science and philosophy of Isaac Newton.

Finding a course through the controversy between the nuts-and-bolts science treatment of UFOs and the conception of UFOs as religious myth, Dr. Downing has argued for the physical reality of the phenomenon, but also for Biblical evidence of ancient UFO events, such as the parting of the Red Sea.[7] This puts him at odds both with religious liberals who tend to see UFOs as a modern myth, and with religious conservatives who tend to see them as demonic if they exist.

Although his book created a little anxiety in the church at the beginning while he was an assistant pastor, Dr. Downing does not preach on UFOs. He tells parishioners that UFOs are a research area for him, and that they are not up there with the Apostles Creed among things to believe in.

Greer, Steven M. is Chairman of the Department of Emergency Medicine at a hospital in North Carolina, and International Director of the Center for the Study of Extraterrestrial Intelligence (CSETI).

Dr. Greer has a strong background not only in medicine, with an M.D. from East Tennessee State University, but also in meditation and religion. He was trained as a Transcendental Meditation teacher and served as the Director of the International Meditation Society in the Bahamas in 1976. He is also active in the Baha'i Faith.

Popular as a lecturer and banquet speaker, Dr. Greer is best known for his CE-V research, attempting to attract UFOs and to develop protocols for interacting with their occupants. Part of the mission of CSETI involves working with world leaders to prepare for friendly diplomatic contact with extraterrestrials.

Haley, Leah A. is a CPA and the author of *Lost Was the Key*[8] and *Ceto's New Friends*[9].

Ms. Haley has an M.A. in Education from the University of North Alabama, and an M.B.A. from Mississippi State University. A certified public accountant, she practiced public accounting and then taught university accounting courses for several years.

Lost Was the Key is an account of her own abduction encounters with aliens and with apparent military personnel. Ms. Haley reports being on board a UFO when it crash-landed on a beach. Although she remained skeptical for quite a while about her own experiences, there

7. Downing, 1994.
8. Haley, 1993.
9. Haley, 1994.

was an accumulation of physical and other evidence to confirm their reality.[10]

Ceto's New Friends is a children's book designed to alleviate fears in young abductees. It is the story of Ceto, an alien boy, and his Earth friends Annie and Seth.

Howe, Linda Moulton is an independent author, television producer and documentary filmmaker (LMH Productions). Her documentaries about unusual phenomena have included: *A Strange Harvest* first broadcast on KMGH-TV (CBS) in 1980 which earned a Regional Emmy Award; *Earth Mysteries: Alien Life Forms* for FOX in Atlanta, Georgia, in September 1990; *UFO Report: Sightings* in 1991 for Paramount and the FOX network; and *Strange Harvests 1993* for the home video market. Her books include *An Alien Harvest: Further Evidence Linking Animal Mutilations and Human Abductions to Alien Life Forms*,[11] *Glimpses of Other Realities, Volume 1: Facts and Eyewitnesses*,[12] and *Glimpses of Other Realities, Vol. 2: High Strangeness.*[13]

Ms. Howe has an M.A. in Communications from Stanford University and has produced many film documentaries on science, medicine and the environment. She had already established her credibility by winning several journalism awards, including Emmies, before working on "A Strange Harvest" in 1979 (first broadcast in 1980), in which she examined the animal mutilation mystery. Although the mutilation subject is controversial, Ms. Howe has built her case carefully on first-hand testimony and is now gathering more scientific evidence through necropsies performed on mutilated animals by veterinarians.

Uncomfortable with the term "ufology, " partly because of the way the concept of "UFO" has been maligned in some circles, Ms. Howe defines her interests as focusing on unidentified and unexplained phenomena. Consequently her work includes not only animal mutilations, but also crop circles, Marian visions and the human abduction syndrome, all of which have been associated with strange lights.

She herself has experienced unusual sky objects since 1979. The first occurred in October 1979 while producing *A Strange Harvest*. "The film crew and I were with a rancher in...Wyoming when all four saw a tomato-red light rise above a butte, move horizontally and vertically for several minutes and then go back to where it had first appeared."

On another occasion, November 5, 1986, she was coming out of a bank in Aurora, Nevada, and headed into the parking lot about 6:00

10. Davenport, 1994.
11. Moulton Howe, 1989.
12. Moulton Howe, 1995.
13. Moulton Howe, 1996.

P.M., when for some reason she spun around and looked up to see an enormous silent object shaped like a boomerang as big as two ten-story buildings joined together. No one else was around.

Her third sighting occurred in Peru in June 1987, at 22,000 feet. Staring at the Southern Cross in the sky she saw a very bright flash that she thought at first might be a satellite. But then there was a second flash and a third forming a triangular arrangement. The same sequence repeated. After that a vivid white line was drawn from the Southern Cross to the triangle of stars or lights and stayed there. By the time she could arouse other people to come out into the extreme cold to see this display, it had disappeared.

Her fourth sighting was with another person while investigating a cattle mutilation report in Mora, New Mexico, in September 1994. About 7:15 P.M. they saw a flash of light over the mountains and watched with binoculars as a bright white light went up and down three times, staying behind the trees but following the line of the hill.

It is interesting that Ms. Howe experienced no physical or psychic reactions after any of these four events. Nor does she try to interpret them as having special meaning for herself as some ufologists do who incorporate sightings into a "sense of mission." She is very scientific and meticulous in her work, however, and tries hard to get people to look beyond the old paradigms.

Jacobs, David M. is Associate Professor of History at Temple University, and the author of *The UFO Controversy in America*[14] and of *Secret Life: Firsthand Accounts of UFO Abductions*[15].

His 1975 book was his Ph.D. dissertation in history at the University of Wisconsin in 1973, and its printing by the Indiana University Press represents the only publication of a pro-ufology book by a university press. This is the classic work on the history of ufology (see Ch. 2).

Secret Life is more controversial academically because it takes abductions as serious, real experiences. When Dr. Jacobs met Budd Hopkins, pioneer and outstanding figure in abduction research, in 1982, he thought that abductions were mainly a psychological phenomenon, but he began doing his own regressions with abductees in 1986.

Dr. Jacobs is concerned about proper methodology, especially when using hypnosis. He watches carefully for signs of confabulation and eliminates cases from his data base that are not confirmed by others. Some critics think that these unusual cases should be included in

---

14. Jacobs, 1975.
15. Jacobs, 199B.

the analysis to prevent a distorted picture and to avoid a standard abduction stereotype.

Another methodological problem involves the formation of a popular culture about abductions that may influence alleged experiencers. Jacobs agrees that this can be a problem as more reports are published, but he observes that most abductees are fully aware of this contamination issue and want to avoid saying things that are just their imagination. Most abductees are naive about the subject, have seen little about it on TV, and are afraid they'll sound crazy when they relate their memories.

Klass, Philip J. is an electrical engineer, avionics journalist and the author of four skeptical books on UFOs, including *UFOs: The Public Deceived*[16] and *UFO-Abductions: A Dangerous Game*[17]. He is also a member of the Executive Council of The Committee for the Scientific Investigation of Claims of the Paranormal (CSICOP) and a member of the Editorial Board of the CSICOP publication *The Skeptical Inquirer*. Since 1989, Klass has published a bimonthly newsletter, called *Skeptics UFO Newsletter* (SUN). It currently has a circulation of more than 400 with subscribers in more than a dozen countries.

Although Mr. Klass is recognized as the top UFO debunker (see Ch. 5), he is also a ufologist in the sense that he investigates UFO cases and attends UFO conferences, looks at the evidence in UFO cases, and, in some cases, has presented his own anomalous explanations involving ball lightning and plasmas.[18] One ufologist told me in an interview that you had better listen to Phil Klass when he discusses electrical phenomena in connection with UFO reports, because he knows what he is talking about.

Mr. Klass has a degree in electrical engineering from Iowa State University, where he also took journalism courses and worked in college radio and with the student engineering magazine. At General Electric for ten years, he trained engineers in aviation electronics. With his background in aviation and writing, he was hired by *Aviation Week* magazine in 1952, where he became avionics editor. Since his retirement in 1986, he still serves as contributing editor.

His first article on UFOs was published in *Aviation Week* in 1953 when he reported the results of the (then) Civil Aviation Administration investigation of the July 19-20, 1952, radar UFO sightings over

---

16. Klass, 1983.
17. Klass, 1988.
18. Clark, 1990, p. 150.

Washington, D.C., that made front-page headlines. The CAA's conclusion was that the radar blips were caused by temperature inversion.

However, Mr. Klass's first active interest in UFO reports came in 1966 when he was impressed with John G. Fuller's book *Incident at Exeter*.[19] Mr. Klass told me that Fuller's account convinced him (Klass) that there was some mysterious electrical phenomenon generating the reports at Exeter, New Hampshire. Mr. Klass thought that UFO believers might welcome his explanation involving ball lightning near high-tension power lines, but he was denounced in UFO journals.

Mr. Klass, who had become the "leading living skeptical investigator" (his words) of UFOs by the mid-1970s after the death of Harvard astronomer Donald Menzel, joined Paul Kurtz and others in a one-day symposium in April 1976, that led to the creation of CSICOP. In regard to UFO coverage, sociologist Marcello Truzzi (who left after one year to start *The Zetetic Scholar*) wanted some pro-UFO involvement, but Klass carried the day with his argument that there were already groups that promoted UFO belief, and that CSICOP should provide a skeptical counterbalance rather than representing both sides.

When I asked Mr. Klass if he weren't like an attorney making a one-sided anti-UFO argument, he responded that, just like Carl Sagan, he would love to find evidence of intelligence-guided craft and would rush to his computer to report it. It would be terrible if he debunked a case and then a craft crashed there to prove him wrong. He would have missed a terrific story for *Aviation Week*. However, his 30-year search for credible evidence has yielded nothing, including not a single physical artifact.

Maccabee, Bruce S. is a research physicist, Chairman of the Fund for UFO Research (FUFOR) and author of numerous articles in physics and in ufology.

Dr. Maccabee has a Ph.D. in physics from American University, and he has worked as a consultant specializing in laser physics and optical data processing for both private industry and government. In ufology, he is best known for his analysis of alleged UFO photographs and for his papers on FBI and other government involvement in UFO cases.

Although he did have his own UFO sighting in Gulf Breeze in 1991, Dr. Maccabee's interest in UFOs dates from reading in his high school years and later when he did volunteer work for NICAP (National Investigations Committee on Aerial Phenomena) in Washington, D.C., in the late 1960s. Since the cases he investigated then were mostly good

19. Fuller, 1966.

ones, he was encouraged to continue, especially during the flap of the summer of 1973.

Dr. Maccabee is associated with some famous UFO cases, including the McMinnville photo of 1950 when he did a rebuttal of skeptical articles about it in 1976, and the New Zealand UFO film of 1978. Perhaps the most important and controversial case involves the Ed Walters UFO photographs in Gulf Breeze, Florida, beginning in 1987.

In addition to his many presentations at UFO conferences, Dr. Maccabee spoke at a *Star Trek* convention once. After his one-hour talk about the New Zealand case, there was little reaction, mostly with the skeptical attitude, "Defend yourself." Contrary to what one might expect, he says, science fiction fans tend to accept conventional scientific wisdom and deny the existence of UFOs. We might note that the late science-fiction writer Isaac Asimov was a member of CSICOP, and that Arthur C. Clarke, author of *2001: A Space Odyssey*, once called Philip Klass's debunking book *UFOs Explained* "a welcome breath of sanity in a field where it is sadly lacking."[20]

Mack, John E. is Professor of Psychiatry at the Cambridge Hospital, Harvard Medical School; member of the Board of Directors of MUFON; author of *Abduction: Human Encounters with Aliens*[21] and Pulitzer Prize winner for *A Prince of Our Disorder*[22], a biography of Lawrence of Arabia.

Dr. Mack is known as the academic currently with the highest prestige to dare to study UFOs, abductions in fact, and to consider them real. He says that there is a race between his credentials convincing people and his losing credibility due to the subject matter.

Perhaps the first important influence in the involvement of Dr. Mack was his interest in holotropic breathwork techniques used by Stanislav Grof to encourage altered states of consciousness.[23] Adding to this introduction to paranormal experience, he read material on UFOs by Keith Thompson and wondered if UFOs were real or merely mythical. When he was about to meet abduction researcher Budd Hopkins in 1990, Mack thought that Hopkins "must be crazy" and that all of his supposed abductees must be crazy, too.

When he came to do his own abduction research, he concluded after working with over 75 people for thousands of hours that there was no psychiatric condition that could explain the recounting of their experiences with such "authentic feeling" other than real events.[24] Fully aware that some of the evidence that he was getting was very strange, Dr. Mack asked Thomas Kuhn, author of *The Structure of Scientific Revolutions*, for advice on how to approach his data. Kuhn suggested that he forget about conventional categories and concepts and just gather information.[25]

Consequently, Mack believes that in order to understand abductions we must stretch our methodology beyond physical evidence and normal science to include such things as the study of altered states. This means the development of other ways of knowing beyond traditional science (see Ch. 10) and that our consciousness must grow to meet the UFO phenomenon.

After an investigation into Dr. Mack's work from summer 1994, to nearly fall 1995, a "Special Faculty Committee" within the Harvard Medical School decided not to censure Dr. Mack for his work with abductees. However, a preliminary report from the committee had criticized him for "affirming the delusions" of his patients.[26] Some faculty supported him on grounds of academic freedom. Mack's legal defense was expected to cost him $130,000.

Parnell, June O. is a counselor and an author of studies on the personality characteristics of UFO experiencers.

Dr. Parnell has a Ph.D. in Counselor Education from the University of Wyoming and has worked as a counselor both at the same university and in a private social services agency. She has been associated with Dr. Leo Sprinkle, who was on her dissertation committee and who co-authored an article with her on "Personality Characteristics of Persons Who Claim UFO Experiences" in the *Journal of UFO Studies*.[27]

When Dr. Parnell entered the graduate program in counselor education, she told the faculty that she was interested in studying UFO experiencers. The chairperson said, "Well, if you do it scientifically, it'll be okay." As she got further into the program, however, professors got more wary and skeptical about how this topic might be handled. Consequently the dissertation, "Personality Characteristics on the MMPI, 16PF, and ACL of Persons Who Claim UFO Experiences,"[28] received considerable scrutiny. As one member of her dissertation committee put it, "This will be looked at by a lot of people." In the end the committee was very collegial, and it was a good experience.

---

24. Mack, 1993B.
25. Mack, 1993A, p. 208.
26. Beam, 1995.
27. Parnell and Sprinkle, 1990.
28. Parnell, 1987.

Dr. Parnell says that she learned to be very cautious and guarded in her statements. Realizing that she had neither the experience nor the academic status of Leo Sprinkle, she could not challenge people openly about the subject of UFO experiences as he did. Of course Dr. Sprinkle (see page 235) received significant opposition at the University of Wyoming, but Dr. Parnell felt that he was respected nonetheless.

Dr. Parnell thought that there might have been some negative feelings about her UFO interests while she worked as a counselor at the university, and she was hired for two, but not for the third, of three positions she applied for. However, she says that there was no problem over UFOs when she worked at a Catholic social services agency. She had learned how to speak to people about UFOs so as not to upset them, and she thought that Catholics can be very open about UFOs because of their ideas about saints and angels.

Ring, Kenneth is recently retired as a professor of psychology but is still on the faculty at the University of Connecticut. His best known work involving UFOs is *The Omega Project: Near-Death Experiences, UFO Encounters, and Mind at Large* [29].

Dr. Ring has a Ph.D. in psychology from the University of Minnesota. More interested in psychological anomalies than in UFOs in particular, he started to get involved in ufology only in 1987 when he read Whitley Strieber's *Communion* and noticed similarities between near-death experiences (NDEs) and UFO experiences.

Noting that he has been academic rather than popular in his approach, and certainly not wild or proselytizing, nevertheless he states that he has had some mildly negative reactions to his research on the paranormal. "As an NDE researcher in academe, I was used to walking uncomfortably close to the edge of professional respectability.... I would have to endure the reproachful and sometimes withering gaze of my department head...."[30] Dr. Ring would refuse to sponsor undergraduate projects on UFOs "and other similar professionally taboo topics."

Calling himself not much of a joiner, he has had a brief involvement with ufology organizations and conferences, and says that he intends to let these associations lapse as he continues his long-standing interest in NDEs and other extraordinary psychological phenomena. Generally, he felt closer to the skeptics in the UFO field.

Nevertheless, a careful reading of *The Omega Project* reveals much more than just the psychological concept of "encounter-prone person-

29. Ring, 1992.
30. Ring, 1992, p. 8.

alities" that are susceptible to both NDEs and UFO experiences. Although Dr. Ring considers a rich mix of skeptical perspectives on the UFO phenomenon, including tectonic strain or "earth light" theories and mythical explanations, some of the possibilities he considers are rather New Age, e.g., Michael Grosso's treatment of global mind or "mind at large" and millennial transformation. Sounding rather like John Mack, and writing before Mack's book on abductions, Ring states, "Ultimately we must decondition ourselves from all conventional knowledge and understanding if we are to penetrate into the...essence [of the UFO mystery]."[31]

Rodeghier, Mark is President and Scientific Director of the J. Allen Hynek Center for UFO Studies (CUFOS) in Chicago, associate editor of the *Journal of UFO Studies*, a contributing editor for *International UFO Reporter*, and author of several UFO articles and editorials.

Dr. Rodeghier has a Ph.D. in sociology, an undergraduate degree in astrophysics and has worked as a statistics and survey-research consultant. He has been interested in UFOs since about age ten, due partly to a best friend's interest and partly to his own curiosity about puzzles that question scientific authority. His involvement was dormant for a while until the 1973 UFO wave, after which, as a resident of Indiana not far from Chicago, and as an undergraduate at Indiana University, he volunteered at the Center for UFO Studies starting in 1974 and became closely associated with Hynek himself.[32]

In his doctoral dissertation, Dr. Rodeghier applied quantitative methods to measure the influence of "social factors" (e.g., age) and "intrinsic factors" (e.g., understanding of the Drake equation estimates on the probability of intelligent ETs) on the attitudes of scientists about the legitimacy of UFO studies. This contrasts with the usual qualitative case-study method used in the sociology of science, which he sees as making "grandiose claims" about what factors influence scientists, claims without sufficient quantitative/statistical evidence.

Although a sociologist, Dr. Rodeghier has a wide range of interest in the UFO phenomenon partly due to his background in astrophysics. He actually sees physical evidence cases as more important than the social and psychological aspects. If it turns out *not* to be a basically physical reality, then the social/psychological questions will still be important, but the physical takes precedence at this point.

Dr. Rodeghier thinks that UFO reports have a complex set of causes,[33] and he wonders how much they can be understood by standard

31. Ring, 1992, p. 246.
32. Clark, 1990, p. 188.

science as opposed to the new physics or even the science of 500 years hence. He suspects that the answer will come from some unsuspected direction, such as from discoveries in the physics of hyperspace. Perhaps ufologists will not be involved in the solution because there is too much amateur ufology and not enough funded research.

Sprinkle, R. Leo is a counseling psychologist in private practice in Laramie, Wyoming; Professor Emeritus, Counseling Services, University of Wyoming; organizer of the Annual Rocky Mountain UFO Conference in Laramie since 1980; and author of numerous articles and book chapters in ufology and counseling psychology. He serves as President and member of the Board of ACCET (Academy of Clinical Close Encounter Therapists).[34]

Dr. Sprinkle has a Ph.D. in counseling psychology from the University of Missouri. Throughout his career at the University of North Dakota (1961-1964) and at the University of Wyoming (1964-1989) he served in various combinations as professor of psychology, professor of counseling services and director of counseling.

Starting as a skeptic, Dr. Sprinkle, as an undergraduate at the University of Colorado in 1949, with a friend, saw an elliptical metallic object covering an area in the sky equivalent to a fingernail held at arm's length. This object, flying faster than a jet could have, confounded his sense of science and religion.

Then in 1956 he and his wife saw a lighted object that he thought was a planet, but then it moved down, hovered, moved again, hovered, etc. Although motorists were honking their horns, evidently seeing the same thing, nothing appeared in the paper about it the next day. At that point, he knew he would have to investigate.

From 1962 to 1988, he served as consultant to Aerial Phenomena Research Organization (APRO). In 1968 he was a psychological consultant to the Condon study and did a survey of the attitudes of people interested in UFOs.[35] Since then he has been a consultant to several mass-media producers of UFO pieces, including his work from 1972 to 1980 on the *National Enquirer* UFO Panel (See "Tabloids" on page 30.), as well as *Playboy Magazine* (January, 1978), *In Search Of* (June, 1978), *20/20* (May, 1979), Linda Moulton Howe's TV documentary *A Strange Harvest* (March, 1980), and *That's Incredible* (July, 1980; September, 1981).

Although Dr. Sprinkle took early retirement from the University of Wyoming in 1989, before he was eligible for pension, he arrived at this

---

33. Clark, 1990, p. 189.
34. Academy of Clinical Close Encounter Therapists; 2826 O Street, Suite 3; Sacramento, CA 95816.
35. Clark, 1990, p. 198.

personal decision based on an "accumulation of straws" and was not forced out. In fact, he was given emeritus status for his good service to the university. However, his openness about his UFO work and about his own UFO experiences resulted in negative pressures, especially in the 1980s, that combined with administrative political conflicts unrelated to ufology and made it difficult for him to do his job.

Much of the resistance to Dr. Sprinkle's work came about as a result of the extensive popular media coverage in such publications as the *National Enquirer* and *Playboy*. Then a Denver newspaper account of one of his UFO presentations at a Colorado State University conference in 1988 "made me look foolish," he says. This led to an anonymous complaint sent to the American Psychological Association that his research was not scientific. Within one year, the ethics committee of the APA had looked at the evidence (including his conference paper and a video of his presentation) and unanimously dropped the charges.

At one point, Dr. Sprinkle was told verbally and in writing to refrain from past-life therapy and UFO investigation during university office hours. He was also forced to take vacation time when holding the Rocky Mountain UFO Conference on campus. All in all, however, most of his colleagues didn't care about his UFO involvement, a few gave strong support, and a few were negative. One mathematics professor who teased him saying, "See any little green men lately?" later became interested and claimed that he hadn't changed his attitude, it was just that the UFO evidence had improved.

Of course, Dr. Sprinkle's use of past-life therapy is controversial even with many ufologists. He says that he stumbled upon it by accident in the 1960s. He asked one man who was afraid of dogs to go back under hypnotic regression to his earliest experience which was connected with his fear of dogs. When the man related a Medieval experience in which he was chased and eaten by wolves, Leo thought it was nonsense.[36] But later a woman who was afraid of drowning told about being keelhauled in a lifetime as a pirate. He hadn't asked for a past life then either.

His approach has been that on one level, if it helps people to heal, then past-life therapy is useful, regardless of its reality status. He always tells people that they should take their apparent experiences for what they are worth personally, and that he does not want to create false memories. He encourages people to "consider" information on UFOs, channeling and past lives without necessarily accepting or rejecting it.

---

36. Sprinkle, 1994B.

In addition to the nature of his work, another factor that made Dr. Sprinkle a controversial figure at the University of Wyoming was his admission in 1980 that he himself was an experiencer or "contactee." He had told people all along about his 1949 and 1956 sightings. However, it was a different matter when he revealed that he had found out in 1980 under hypnotic regression that he had been on a craft as a youth and told, "Leo, learn to read and write well; when you grow up you can help other people learn more about their purpose in life."[37]

Leo Sprinkle is one ufologist who clearly has a "sense of mission" (see page 68) that makes him controversial especially among "nuts-and-bolts" ufologists. Jerome Clark refers to him as "a genial New Ager with a strong interest in reincarnation...but [who] also has encouraged his colleagues in the mental health field to study the psychological makeup of contactees."[38]

One of my interviewees, while criticizing Dr. Sprinkle's methods of studying abductees, nevertheless said that "Leo is arguably the nicest man in America." His caring work with experiencers (he never calls them "abductees") at the Rocky Mountain UFO Conference and in his voluminous personal correspondence is dedicated to the transformational (New Age) view of the UFO experience, and it is the core of his sense of mission. However, he also sees UFOs as *both* physical and psychical phenomena, and even the "New Agers" at his conference ask lots of technical questions of the "nuts-and-bolts" speakers.

Dr. Sprinkle is the author of the forthcoming book, *Soul Samples,*[39] from Wild Flower Press.

Swords, Michael D. is professor of natural sciences at Western Michigan University, editor of the *Journal of UFO Studies* until 1996, and the author of several scholarly articles in UFO journals.

Dr. Swords received a Ph.D. in the history of science and technology from Case Western Reserve. At this writing he was on sabbatical to do an update of David M. Jacobs' classic work on the history of UFO studies, *The UFO Controversy in America.*[40]

His undergraduate chemistry degree and master's degree in biochemistry combines with his interdisciplinary history Ph.D. to give him a strong perspective on the history/philosophy/sociology of science. He has taught "human biology, environmental planning, history and philosophy of science...cosmic evolution, and...a class on scientific methodology (involving UFOs and other anomalies)."[41]

---

37. Sprinkle, 1994A.
38. Clark, 1990, p. 198.
39. Sprinkle, 1998.
40. Jacobs, 1975.

Not only has he edited the *Journal of UFO Studies*, but he also is an avid writer whose love of the subject shows through in his work in every issue of the journal. Perhaps his most significant article has been "Science and the Extraterrestrial Hypothesis in Ufology,"[42] discussed here in Chapter 4, in which he reviews the literature by astronomers and others in evaluating the plausibility of the ETH for ufology.

Interestingly, although he did have his own UFO experience at the age of 18, a rather exciting view of a revolving disk with dome and lights seen by about 100 witnesses and described later in the media, he says that he was not "blown away" by it, and it did not increase his interest that much from what he had already developed through reading. A true intellectual, however, he was "astounded" by what he heard at a UFO conference in Chicago featuring Hynek and others in 1976. After that, he subscribed to journals and slowly increased his involvement until 1986 when he began to make his own contribution to the literature.

Webb, Walter N. is author of *Encounter at Buff Ledge*,[43] was Assistant Director of the Hayden Planetarium at Boston's Museum of Science, and has contributed numerous articles and case reports in ufology, including currently the regular feature "The Night Sky" in the *MUFON UFO Journal*.

In addition to his B.S. in biology, Mr. Webb served under the late astronomer J. Allen Hynek in 1957-58 as a camera operator at the Smithsonian Astrophysical Observatory satellite tracking station in Maui, Hawaii. Since then he worked not only with the Hayden Planetarium, but also as advisor and consultant to three of the major national UFO organizations (NICAP, APRO and MUFON) and as research associate to another (CUFOS).

Although he has had half a dozen of his own sightings, mainly distant unexplained lights, he is no true believer. In fact, he has been a tough case investigator involved with several famous cases. He was the first person to investigate the Barney and Betty Hill encounter that was the subject of *The Interrupted Journey*[44] by John Fuller. Over the years he has been asked to evaluate many UFO reports for which he has found conventional explanations. And he still thinks that there are a lot of holes in the Ed Walters case, although many others besides Ed have reported sighting UFOs in Gulf Breeze, Florida.

---

41. Clark, 1990, p. 203.
42. Swords, 1989.
43. Webb, 1995.
44. Fuller, 1966B.

Especially interested in CE-III (UFO occupant) cases, Mr. Webb worked as a member of the NICAP "occupant panel" to examine these controversial cases that NICAP had previously "sat on" because they had seemed too strange. More recently, he served on the planning committee for the 1992 Abduction Study Conference held at MIT, a landmark scientific gathering on UFO abductions. And he was hired for six months in 1995 as a full-time investigative consultant for a coalition of CUFOS, FUFOR (The Fund for UFO Research) and MUFON. His other major interest is in the analysis of scientific and governmental behavior that has defined ufology as illegitimate.

Wood, Robert M. is Director of Research for MUFON, worked in research and development management for McDonnell Douglas until 1993, and is the author of articles on the extraterrestrial hypothesis and on possible UFO propulsion systems.

Dr. Wood has a Ph.D. in physics from Cornell University, a degree he pursued to become a better engineer. Working mainly for Douglas Aircraft and McDonnell Douglas, he helped develop missile systems and, later on, became involved in space-station projects.

Dr. Wood's interest in UFOs began in 1967 when he read a debunking book by Donald Menzel, found it unconvincing, and then read a hundred other books about UFOs. Taking a very practical approach, he got the management of McDonnell Douglas to fund a small project in which they explored the potential for gravity propulsion systems such as those possibly used in UFOs.[45] This program was discontinued in 1969 after he decided that such a system would not be feasible in the near future with foreseeable technology, although in principle it should work.

Management was "not so ultraconservative" because if a project could make money, it would be okay, even if it lay outside accepted academic paradigms. As discussed in Chapter 2, the Condon study group, or actually Condon himself, was not so open-minded when Dr. Wood presented his ideas there.

Although Dr. Wood's experience has been most directly involved with technical matters, his interest is not strictly nuts-and-bolts. He thinks it not unlikely that some UFO research will head towards a broader scope of study. This does not necessarily mean a New Age or paranormal emphasis, because parapsychological research may show psychic phenomena to be continuous with other phenomena currently considered normal.

---

45. Wood, 1993.

About the Author

Charles F. Emmons was born in 1942 and was raised in Erie, Pennsylvania. He attended Gannon University in Erie as an undergraduate, and received an M.A. in anthropology in 1966 from the University of Illinois, Urbana. In 1971 he completed a doctorate in sociology at the University of Illinois, Chicago. He is currently Professor of Sociology at Gettysburg College in Pennsylvania, where he has taught since 1974.

His other writings include the books *Chinese Ghosts and ESP: A Study of Paranormal Beliefs and Experiences* (1982), and *Hong Kong Prepares for 1997* (1988). He has widely varying interests. He has taught Latin and Greek, and he currently speaks eight foreign languages. He is interested in mass media and popular culture, the sociology of science and the paranormal. He plays the cello and loves music, especially classical and progressive rock. He has been involved in college radio for over 20 years.

Charles F. Emmons, Ph.D.

Glossary

abductee - an individual who has allegedly been taken unwillingly on board a UFO and/or examined or manipulated by alien beings (see "experiencer")

academe - the institution of higher leaning, including the community of professional scholars at colleges and universities

alien - UFO occupant, usually assumed to be extraterrestrial (if not, other term like "visitor" may be used)

animal mutilations - precise excisions of parts of animals, especially cattle, allegedly done by aliens

black helicopters - craft, usually unmarked, that seem to be associated with UFOs, possibly either disguised UFOs or military craft investigating UFOs

channeling - receiving telepathic messages (from UFO intelligences), often at a great distance; similar to spirit mediumship

confabulation - distortions or false elements given under hypnosis, possibly to please the therapist (see "false memory syndrome")

"Cosmic Watergate" - a phrase used especially by Stanton Friedman to refer to a cover-up of government knowledge of UFOs.

crop circles - complex artificial patterns formed in field of grain in England and elsewhere, often considered related to the UFO phenomenon

debunker - extreme skeptic involved in discrediting what defenders of normal science consider pseudoscience

entity - a being considered to be associated with UFOs; either a humanoid or some other animal or robotic form

ESP - extrasensory perception, including telepathy, thought to be the basis for alien communication

experiencer - a person who has had a UFO experience, especially of a close encounter; often a euphemism for "abductee"

extraterrestrial hypothesis (ETH) - the theory that UFOs are visitors to the Earth from elsewhere

false-memory syndrome (FMS) - the production of erroneous recall through   hypnosis (see "confabulation")

flap - a rash of UFO sightings, also known as a "wave"

humanoid - a presumably living human-like being, or possibly a partly bionic   or robotic being, associated with UFOs

hyperspace - extra dimension(s) of physical reality beyond the three commonly   experienced by humans

hypnagogic (and hypnopompic) hallucinations - dream-like imagery experienced by   people falling asleep (or waking up)

implants - tiny devices allegedly hidden in the bodies of abductees by alien   abductors, possibly for monitoring or control purposes

"missing time" - Budd Hopkins' phrase referring to forgotten or re-pressed   memory of the time during which an apparent abduction has taken place

NDEs - "near-death (or "beyond-and-back") experiences," in which in-dividuals   have a sensation of traveling to "the light" and/or see-ing spirit beings   before reviving (related to "OBEs")

New Age - a diffuse social movement directed toward a spiritual transformation   of humans and a holistic approach to nature

normal science - knowledge production that is approved by main-stream "academe"   (see "pseudoscience")

"nuts-and-bolts" - the approach in ufology that emphasizes the search for   especially physical evidence and the use of rigorous scientific methodology

OBEs - "out-of-body experiences," in which individuals have the sen-sation of   their consciousness leaving their physical body (related to "NDEs")

paradigm shift - a major change from one theoretical point of view to another

probes - small lights or craft too small for humanoid occupants but seemingly   associated with UFOs, often presumed to gather in-formation

pseudoscience - knowledge production that seems scientific to some, but that is   rejected as invalid by "normal science"

"reality tunnel" - phrase used by Robert Anton Wilson to illustrate the   narrowness of any restricted point of view, scientific or oth-erwise

"sense of mission" - phrase used by Richard and Lee Boylan to re-fer to the   dedication of UFO experiencers and/or researchers to the cause of human   transformation through UFO contact

SETI- the Search for Extraterrestrial Intelligence; a program of attempting to   contact extraterrestrial intelligence by sending radio signals into outer   space and looking for incoming signals

skeptic - one who doubts, in the spirit of the scientific method of testing   claims by gathering data as evidence; however, often used in the sense of   "debunker"

sleep paralysis - inability to move in the hypnagogic (or hypnopompic) state

synchronicity - meaningful coincidence, considered in a New Age context to   show direction or mission in one's life

true believer - one who is certain that something exists or is true with little   or no evidence; opposite of debunker

UBOs - "unidentified bright objects," or lights in the sky that astronomers   cannot account for

ufology - the study of UFOs and of UFO reports and experiencers

UFOs - literally "unidentified flying objects," but used popularly to mean   unknown, intelligently guided vehicles, posssibly extraterrestrial in origin

wave - a rash of UFO sightings, also known as a "flap"

wormholes - shortcuts through hyperspace

Bibliography

Abbot, Edwin. *Flatland: A Romance of Many Dimensions by a Square.* Oxford: Blackwell, 1884.

Adamski, George. *Inside the Space Ships.* NY: Abelard-Schuman, 1955.

Ajaja, Vladimir G. "Ufology: New Approaches," *MUFON 1992 International UFO Symposium Proceedings,* Seguin, TX: MUFON, 1992, pp. 196-204.

Alexander, Victoria. "New Protocol for Abduction Research," *MUFON UFO Journal,* pp. 7-10, 1993, Nov. 1993.

Andrus, Walter H. "Re-Opening the Ed Walters Case," *MUFON UFO Journal,* p. 24, June 1991.

——"The Role of the Mutual UFO Network in UFO Research," *MUFON 1992 International UFO Symposium Proceedings,* Seguin, TX: MUFON, 1992, pp. 89-100.

——"Director's Message," *MUFON UFO Journal,* pp. 24, 23, July 1993.

Appelle, Stuart. Review of *They Call it Hypnosis* (1990) and *Hidden Memories* (1992) both by Robert Baker, *Journal of UFO Studies,* N.S. 4, 1992, pp. 175-180.

——"Scientific Credibility," *MUFON UFO Journal,* March 1994, pp. 16-17.

Aronowitz, Stanley. *Science As Power: Discourse and Ideology in Modern Society.* Minneapolis: University of Minnesota Press, 1988.

Baigent, Michael and Richard Leigh. *The Dead Sea Scrolls Deception.* NY: Simon and Schuster, 1991.

Baigent, Michael, Richard Leigh, and Henry Lincoln. *Holy Blood, Holy Grail.* NY: Dell Publishing, 1982.

Baker, Robert A. "An Anomalous Minority," *Journal of UFO Studies,* N.S. 3, 1991, pp. 142-148.

Ballester Olmos. "Spanish Air Force UFO Files: The Secret's End," *MUFON 1993 International Symposium Proceedings,* Seguin, TX: MUFON, 1993, pp. 126-168.

Barclay, David and Therese Marie Barclay (eds.) *UFOs: The Final Answer?: Ufology for the 21st Century.* London, England: Blandford, 1993.

Bartholomew, Robert E. and Keith Basterfield. "Fantasy-Prone and UFO Contact Percipients Still an Untested Hypothesis," *Journal of UFO Studies,* N.S. 2, 1990, pp. 184-185.

Basterfield, Keith. "Implants," *International UFO Reporter,* Jan./Feb. 1992, pp. 18-20.

——"Abduction Research in Australia," *MUFON UFO Journal,* July 1994, pp. 6-8.

Basterfield, Keith, Vladimir Godic, Pony Godic, and Mark Rodeghier. "Australian Ufology: A Review," *Journal of UFO Studies,* N.S. 2, 1990, pp. 19-44.

Beam, Alex. "'Mack Attack': Harvard Takes No Action," *MUFON UFO Journal,* Sept. 1995, pp. 13, 15, 19.

Becker, Barbara. "The Invention of a Gulf Breeze UFO," *International UFO Reporter,* March/April 1992, pp. 19-21, 23.

Berliner, Don. "Why the Press Acts that Way," *IUR,* Sept./Oct. 1992, pp. 16-18.

Boeche, Raymond W. "Public Reaction to Alien Contact: A Study," *MUFON 1988 International Symposium Proceedings,* Seguin, TX: MUFON, 1988, pp. 73-85.

Bohm, David. *Wholeness and the Implicate Order.* London: Routledge & Kegan Paul, 1980.

Boras, David. Review of *Lost Was the Key* by Leah Haley, *International UFO Reporter,* July/Aug. 1993, p. 10.

Boylan, Richard J. and Lee K. Boylan. *Close Extraterrestrial Encounters: Positive Experiences with Mysterious Visitors.* Mill Spring, NC: Wild Flower Press, 1994.

de Brosses, Marie-Therese. "An Interview with Professor Jean-Pierre Petit," *MUFON UFO Journal,* Jan. 1991, pp. 3-9.

Bryant, Alice and Linda Seebach. *Healing Shattered Reality: Understanding Contactee Trauma.* Mill Spring, NC: Wild Flower Press, 1991.

Bullard, Thomas E.."Hypnosis and UFO Abductions: A Troubled Relationship," *Journal of UFO Studies,* N.S. 1, 1989, pp. 3-40.

——"Folkloric Dimensions of the UFO Phenomenon," *Journal of UFO Studies,* N.S. 3, 1991, pp. 1-57.

Burnham, John C. *How Superstition Won and Science Lost: Popularizing Science and Health in the United States.* New Brunswick, N.J.: Rutgers University Press, 1987.

Cantril, Hadley. *The Invasion from Mars.* NY: Harper and Row, 1966.

Capra, Fritjof. *The Tao of Physics.* NY: Bantam, 1976.

Carpenter, John S. "Double Abduction Case: Correlation of Hypnosis Data," *Journal of UFO Studies*, N.S. 3, 1991A, pp. 91-114.

——"The Reality of the Abduction Phenomenon," *MUFON 1991 International UFO Symposium Proceedings*, Seguin, TX: MUFON, 1991B, pp. 149-172.

——"Cattle Mutilations and UFOs" (letter to the editor), *IUR*, May/June 1992, pp. 20-21.

——"Abduction Notes: Therapeutic Ideas for Coping," *MUFON UFO Journal*, Jan. 1993A, pp. 6-8.

——"Abduction Notes: 'Reptilians and Other Unmentionables,'" *MUFON UFO Journal*, April 1993B, pp. 10-11.

——"Abduction Notes: Educating Mental Health Professionals," *MUFON UFO Journal*, June 1993C, pp. 18-19.

——"Abduction Notes: Still More Explanations (Part Two)," *MUFON UFO Journal*, Oct. 1993D, pp. 14-16.

——"Abduction Notes: Alien Mistakes: Humorous Evidence," *MUFON UFO Journal*, Sept. 1994, pp. 17-18.

Casteel, Sean. "Encountering...'The Watchers'—Q&A: Raymond Fowler," *UFO*, Vol. 6, No. 4, 1991A, pp. 25-29.

——"Q & A: Encounters of Betty Luca," *UFO*, Vol. 6, No. 6, 1991B, pp. 23-25.

Chiang, Hoang-Yung. "UFO Sightings and Research in Modern China," *1993 MUFON International UFO Symposium Proceedings*, Seguin, TX: MUFON, 1993, pp. 42-58.

Chorost, Michael (ed.). *Report on the Results of Project Argus: An Instrumented Study of the Physical Materials of Crop Circles*. Durham, N.C.: Project Argus Report, 1993.

Christensen, Marge. "Scientists, UFOs, and Anti-Scientific Thinking," *MUFON 1986 International Symposium Proceedings*, Seguin, TX: MUFON, 1986, pp. 12-17.

——"Hynek's Last Wish for Ufology," *MUFON 1988 International UFO Symposium Proceedings*, Seguin, TX: MUFON, 1988, pp. 13-17.

Clark, Jerome. "The Fall and Rise of the Extraterrestrial Hypothesis," *MUFON 1988 International UFO Symposium Proceedings*, Seguin, TX: MUFON, 1988, pp. 59-72.

——*UFOs in the 1980s: The UFO Encyclopedia, Vol. I*. Detroit, MI: Apogee Books, 1990.

——"Editorial: That's the Way the Committee Crumbles," *IUR*, March/April 1992, pp. 3, ff.

——"Up in the Air," *International UFO Reporter*, Jan./Feb. 1993A, pp. 3, 22-23.

——"A Catalog of Early Crash Claims," *International UFO Reporter*, July/Aug. 1993B, pp. 11-18, 24.

——"Into the Mystic." *International UFO Reporter*, Sept./Oct. 1993C, p. 3.

——"Wagging the Dog," *International UFO Reporter*, Jan./Feb. 1994A, pp. 3, 22-24.

——"Big (Space) Brothers," *International UFO Reporter*, March/April 1994B, pp. 7-10.

Clark, Jerome and others. Various articles on the "Linda case," *IUR*, Vol. 18, No. 2, 1993, pp. 3-17, 21-24.

Clarke, Arther C. *Profiles of the Future: An Inquiry into the Limits of the Possible*. NY: Harper and Row, 1973.

Condon, Edward University *Scientific Study of Unidentified Flying Objects*. NY: Bantam Books, 1969.

Connecting Link, Oct., Nov. 1992 issues.

Conroy, Ed. *Report on Communion*. NY: Avon Books, 1989.

Cooper, Topher. "Anomalous Propagation," *Journal of Scientific Exploration*, Vol. 8, No. 1, 1994A, pp. 119-123.

——"Anomalous Propagation," *Journal of Scientific Exploration*, Vol. 8, No. 2, 1994B, pp. 269-273.

Corbin, Mike. "People in Focus...Scott Corder," *UFO*, Vol. 4, No. 4, 1989, p. 10.

Cortile, Linda. "Budd Hopkins' 'Linda' Case: A Look Behind the Experience," *MUFON 1994 International UFO Symposium Proceedings*, Seguin, TX: MUFON, 1994, pp. 239-255.

Coyne, George. "Current Case Log," *MUFON UFO Journal*, July 1992, p. 19.

Crawford, Forest. "The Revealing Science of Ufology: An Anatomy of Abduction Correlations," *MUFON UFO Journal*, Dec. 1991, pp. 10-15.

Cremo, Michael A. and Richard L. Thompson. *Forbidden Archaeology*. San Diego, CA: Govardhan Hill Publishing, 1993.

Crystall, Ellen. *Silent Invasion: The Shocking Discoveries of a UFO Researcher*. NY: Paragon House, 1991.

Davenport, Marc. *Dear Mr. President: 100 Earth-Saving Letters*. Citadel Press, 1992A.

——*Visitors from Time: The Secret of the UFOs*. Murfreesboro, TN: Greenleaf Publications, 1992B.

——Review of *Lost Was the Key* by Leah A. Haley, *MUFON UFO Journal*, June 1994, p. 17.

Dawes, Robyn M. and Matthew Mulford. "Diagnoses of Alien Kidnappings That Result from Conjunction Effects in Memory," *Skeptical Inquirer*, Fall 1993, pp. 50-51.

Dean, Robert O. "UFOs and World History," *MUFON 1994 International Symposium Proceedings*, Seguin, TX: MUFON, 1994, pp. 91-107.

DiCarlo, Russell E. *Towards a New World View: Conversations at the Leading Edge*. Erie, PA: Epic Publishing, 1996.

Dormer, Joseph. "All in the Eye of the Beholder?" Chapter 7, pp. 130-153 in Barclay and Barclay (eds.), 1993.

Downing, Barry H. *The Bible and Flying Saucers*. NY: Berkley Books, 1968.

——"UFOs and Religion: Of Things Visible and Invisible," *MUFON 1994 International Symposium Proceedings*, Seguin, TX: MUFON, 1994, pp. 34-48.

Drake, Frank D. "On Hands and Knees in Search of Elysium," *Technology Review*, Vol. 78, June 1976, pp. 22-29.

Drasin, Daniel. "Ridicule Is No Laughing Matter: The Anatomy of Debunking," presented to the International Association for New Science Conference on UFOs. Denver, CO: May 25, 1992.

Druffel, Ann. "Resisting Alien Abductions: An Update," *MUFON UFO Journal*, March 1992, pp. 3-7.

——"Remembering James McDonald," *IUR*, Sept./Oct. 1993, pp. 4-6, 23-24.

Durant, Robert J. "Evolution of Public Opinion on UFOs," *IUR*, Nov./Dec. 1993, pp. 9-13, 20-23.

Earley, George W. "Crashed Saucers and Pickled Aliens" *Fate Magazine*, March/April 1981.

——Review of *The Watchers* by Raymond E. Fowler, *UFO*, Vol. 5, No. 6, 1990, pp. 36-37.

——"Hopkins Rates Mini-Series: 'B+,'" *UFO*, Vol. 7, No. 4, 1992, p. 11.

Ellison, Wesley E. "Detection and Analysis of Aerial Phenomenon," *MUFON 1993 International UFO Symposium Proceedings*, Seguin, TX: MUFON, 1993, pp. 114-125.

Emmons, Charles F. *Chinese Ghosts and ESP: A Study of Paranormal Beliefs and Experiences*. Metuchen, N.J.: Scarecrow Press, 1982.

——"Ufology and Religion: Then and Now," presented at the Popular Culture Association annual meeting. New Orleans, LA: April 15, 1993.

Faile, Samuel P. "Notice of Disclaim for Anti-UFO Abduction Device," unpublished photocopy, June 13, 1994.

Ferryn, Patrick. "The Belgian Wave," *International Association for New Science UFO Conference*, Denver, CO: May 24, 1992; .

Festinger, Leon, Henry W. Riecken and Stanley Schachter. *When Prophecy Fails: A Social and Psychological Study of a Modern Group that Predicted the Destruction of the World*. NY: Harper and Row, 1956.

Forrest, Rick. "'60s UFO Films: Decade in Transition," *UFO*, Vol. 2, No. 4, 1987, pp. 35-37.

Fowler, Raymond E. *Casebook of a UFO Investigator.* (WFP reprint forthcoming) Englewood Cliffs, NJ: Prentice Hall, Inc., 1981.

——*The Andreasson Affair: The Documented Investigation of a Woman's Abduction Aboard a UFO*. Englewood Cliffs, NJ: Prentice-Hall, Inc., 1979. Reprint Mill Spring, NC: Wild Flower Press, 1994.

——*The Andreasson Affair Phase Two: The Continuing Investigation of a Woman's Abduction By Extraterrestrials*. Englewood Cliffs, NJ: Prentice-Hall, Inc., 1982. Reprint Mill Spring, NC: Wild Flower Press, 1994.

——*The Watchers: The Secret Design Behind UFO Abduction*. NY: Bantam Books, 1990.

——*The Watchers II: Exploring UFOs and the Near-Death Experience.*. Mill Spring NC: Wild Flower Press, 1995.

——*The Allagash Abductions: Undeniable Evidence of Alien Intervention*. Mill Spring, NC: Wild Flower Press, 1993.

Frazier, Kendrick. "UFOs and the Tabloids: The Education of a Writer," *The Skeptical Inquirer*, Summer 1982, pp. 7-8.

——"NOVA's Look at UFOs," *The Skeptical Inquirer*, Winter 1982-83, pp. 6-7.

Friedman, Stanton T. "E-T Artifact Testing," *MUFON UFO Journal*, Dec. 1993, pp. 10-11, 14.

Friedman, Stanton and Don Berliner. *Crash at Corona*. NY: Paragon House, 1992.

Fuller, John G. *Incident and Exeter*. NY: G.P. Putnam's Sons, 1966A.

——*The Interrupted Journey*. NY: Dial Press, 1966B.

Garner, W. L., Jr. "MUFON Versus the New Age," *MUFON UFO Journal*, Dec. 1993, pp. 13-14.

Good, Timothy. *Above Top Secret: The Worldwide UFO Cover-up*. NY: Quill, Wm. Morrow, 1988.

Gordon, James S. "Someone to Watch Over Us," review of *Abduction* by John E. Mack, *The NY Times Book Review*, May 1, 1994, pp. 13-14.

Gotlib, David. "Who Speaks for the Witness?" *MUFON 1990 International UFO Symposium Proceedings*, Seguin, TX: MUFON, 1990, pp. 25-35.

——"False Memory Syndrome," *MUFON UFO Journal*, July 1993, pp. 12-14.

Greco, Samuel and Stan Gordon "Williamsport Wave," *MUFON UFO Journal*, June 1992, pp. 3-10.

Greenwood, Barry. "Ufology in Crisis: Two Views," *International UFO Reporter*, Nov./Dec. 1991, pp. 3, 19.

Greer, Steven M. Untitled compilation of papers, Asheville, NC: CSETI, 1992.

Gresh, Bryan. "Soviet UFO Secrets," *MUFON UFO Journal*, Oct. 1993, pp. 3-7.

Gribble, Robert and Donald Ware. "Current Cases," *MUFON UFO Journal*, Dec. 1992, pp. 18-19.

Grosso, Michael. "Transcending the 'ET Hypothesis,'" *California UFO* 3, no. 3, 1988, pp. 9-11.

Haines, Richard F. "A Scientifically Based Analysis of an Alleged UFO Photograph," *MUFON 1986 UFO Symposium Proceedings*, Seguin, TX: MUFON, 1986, pp. 112-129.

——"A 'Three Stage Technique' (TST) to Help Reduce Biasing Effects During Hypnotic Regression," *Journal of UFO Studies*, N.S. 1, 1989, pp. 163-167.

——"Encounter over Siberia," *IUR*, Nov./Dec. 1991, pp. 12 ff.

——"Fifty-Six Aircraft Pilot Sightings Involving Electromagnetic Effects," *MUFON 1992 International UFO Symposium Proceedings*, Seguin, TX: MUFON, 1992, pp. 102-131.

——"Insights from Studying Groups of UFOs," *MUFON 1994 International Symposium Proceedings*, Seguin, TX: MUFON, 1994A, pp. 154-172.

——"Get Involved and Make a Difference!" *MUFON UFO Journal*, Sept. 1994B, pp. 14-15.

Haley, Leah A. *Lost Was the Key*. Murfreesboro, TN: Greenleaf Publications, 1993.

——*Ceto's New Friends*. Murfreesboro, TN: Greenleaf Publications, 1994.

Hall, Richard H. "NICAP and Lessons from the Past," *International UFO Reporter*, May/June 1992A, pp. 17, 24.

——"Hall's Corner," *UFO*, Vol. 7, No. 4, 1992B, p. 13.

——"Hall's Corner," *UFO*, Vol. 8, No. 1, 1993A, pp. 12-13.

——"The Future of Ufology," *International UFO Reporter*, Sept./Oct. 1993B, pp. 7, 24.

——"The Quest for Truth about UFOs: A Personal Perspective on the Role of NICAP," *MUFON 1994 International UFO Symposium Proceedings*, Seguin, TX: MUFON, 1994, pp. 186-222.

Hall, Robert L., Donald A. Johnson and Mark Rodeghier. "UFO Abduction Survey: A Critique," *MUFON UFO Journal*, July 1993, pp. 9-11, 14.

Hall, Robert L., Mark Rodeghier and Donald A. Johnson. "On Mass Panic and Other Favorite Myths," *MUFON 1990 International Symposium Proceedings*, Seguin, TX: MUFON, 1990, pp. 61-71.

——"The Prevalence of Abductions: A Critical Look," *Journal of UFO Studies*, N.S. 4, 1992, pp. 131-135.

Hamilton, Bill. "Skydancer over Antelope Valley," *MUFON UFO Journal*, April 1994, pp. 10 ff.

Harder, James A. "The Aerial Phenomena Research Organization, Inc. and the Future of Ufology," *MUFON 1994 International UFO Symposium Proceedings*, Seguin, TX: MUFON, 1994, pp. 224-237.

Heaton, Timothy H. Review of *Abduction* by John E. Mack, *MUFON UFO Journal*, July 1994, pp. 13-15.

Hess, David J. *Science in the New Age: The Paranormal, Its Defenders and Debunkers, and American Culture*. Madison, Wisc.: University of Wisconsin Press, 1993.

Hind, Cynthia. "Abductions in Africa--Worldwide Similarities," *MUFON 1993 International UFO Symposium Proceedings*, Seguin, TX: MUFON, 1993, pp. 17-25.

Holt, Alan C. "Interstellar Spaceports and Transportation Systems," *MUFON 1986 UFO Symposium Proceedings*, Seguin, TX: MUFON, 1986, pp. 82-99.

Holton, Gerald. *Science and Anti-Science*. Cambridge: Harvard University Press, 1993, pp. 146-147.

——"The Antiscience Problem," *Skeptical Inquirer*, Vol. 18, 1994, pp. 264-265.

Hopkins, Budd. *Intruders: The Incredible Visitations at Copley Woods*. NY: Random House, Inc., 1987.

——"One Ufologist's Methodology," *UFO*, Vol. 4, No. 2, 1989, pp. 26-30.

——Letter to Editor, *MUFON UFO Journal*, Feb. 1992A, p. 18.

——"Abduction Observed by Independent Witnesses," presented at MUFON 1992 International UFO Symposium, Albuquerque, New Mexico: July 11, 1992B.

——"The Linda Cortile Abduction Case," *MUFON UFO Journal*, Sept. 1992C, pp. 12-16.

——"Invisibility and the UFO Abduction Phenomenon," *MUFON 1993 International UFO Symposium Proceedings*, Seguin, TX: MUFON, 1993A, pp. 183-201.

———"Invisibility and the UFO Abduction Phenomenon," presented at MUFON International UFO Symposium, Richmond, VA: July 4, 1993B.

———"New Revelations about Alien Abductions," presented at The UFO Experience Conference, North Haven, CT: Oct. 9, 1993C.

———"Losing a Battle While Winning the War," *MUFON UFO Journal*, June 1994A, pp. 10-12.

———"New Research on Implants and Group Abductions," presented at the Second Annual Gulf Breeze UFO Conference, Pensacola, FL: Oct. 14, 1994B.

———"Science Is Not Always What Science Programs Do: A Response to *Nova's* Program on UFO Abductions," *MUFON UFO Journal*, March 1996A, pp. 17-20.

———"Budd Hopkins' Response to the UFO Abduction Phenomenon," *Contact Forum*, March/April, 1996B, p.1.

———Hopkins, Budd. *Witnessed: The True Story of the Brooklyn Bridge UFO Abductions*. New York: Pocket Books, 1996C.

———, David Jacobs, and Ron Westrum. *Unusual Personal Experiences*. Las Vegas, NV: Bigelow Holding Corporation, 1992.

Horn, Arthur David. *Humanity's Extraterrestrial Origins: ET Influences on Humankind's Biological and Cultural Evolution*. Mount Shasta, CA: A & L Horn, 1994.

Howe, Linda Moulton. *An Alien Harvest: Further Evidence Linking Animal Mutilations and Human Abductions to Alien Life Forms*. Huntingdon Valley, PA: LMH Productions, 1989.

———"Further Evidence Linking Animal Mutilations and Human Abductions to Alien Life Forms," *MUFON 1991 International UFO Symposium Proceedings*, Seguin, TX: MUFON, 1991, pp. 134-147.

———"The UFO Jigsaw," *MUFON 1992 International UFO Symposium Proceedings*, Seguin, TX: MUFON, 1992, pp. 16-36.

———"Moving Lights, Disks and Animal Mutilations in Alabama," *MUFON 1993 International UFO Symposium Proceedings*, Seguin, TX: MUFON, 1993A, pp. 27-40.

———*Glimpses of Other Realities, Vol. 1: Facts and Eyewitnesses*. Huntingdon Valley, PA: LMH Productions, 1993B.

———"Exploring Other Realities with Facts and Eyewitnesses," presented at International Forum for New Science Conference, Fort Collins, CO: Sept. 16, 1994.

———*Glimpses of Other Realities, Vol. 2: High Strangeness*. Huntingdon Valley, PA: LMH Productions, 1996.

Hufford, Art. "Ed Walters, the Model and Tommy Smith," *MUFON UFO Journal*, Jan. 1993, pp. 9-13.

Hufford, David J. *The Terror That Comes in the Night: An Experience-Centered Study of Supernatural Assault Traditions.* Philadelphia: University of PA Press, 1982.

Huneeus, J. Antonio. "Red Skies: The Great 1989 UFO Wave in the UniversityS.S.R.," *MUFON 1990 International Symposium Proceedings,* Seguin, TX: MUFON, 1990, pp. 170-201.

——"Global Ufology: Worldwide Cases, Official Policies and Ufological Attitudes," *MUFON 1992 International Symposium Proceedings,* Seguin, TX: MUFON, 1992, pp. 173-190.

Hynek, J. Allen. "The Condon Report and UFOs," *Bulletin of the Atomic Scientists,* 25, April 1969, pp. 39-42.

——*The UFO Experience: A Scientific Inquiry.* NY: Ballantine, 1972.

Hynek, J. Allen, Philip J. Imbrogno, and Bob Pratt. *Night Siege: The Hudson Valley UFO Sightings.* NY: Ballantine Books, 1987.

Imbrogno, Philip. "UFOs and the Stone Chambers of the Hudson Valley," presented at The UFO Experience Conference; North Haven, CT: Oct. 9-10, 1993.

Jacobs, David M. *The UFO Controversy in America.* Bloomington, Indiana: Indiana University Press, 1975.

——"On Studying the Abduction Phenomenon without Knowing What It Is," *Journal of UFO Studies,* N.S. 3, 1991, pp. 153-163.

——"What Do Sightings Mean?" *International UFO Reporter,* Jan./Feb. 1992A, pp. 13-17, 23.

——*Secret Life: Firsthand Accounts of UFO Abductions.* NY: Simon & Schuster, 1992B.

—— and Budd Hopkins. "Suggested Techniques for Hypnosis and Therapy of Abductees," *Journal of UFO Studies,* N.S. 4, 1992, pp. 138-150.

—— and Michael D. Swords. "Faking History," *IUR,* July/Aug. 1994, pp. 7-10, 23.

Johnson, Donald A. "UFO Car Pursuits: Some New Patterns from Old Data," *MUFON 1989 International UFO Symposium Proceedings,* Seguin, TX: MUFON, 1989, pp. 136-146.

Johnson, Jerold R. "Current Cases," *MUFON UFO Journal,* Feb. 1994, p. 18.

Johnson, Vince. "Time Travelers: An Alternative to the ET Hypothesis," *MUFON UFO Journal,* Jan. 1993, pp. 4-5.

Jung, Carl G. "Flying Saucers: A Modern Myth of Things Seen Flying in the Sky," *The Collected Works of C.G. Jung,* Princeton, NJ: Princeton University Press, Vol. 10, 1970, pp. 307-333 .

Kaku, Michio. *Hyperspace: A Scientific Odyssey through Parallel Universes, Time Warps, and the Tenth Dimension.* NY: Oxford University Press, 1994.

Kannenberg, Ida M. *UFOs and the Psychic Factor.* Mill Spring, NC: Wild Flower Press, 1992.

Kasher, Jack. "A Scientific Analysis of the Videotape Taken by Space Shuttle Discovery on Shuttle Flight STS-48," *MUFON 1994 International UFO Symposium Proceedings*, Seguin, TX: MUFON, 1994, pp. 109-136.

Keel, John A. "The Man Who Invented Flying Saucers," *The Fringes of Reason: A Whole Earth Catalog*, ed. Ted Schultz, NY: Harmony Books, 1989, pp. 138-145.

Kerth, Linda. "In Defense of Memory," *International UFO Reporter*, May/June 1992, pp. 15-16, 23-24.

Kerth, Linda and Richard F. Haines. "How Children Portray UFOs," *Journal of UFO Studies*, N.S. 4, 1992, pp. 39-77.

Kinder, Gary. *Light Years.* NY: Pocket Books, 1987.

Kitcher, Philip. *The Advancement of Science: Science without Legend, Objectivity without Illusions.* NY: Oxford University Press, 1993.

Klass, Philip J. *UFOs Explained.* NY: Vintage Books, 1976.

——"Hypnosis and UFO Abductions," *Skeptical Inquirer*, Spring 1981, 1981, pp. 16-24.

——*UFOs: The Public Deceived.* Buffalo, NY: Prometheus Books, 1983.

——"Radar UFOs: Where Have They Gone?" *Skeptical Inquirer*, Spring 1985, pp. 257-260.

——*UFO-Abductions: A Dangerous Game.* Buffalo, NY: Prometheus Books, 1988.

——"*Time* Challenges John Mack's UFO Abduction Efforts," *Skeptical Inquirer*, Summer 1994, pp. 340-342.

——"Nova's TV Documentary on UFO Abductions Evokes Harsh Criticism from Abduction Guru Hopkins," *Skeptics UFO Newsletter*, March 1996, pp.1-4.

Knapp, George. "What the Russians Know about UFOs," *MUFON 1994 International UFO Symposium Proceedings*, Seguin, TX: MUFON, 1994, pp. 276-306.

Komar, John and Pete Theer. "Connecting By Computer," *MUFON UFO Journal*, Nov. 1992, pp. 9-11.

Kuhn, Thomas. *The Structure of Scientific Revolutions.* Chicago: The University of Chicago Press, 1962.

Kulikowski, Stan, II. "Infernal UFOs: Bigger Inside than Out?" *MUFON UFO Journal*, May 1994, pp. 9-12, 14.

Kurtz, Paul. "The Growth of Antiscience," *Skeptical Inquirer*, Vol. 18, Spring 1994, pp. 255-263.

Larry King Live. "UFO Coverup?" TNT, Oct. 2, 1994.

Lederman, Leon with Dick Teresi. *The God Particle: If the Universe Is the Answer, What Is the Question?* Boston: Houghton Mifflin Co., 1993.

Loftus, Elizabeth. "Remembering Dangerously," *Skeptical Inquirer*, March/April 1995, pp. 20-29.

Lorenzen, Coral and Jim Lorenzen. *Encounters with UFO Occupants.* NY: Berkeley Publishing Co., 1976.

von Ludwiger, Illobrand. "The Most Significant UFO Sightings in Germany," *MUFON 1993 International UFO Symposium Proceedings*, Seguin, TX: MUFON, 1993, pp. 240-303.

Maccabee, Bruce S. "Still in Default," *MUFON 1986 UFO Symposium Proceedings*, Seguin, TX: MUFON, 1986, pp. 131-158.

——"A History of the Gulf Breeze, Florida Sighting Events," *MUFON 1988 International UFO Symposium Proceedings*, Seguin, TX: MUFON, 1988, pp. 114-204.

——"Gulf Breeze Without Ed," *MUFON 1991 International UFO Symposium Proceedings*, Seguin, TX: MUFON, 1991A, pp. 186-267.

——Letter to the editor on "Ed type" UFOs, *MUFON UFO Journal*, Aug. 1991B, pp. 20-21.

——"Hiding the Hardware," *IUR*, Sept./Oct. 1991C, pp. 4-10, 23.

——"Strange Lights over Gulf Breeze," *MUFON UFO Journal*, Dec. 1991D, pp. 16-17.

McCampbell, James M. "Interpreting Reports of UFO Sightings," *MUFON 1975 UFO Symposium Proceedings*, Seguin, TX: MUFON, 1975, pp. 78-91.

Mack, John E. *A Prince of Our Disorder: The Life of T.E. Lawrence.* Boston, MA: Little, Brown, 1977.

——"Helping Abductees," *International UFO Reporter*, July/Aug. 1992, pp. 10-15, 20.

——"The UFO Abduction Phenomenon: What Might it Mean for the Human Future?" *MUFON 1993 International UFO Symposium Proceedings*, Seguin, TX: MUFON, 1993A, pp. 203-213.

——"Alien Abductions: Exploring Possible Meanings in Human Evolution," presented at The UFO Experience Conference, North Haven, CT: Oct. 10, 1993B.

——*Abduction: Human Encounters with Aliens.* NY: Charles Scribner's Sons, 1994A.

——"Alien Reckoning," *The Washington Post*, Outlook: Commentary and Opinion, Sunday, April 17, 1994B, pp. C1, C4.

——"'Alien Abduction:' Possible Implications for Human Evolution," presented at the Fifteenth Rocky Mountain UFO Conference, Laramie, WY: June 25, 1994C.

——"John Mack's Letter to Nova in Advance of the Program," *Contact Forum*, March/April, 1996, p.1.

McDaniel, Stanley V. *The McDaniel Report*. Berkeley, CA: North Atlantic Books, 1993.

McDonald, James E. "UFOs: Greatest Scientific Problem of Our Times?" presented at annual meeting of the American Society of Newspaper Editors, WAshington, D.C.: April 22, 1967.

Mahoney, Michael J. "Psychology of the Scientist: An Evaluation Review," *Social Studies of Science*, Vol. 9, 1979, pp. 349-375.

Marciniak, Barbara. *Bringers of the Dawn: Teachings from the Pleiadians*. Santa Fe, New Mexico: Bear & Co. Publishing, 1992.

——Pleiadian Workshop, Lily Dale, NY: Aug. 19, 1994.

Menzel, Donald H. and Lyle G. Boyd. *The World of Flying Saucers*. Cambridge: Harvard University Press, 1963.

Merton, Robert K. *Social Theory and Social Structure*. NY: Free Press, 1949.

Meyer, Ginna. "Abductee Memory Loss," *MUFON UFO Journal*, March 1992, p. 12.

Moore, Robert. "Science V. Saucery," Ch. 4 in Barclay and Barclay (eds.), 1993.

Moore, William L. and Stanton T. Friedman. "MJ-12 and Phil Klass: What Are the Facts?" *MUFON 1988 International UFO Symposium Proceedings*, Seguin, TX: MUFON, 1988, pp. 206-241.

Morris, M.S. and K.S. Thorne. "Wormholes in Space and Their Use for Interstellar Travel: A Tool for Teaching General Relativity," *American Journal of Physics*, 56, 1988, p. 411.

Morris, M.S., K.S. Thorne and U. Yurtsever. "Wormholes, Time Machines, and the Weak Energy Condition," *Physical Review Letters*, 61, 1988, p. 1446.

Mundy, Jean. "A Case of 'Unnatural' Pregnancy," *UFO*, Vol. 6, No. 4, 1991, pp. 23-24, 44.

Neal, Richard M., Jr. "Paralysis by Microwaves," *MUFON UFO Journal*, Nov. 1991, pp. 13-16, 22.

——"The Missing Embryo/Fetus Syndrome," *MUFON 1992 International UFO Symposium Proceedings*, Seguin, TX: MUFON, 1992, pp. 214-229.

Neimark, Jill. "The Harvard Professor and the UFOs," *Psychology Today*, March/April 1994, pp. 46, ff.

Nickell, Joe. "UFO 'Dogfight': A Ballooning Tale," *Skeptical Inquirer*, Fall 1993,pp. 3-4.

Noyes, Ralph (ed.). *The Crop Circle Enigma*. Bath, England: Gateway, 1991.

O'Leary, Brian. *Exploring Inner and Outer Space: A Scientist's Perspective on Personal and Planetary Transformation*. Berkeley, CA: North Atlantic Books, 1989.

Parnell, June O. "Personality Characteristics on the MMPI, 16PF, and ACL of Persons Who Claim UFO Experiences." Ph.D. dissertation, University of Wyoming (University Microfilms, order no. DA 8623104), 1987.

Parnell, June O. and R. Leo Sprinkle. "Personality Characteristics of Persons who Claim UFO Experiences," *Journal of UFO Studies*, N.S. 2, 1990, pp. 45-58.

Petit, Jean-Pierre. "Has Science Something to Do with UFOs?" *MUFON 1991 International UFO Symposium Proceedings*, Seguin, TX: MUFON, 1991, pp. 40-49.

Phillips, K.W.C. "The Psycho-Sociology of Ufology," Ch. 3 in Barclay and Barclay (eds.), 1993.

Phillips, Ted R. "Close Encounters of the Second Kind: Physical Traces," *MUFON 1981 UFO Symposium Proceedings*, Seguin, TX: MUFON, 1981, pp. 93-129.

Pritchard, David E. "Introductory Remarks at the Conference," *Alien Discussions: Proceedings of the Abduction Study Conference held at MIT, Cambridge, MA*, Cambridge, MA: North Cambridge Press, 1994.

Puhalski, Roberta. "Abductions: State of Siege—Or Mind?" *MUFON UFO Journal*, May 1994, pp. 15-17.

Randle, Kevin D. and Donald R. Schmitt. *UFO Crash at Roswell*. NY: Avon Books, 1991.

——*The Truth about the UFO Crash at Roswell*. NY: M. Evans, 1994.

Randles, Jenny. "Round and Round in the Circle Game," *IUR*, Nov./Dec. 1991, pp. 17-18, 22-23.

Randles, Jenny and others. *Sky Crash*. London: Neville Spearman, 1984.

Randles, Jenny and Peter Warrington. *Science and the UFOs*. Oxford, England: Basil Blackwell Ltd., 1985.

Raphael (Ken Carey). *The Starseed Transmissions: An Extraterrestrial Report*. Kansas City, Mo.: Uni-Sun, 1982.

Redfield, James. *The Celestine Prophecy: An Adventure*. NY: Warner Books, 1993.

Ring, Kenneth. "Fantasy Proneness and the Kitchen Sink," *Journal of UFO Studies*, N.S. 2, 1990, pp. 186-187.

——*The Omega Report: Near Death Experiences, UFO Encounters, and Mind at Large*. NY: Wm. Morrow & Co., 1992.

Ring, Kenneth and Christorpher J. Rosing. "The Omega Project: A Psychological Survey of Persons Reporting Abductions and Other UFO Encounters," *Journal of UFO Studies*, N.S. 2, 1990, pp. 59-98.

Rodeghier, Mark and Mark Chesney. "The Air Force Report on Roswell: An Absence of Evidence," *IUR*, Sept./Oct. 1994, pp. 3, 20-24.

Rodeghier, Mark, Jeff Goodpaster and Sandra Blatterbauer. "Psychosocial Characteristics of Abductees: Results from the CUFOS Abduction Project," *Journal of UFO Studies*, N.S. 3, 1991, pp. 59-90.

Rothman, Milton A. *The Science Gap: Dispelling the Myths and Understanding the Reality of Science*. Buffalo, NY: Prometheus Books, 1992.

Rutkowski, Chris A. "The TST: Down for the Count," *Journal of UFO Studies*, N.S., Vol. 2, 1990, pp. 166-168.

——"Will the Circles Be Broken?" *IUR*, Jan./Feb. 1993, pp. 11-12, 23.

Sagan, Carl. "Direct Contact among Galactic Civilizations by Relativistic Interstellar Spaceflight," in Donald Goldsmith, *The Quest for Extraterrestrial Life*, Mill Valley, CA: University Science Books, 1980.

——*Contact*. NY: Simon and Schuster, 1985.

——"The Search for Signals from Space," *Parade Magazine*, Sept. 19, 1993, pp. 4-6.

Sainio, Jeffrey W. "Photo Analysis: A Pictorial Primer," *MUFON 1992 International UFO Symposium Proceedings*, Seguin, TX: MUFON, 1992, pp. 133-165.

——"Video Analysis," *MUFON 1993 International UFO Symposium Proceedings*, Seguin, TX: MUFON, 1993, pp. 86-111.

Salisberry, Carol and Rex Salisberry. Letter to the editor on Walters' photographs, *MUFON UFO Journal*, June 1991, pp. 17-18.

Sarasohn, Judy. *Science on Trial: The Whistle-Blower, the Accused, and the Nobel Laureate*. NY: St. Martin's Press, 1993.

Schroth, David A. Review of *UFO...Contact from the Pleiades, Vol. 1* by Lee J. Elders and others, *Skeptical Inquirer*, Fall 1980, pp. 74-77.

Schuessler, John F. "MUFON: A World Leader in Ufology," *MUFON 1994 International UFO Symposium Proceedings*, Seguin, TX: MUFON, 1994, pp. 174-184.

Schuessler, John F. and Edward F. O'Herin. "Truck Driver Injured by UFO: The Eddie Doyle Webb Case," *MUFON 1993 International UFO Symposium Proceedings*, Seguin, TX: MUFON, 1993, pp. 60-84.

Schwarz, Berthold E. *UFO Dynamics: Psychiatric and Psychic Aspects of the UFO Syndrome*. Moore Haven, Florida: Rainbow Books, 1983.

Sedona, Oct. 1994

Sheaffer, Robert. Review of *The Hynek UFO Report* by J. Allen Hynek, *Skeptical Inquirer*, Winter 1978, pp. 64-67.

——Review of *Project Identification* by Harley D. Rutledge, *Skeptical Inquirer*, Spring 1982, pp. 68-69.

——"Psychic Vibrations: Unreal with Rael...", *Skeptical Inquirer*, Summer 1994, pp. 363-364.

Simon, Armando. Review of *Observing UFOs* by Richard F. Haines, *Skeptical Inquirer*, Summer 1980, pp. 52-53.

——"Psychology and UFOs," *Skeptical Inquirer*, Summer 1984, pp. 355-367.

Sims, Derrel and Mary Jo Florey. "Evidence for and Implications of Medically Unexplained Implants in Abductees," presented at International Forum for New Science, Fort Collins, CO: Sept. 17, 1994.

Smith, Willy. "On UFO Noises," *International UFO Reporter*, July/Aug. 1993, pp. 19-20, 24.

Snow, C.P. *The Two Cultures and the Scientific Revolution*. NY: Cambridge University Press, 1991.

Spanos, Nicholas P. *et al.* "Close Encounters: An Examination of UFO Experiences," *Journal of Abnormal Psychology*, Vol. 102, No. 4, 1993, pp. 624-632.

Spataford, Guy. "The Abduction/Out-Of-Body Connection," *UFO*, Vol. 8, No. 2, 1993, pp. 17-20.

Speiser, Jim. "TV Drama Fell Short, Some Witnesses Charge," *UFO*, Vol. 6, No. 6, 1991, pp. 18-19.

Spencer, John L. "The Differences between Perceptions of Ufology in America and Europe," *MUFON 1990 International Symposium Proceedings*, Seguin, TX: MUFON, 1990, pp. 37-44.

Sprinkle, R. Leo. "UFO Research: Problem or Predicament?" *MUFON 1975 UFO Symposium Proceedings*, Seguin, TX: MUFON, 1975, pp. 37-49.

——"Physical and Spiritual Evidence," letter to the editor, *International UFO Reporter*, May/June 1992, p. 20.

——Hypnosis Workshop, 15th Annual Rocky Mountain UFO Conference, Laramie, WY: June 22, 1994A.

——"A Model of Reincarnation and UFO Activity," presented at Second Annual Gulf Breeze UFO Conference, Pensacola, FL, Oct. 16, 1994B.

——*Soul Samples: Personal Exploration in Reincarnation and UFO Experiences*. Mill Spring, NC: Wild Flower Press, forthcoming 1998.

Stacy, Dennis. "The Circles of Summer," *MUFON UFO Journal*, Sept. 1992, pp. 3-11.

——"Military Retrieval of Crashed UFOs," Presented at The UFO Experience Conference, North Haven, CT:, Oct. 9, 1993.

——"Cosmic Conspiracy: Six Decades of Government UFO Cover-ups," *Omni*, monthly, April through Sept. 1994.

Stark, Sherie. "UFO Documentaries: Behind the Scenes," *UFO*, Vol. 3, No. 4, 1988, pp. 18-24.

Stock, Debbie. "Leno Laughs at UFOs," *MUFON UFO Journal*, July 1994, pp. 9-10.

Story, Ronald D. *UFOs and the Limits of Science*. NY: Wm. Morrow & Co., 1981.

——"UFOs on NOVA," *Skeptical Inquirer*, Spring 1983, pp. 70-72.

Strentz, Herbert. "An Analysis of Press Coverage of Unidentified Flying Objects, 1947-1966," Ph.D. dissertation, Evanston, IL: Northwestern University, 1970.

Strieber, Whitley. *Communion: A True Story*. NY: Morrow/Beech Tree Books, 1987.

Sturrock, Peter A. "Report on a Survey of the Membership of the American Astronomical Society Concerning the UFO Problem: Part 1," *Journal of Scientific Exploration*, Vol. 8, No. 1, 1994A, pp. 1-45.

——"Guest Column: A Survey and a Society," *Journal of Scientific Exploration*, Vol. 8, No. 1, 1994B, pp. 129-134.

Swords, Michael D. "The Case for E.T.: Within the Mainstream of Science," *MUFON 1986 UFO Symposium Proceedings*, Seguin, TX: MUFON, 1986, pp. 19-43.

——"Science and the Extraterrestrial Hypothesis in Ufology," *Journal of UFO Studies*, N.S. 1, 1989, pp. 67-102.

——"Modern Biology and the Extraterrestrial Hypothesis," *MUFON 1991 International UFO Symposium Proceedings*, Seguin, TX: MUFON, 1991, pp. 51-78.

——Review of *Anomalous Experiences and Trauma* by Rima E. Laibow *et al.*, *Journal of UFO Studies*, N.S. 4, 1992A, pp. 201-205.

——"Michael Swords Replies," *MUFON UFO Journal*, June 1992B, pp. 12-13.

——"Does the ETH Make Sense?" *International UFO Reporter*, Sept./Oct. 1992C, pp. 6-8, 12.

——"Could Extraterrestrial Intelligences Be Expected to Breathe Our Air?" *Journal of Scientific Exploration*, Vol. 9, No. 3, 1994, pp. 1-14.

——"Donald Keyhoe and the Pentagon: The rise of interest in the UFO phenomenon and what the government really knew," *Journal of UFO Studies*, Vol. 6, 1996A.

——"The University of Colorado UFO Project: The 'scientific study of UFOs.'" *Journal of UFO Studies*, Vol. 6, 1996B.

Swords, Michael D. and Erol Faruk. "Research Note: Delphos, Kansas, Soil Analysis," *Journal of UFO Studies*, N.S. 3, 1991, pp. 115-137.

Swords, Michael D. *et al.* "Analysis of Alleged Fragments from an Exploding UFO near Ubatuba, Brazil," *Journal of UFO Studies*, N.S. 4, 1992, pp. 1-37.

Talbot, Michael. *The Holographic Universe*. NY: HarperCollins, 1991.

Taylor, Lee Roger, Jr., and Michael R. Dennett. "The Saguaro Incident: A Study in CUFOS Methodology," *Skeptical Inquirer*, Fall 1985, pp. 69-82.

Thompson, Keith. *Angels and Aliens: UFOs and the Mythic Imagination*. NY: Fawcett Columbine, 1991.

Thompson, Richard L. *Alien Identities*. San Diego, CA: Govardhan Hill, Inc., 1993.

Thorne, Kip S. *Black Holes and Time Warps: Einstein's Outrageous Legacy*. NY: W.W. Norton and Co., 1994.

Tilly, Virginia M. "Resisting Resisting," *MUFON UFO Journal*, Aug. 1992, pp. 11-12.

Tipler, Frank J. "Extraterrestrial Beings Do Not Exist," *Quarterly Journal of the Royal Astronomical Society*, Vol. 21, 1980, pp. 267-281.

Torme, Tracy. Letter to "MUFON Forum," *MUFON UFO Journal*, Feb. 1993, p. 18.

Trefil, James. *The Moment of Creation*. NY: Macmillan, 1983.

Turner, Karla. *Into the Fringe: A True Story of Alien Abduction.* NY: Berkley Books, 1992.

——"Encounter Phenomena Defy 'Set Pattern,'" *UFO*, Vol. 8, No. 1, 1993, pp. 26-30.

——*Taken: Inside the Alien-Human Abduction Agenda*. Roland, Arkansas: Kelt Works, 1994A.

——"Expanding the Parameters of the Alien-Human Abduction Agenda," *MUFON 1994 International UFO Symposium Proceedings*, Seguin, TX: MUFON, 1994B, pp. 20-32.

UFO Journal
"Chemical Analysis Reveals 'UFO Ash' As Potassium Chloride," Vol. 4, No. 2, 1989, p. 9.
"Gulf Breeze Sightings: The UFO Model," Vol. 5, No. 5, 1990, p. 33.
"News: Experts Assail Brits' Hoax Claims," Vol. 6, No. 6, 1991, pp. 6-7.

Vallée, Jacques. *Messengers of Deception*. Berkeley, CA: And/Or Press, 1979.

——*Messengers of Deception*. NY: Bantam Books, Inc., 1980.

———"Recent Field Investigations into Claims of UFO Related Injuries in Brazil," *MUFON 1989 International UFO Symposium Proceedings,* Seguin, TX: MUFON, 1989, pp. 32-41.

———*Revelations: Alien Contact and Human Deception.* NY: Ballantine Books, 1991.

———*Forbiddem Science: Journals 1957-1969.* Berkeley, CA: North Atlantic Books, 1992A.

———"The Hybridization Question," *MUFON UFO Journal,* June 1992B, pp. 11-12.

———"Forbidden Science: The UFO Phenomenon and the Research Community," *MUFON 1992 International Symposium Proceedings,* Seguin, TX: MUFON, 1992C, pp. 56-67.

———"Anatomy of a Hoax: The Philadelphia Experiment Fifty Years Later," *Journal of Scientific Exploration,* Vol. 8, No. 1, 1994, pp. 47-71.

Vaughn, Erik. "Chronicles of Credulity," Review of *UFO Chronicles of the Soviet Union* by Jacques Vallée, *Skeptical Inquirer,* Fall 1993, pp. 82-85.

Velasco, Jean-Jacques. "Scientific Approach and Results of Studies into Unidentified Aerospace Phenomena in France," *MUFON 1987 International UFO Symposium Proceedings,* Seguin, TX: MUFON, 1987, pp. 51-58.

Wagner, Mahlon W. "What can ufologists learn from parapsychology?" *International UFO Reporter,* Sept./Oct. 1991, pp. 16-18.

Walters, Ed and Frances Walters. *The Gulf Breeze Sightings.* NY: Wm. Morrow, 1990.

———*UFO Abductions in Gulf Breeze.* NY: Avon Books, 1994.

Walton, Travis and Mike Rogers. "Fire in the Sky: My 5-Day UFO Abduction," Presented at The UFO Experience Conference, North Haven, CT: Oct. 10, 1993.

Ware, Donald. "Current Case Log," *MUFON UFO Journal,* Aug. 1991, pp. 14-15.

———"Current Cases," *MUFON UFO Journal,* March 1992A, pp. 17-19.

———"Current Cases," *MUFON UFO Journal,* May 1992B, p. 15.

———"Current Cases," *MUFON UFO Journal,* Jan. 1993A, p. 16.

———"Current Cases," *MUFON UFO Journal,* Feb. 1993B, p. 16.

———"Current Cases," *MUFON UFO Journal,* July 1993C, p. 19.

Webb, Walter N. "Inside Building 263: A Visit to Blue Book, 1956," *IUR,* Sept./Oct. 1992, pp. 3-5.

———"Sleep Paralysis in Abduction Cases," *UFO,* Vol. 8, No. 2, 1993, pp. 21-25.

———*Encounter at Buff Ledge.* Chicago: Center for UFO Studies, 1995.

Webster, Andrew. *Science, Technology, and Society*. New Brunswick, NJ: Rutgers University Press, 1991.

Weiner, Jim, Jack Weiner, Charlie Foltz, and Chuck Rak. "The Allagash Abductions," presented to Second Annual Gulf Breeze UFO Conference, Oct. 14, 1994.

Westrum, Ron. "Post Abduction Syndrome," *MUFON UFO Journal*, Dec. 1986, pp. 5-6.

White, John. "The 'Seeding' of the Cosmos," *UFO*, Vol. 4, No. 4, 1989, p. 14.

Whiting, Fred. "Conflict or Collaboration?" *MUFON UFO Journal*, Nov. 1992, pp. 12-13.

——"The Background of the GAO Investigation," *MUFON UFO Journal*, March 1994, pp. 11-13.

Wieder, Irwin. "The Willamette Pass Photo Explained," *International UFO Reporter*, Nov./Dec. 1993, pp. 18-19.

Willwerth, James. "The Man from Outer Space," *Time*, April 25, 1994.

Wilson, John P. "Post-Traumatic Stress Disorder (PTSD) and Experienced Anomalous Trauma (EAT): Similarities in Reported UFO Abductions and Exposure to Invisible Toxic Contaminants," *Journal of UFO Studies*, N.S. 2, 1990, pp. 1-17.

Wilson, Robert Anton. *The New Inquisition: Irrational Rationalism and the Citadel of Science*. Scottsdale, Arizona: New Falcon Publications, 1991.

Wingfield, George. "Crop Circles: Is There a UFO Connection?" *MUFON 1994 International UFO Symposium Proceedings*, Seguin, TX: MUFON, 1994, pp. 257-274.

Wolf, Fred Alan. *The Eagle's Quest*. NY: Touchstone, 1991.

Wood, Robert M. "A Little Physics...A Little Friction: A Close Encounter with the Condon Committee," *IUR*, July/Aug. 1993, pp. 6-10.

Wright, Dan. "Gulf Breeze Update," *MUFON UFO Journal*, Feb. 1991, pp. 8, 22.

——"The Entities: Initial Findings of the Abduction Trancription Project: Part I," *MUFON UFO Journal*, Feb. 1994A, pp. 3-7.

——"The Entities: Initial Findings of the Abduction Transcription Project, Part II," *MUFON UFO Journal*, March 1994B, pp. 3-7.

Zeidman, Jennie. "The Mansfield Helicopter Case," *MUFON 1989 International UFO Symposium Proceedings*, Seguin, TX: MUFON, pp. 13-30, 1989.

Index

A scholarly source of material on
scientific investigation of
phenomona outside the current boundaries
of mainstream science
is the quarterly

Jouznal of Scientific Explozation

P.O. Box 5848

Stanford, CA 94309-5848

phone: 415-593-8581

fax: 415-595-4466

email: < sims@jse.com>

Website: <www.jse.com>

The God Hypothesis

Extraterrestrial Life and Its Implications for Science and Religion

ISBN 0-926524-40-2

348 pages

$18.95

Wild Flower Press

800/366-0264

- **Dr. John Mack:** *Lewels has written an important book. He is a prominent and distinguished figure in his El Paso community who has courageously marshalled data from many sources to confirm that the Earth and its citizens are being visited by beings whose origins are not known. Clearly written, his book should contribute to overcoming the official denial of this extraordinary phenomenon, which carries such vast implications for all of our lives. Furthermore, Lewels is not afraid to link science with spirituality and to discuss the profound spiritual and religious implications of alien encounters. This clearly written work will surely put further "rips in the fabric" of the strictly materialist world view that still dominates so much of Western thought.*

- **Whitley Strieber:** *Finally, a book that seriously addresses the question of what the possibility of an alien presence does to religion. It's an exciting, pioneering look at what is almost certainly about to become the burning question of the age, indeed, of all ages. Lewels addresses the issues of belief and meaning with incisive intelligence and an intellectual dynamism that is as refreshing as it is exciting. Altogether, an important, useful and timely effort by an articulate and pioneering thinker.*